Ecclesiastes: The Mid-Life Crisis

Ecclesiastes: The Mid-Life Crisis

Don Anderson

LOIZEAUX BROTHERS
Neptune, New Jersey

First Edition, January 1987

Printed in the United States of America

A publication of Loizeaux Brothers, Inc.
A nonprofit organization devoted to the Lord's work and to the spread
of His truth.

All Scripture quotations, unless otherwise noted, are from the *Holy
Bible, New International Version,* copyright 1973, 1978, 1984 by the
International Bible Society and are used by permission.
References noted NASB are from the *New American Standard Bible,*
copyright The Lockman Foundation 1960, 1962, 1963, 1968, 1971,
1972, 1973, 1975, 1977 and are used by permission.
References noted TLB are from *The Living Bible,* copyright 1971 by
Tyndale House Publishers, Wheaton, Illinois, and are used by
permission.
References noted KJV are from the *Authorized King James Version.*

Library of Congress Cataloging-in-Publication Data

Anderson, Don, 1933-
    Ecclesiastes—the mid-life crisis.

    1. Bible.   O.T.   Ecclesiastes—Meditations.
2. Middle age—Religious life—Biblical teaching.
I. Rodgers, Jane.   II. Title.   III. Title: Ecclesiastes.
BS1475.4.A53   1987   223'.806   86-20855
ISBN 0-87213-001-0

The author wishes to acknowledge the editorial assistance of Jane
Rodgers.

Dedication

To all those who have experienced a blowout on the freeway of life, and who are wanting and waiting for help so their journey can continue.

אֲנִי לְדוֹדִי וְדוֹדִי לִי

I am my beloved's, and my beloved is mine
Song of Solomon 6:3

πάντα χαὶ ἐυ πᾶσιυ Χφιστός

Christ is all and in all
Colossians 3:11

Contents

Foreword

I believe that I am qualified to judge the value of what my good friend Don Anderson has to say on the subject of the mid-life crisis. I've experienced World War II, and two marriages—including the death of my first wife from lung cancer; I've raised six children (some obedient, some rebellious, but all loved), and so far have been blessed with four grandchildren; my career positions have been too numerous to mention—all have ended in either promotion or firing as the result of corporate mergers.

I thought I was pretty well through the various stages of my mid-life crisis almost a decade ago, when Don became my pastor at the Emerald Bay Community Church in East Texas. I had been going to church off and on all my life, but for the first time I found myself looking forward to Sunday mornings—not only for what Charles Kuralt would be reporting on the news, but more importantly, for what new insights into life Don Anderson was going to give my family and me from the pulpit. Hungry for more, I joined Don and his wife, Pearl, at every opportunity. Eventually, I came to know and accept Christ.

When Don was teaching on Ecclesiastes and Solomon's mid-life crisis, I sat on the edge of my seat during the entire eight-week series. I can recall making comments such as these to myself or to my wife, Barbara: "Do you remember that? . . . You can say that again! . . . If I'd only known then when I know now! . . . You mean other people have that problem?"

I am so pleased that through *Ecclesiastes: The Mid-Life*

Crisis more people will have the opportunity to become acquainted with Don and his tremendous ability to communicate God's Word. Learning to understand the Scriptures through Don is truly a privilege—one which I am happy for others to share.

LAMAR MUSE
FORMER PRESIDENT, SOUTHWEST AIRLINES
FORMER CEO, MUSEAIR

A Few Words First

We live our lives at breakneck speed in America. Year after year passes, and the events of each melt into bittersweet memory. The little boy next door too rapidly progresses from Big Wheels to Hot Wheels to ten-speeds to speeding tickets. At eighteen, he goes to college, emerges at twenty-one with a degree and a seemingly endless road in front of him. He enters the marketplace and begins to climb the proverbial corporate ladder. Somewhere along the way he marries. As salary increases come, so do babies and medical bills and insurance premiums. Promotions are accompanied by larger mortgages, fatter car loans, piano lessons, and soccer practice. As his kids grow, so does our hero's checking account—at least at the first of each month. Then around the time his youngest is ready for braces and his oldest for college, the crisis hits.

Psychologists tell us this mid-life crisis is to some extent unavoidable for most men. In his book *Men in Mid-Life Crisis*, Jim Conway, a well-known Christian pastor and author, says: "The truth is that nearly all men in mid-life experience some trauma" (Conway 1979, 25). The crisis can be a devastating period. Few men and families emerge from such trauma unchanged, or at its worst, unscathed. At the very least, *middlescence* (as middle age is sometimes called) is a turning point in the life of an adult. No longer considered young, except by his parents, the middle-aged man begins to round the corner toward old age.

At this important stage in his development, the middle-ager and those close to him need instruction, counsel, guidance, and comfort. In recent years many secular and a few Christian books have been written concerning the crisis. Conway's book is an especially good one for helping Christians cope with the problems of mid-life. Though that book and others may prove to be of great assistance to the man in crisis, there is an even better place to find help.

After all, what greater source of counsel is there than the Word of God? The Bible is far from silent on the subject of mid-life difficulty. In fact, it is my thesis that the Lord, in His infinite wisdom, has provided us with an entire book on the subject: the book of Ecclesiastes. I believe that in Ecclesiastes, Solomon writes about a time in his life when everything has broken loose. He describes and offers solutions to a very real problem in his own life: the mid-life crisis.

Mine is something of a maverick interpretation of Ecclesiastes. Most evangelical authors take the three books of the Bible written by Solomon and sequence them this way. Many feel that Song of Solomon was written when the king was young and in love; Proverbs was written when Solomon was truly living a life in fellowship with God; and, according to most scholars, Ecclesiastes was the product of an old man who had become bitter and resentful about life. (A notable exception is Walter W. Kaiser's position in *Ecclesiastes: Total Life,* published by Moody Press.)

My view differs. Song of Solomon is, in my opinion, the story of Solomon and Shulamith, the little country girl from Lebanon. It tells of the king's first love experience. The book is *the* manual on physical and sexual love in the marriage relationship and should not be allegorized into something other than what it really is. God created love; God created sex, and He gives us a practical design for physical love between a husband and wife. I feel that Solomon writes Proverbs when he is an old man, musing, looking back. He's getting close to the end of his days, so he passes on his wisdom and insights through the vehicle of the Proverbs. He has earned the right to write.

And finally, I believe that Solomon writes Ecclesiastes when in the middle of his life. The pressures of the kingdom are crushing him. He has all the fame, power, money, and success he will ever need, and it's not enough. In essence, he can write his own check as far as the rest of his life is concerned, but he is not a happy or fulfilled man. In Ecclesiastes, he has reached that stage in his development where he is wondering, "Is it worth it?" "Is there any meaning or purpose to life?" Solomon, like the rest of us, has to answer those questions before he can run the last half.

So, for the purposes of this study, we are going to drop Ecclesiastes into the mid-life. I think we'll see each verse we consider become vibrantly real when examined in the light of the mid-life theory. Since God's Word, unaltered, intact, fully ministers to all our needs, we'll be taking an essentially verse-by-verse approach to the text. As he grapples with crisis, Solomon echoes himself often, but even in this repetition we'll sense change . . . and growth. We'll observe him as he sorts out the perplexing issues of life. And as we study Solomon's words, I pray that we, too, as Christian men and women, will come to grips with the often confusing (and hazardous) stage of life known as middle age. If we are receptive, the lessons of Ecclesiastes will teach us how to survive—and surmount—the crisis.

I make that last statement with confidence because the book of Ecclesiastes came alive for me during the years when I underwent a mid-life crisis of sorts. At age forty, I experienced a traumatic job loss. The fear of failure, coupled with the fact that I had to support a wife and five children—three of whom were ready for college—prompted me to engage in a workaholic lifestyle in order, I thought, to survive. I reached age fifty with a small measure of success and the gripping apprehension that I was missing out on a great deal of what life had to offer. Trouble surfaced in my marriage as the kids left home, and I realized that my wife and I had lost touch with each other amid the hustle and bustle of raising our family and ministering to others.

The question for me at that time was not, "How can I cope?" but rather, "Can I really trust God and depend upon

His Word?" And the answer was a resounding, "Yes, yes!" My study of Ecclesiastes lifted me from the pit. I thank God that He is so gracious to give us a book which effectively traces our mid-life pilgrimage and shows us the way—His way.

Proverbs 3:5-6

The Mid-Life Crisis

Once a person reaches his forties and fifties, he finds himself the brunt of countless jokes. The middle years have provided many a would-be comedian with ammunition for his barbs. We've all heard them.

One such fellow has called middle age that perplexing time of life when we hear two voices calling us. One says, "Why not?" And the other tells us, "Why bother?" I love what Ogden Nash had to say about the mid-years. According to Nash, middle age is "when you're sitting at home on Saturday night and the telephone rings and you hope it isn't for you." Yet another comic has added his two cents' worth of humor on the subject: "Middle age is when you try to use everything Mother Nature gave you before God takes it away."

While we fervently hope the last statement isn't true, the fact is that the approach of middle age sets off a panic signal in many people. Middlescence is a time of questioning, reevaluation, and reexamination. Sometimes the middle-ager feels exactly like Aliterus, a character in *The Tenth Measure*, Brenda Lesley Segal's novel about Masada. Aliterus is a Roman actor who, when he arrives in Jerusalem for the first time, makes a statement which I think aptly describes the attitude of more than a few middle-aged individuals. He says:

> I have come here . . . like one aspiring to an audition, an actor in search of a role. Meanwhile, the playwright has vanished. God of Josephus and of my own mother as well, You had better provide me with a stage direction now, or cue me, if You please. The fact is, I

> *have lost my place in this script or wandered foolishly into the wrong theater* (Segal 1980, 276).

That's really not too different from how a middle-aged man may often feel. It sometimes seems that he has lost his place in life's script as he begins to question the goals he once pursued with cocksureness, clarity, and drive. He wonders, "Why am I here? What am I doing? Is there any true meaning or purpose to life? Does what I'm doing really count for anything?" Like Aliterus, he may feel he has blindly strolled into the wrong theater.

You'll notice I've used the pronoun "he" quite a bit. I do not mean to imply that women never experience mid-life trauma. On the contrary, they do, although as one wife I know puts it: "My life is a lot like a hamster habit trail. I'm busier than the dickens, but I just keep covering the same ground. Running up this tube, now that one: make the beds, bake the cookies, wash the clothes, clean the house, buy the groceries, drive the carpool, call the plumber, fix the lunches, bathe the kids." She says, "Mothers don't have time to have a mid-life crisis!" And she means it!

I can't comment on that, but let me in the next few pages describe some things that I have learned about women in mid-life. This information has been gleaned from various sources, particularly Jim Conway's book *Men in Mid-Life Crisis.*

The Woman's Crisis

Most specialists in the study of adult development agree that women encounter periods of self-doubt and questioning at different times than men. Women, it seems, experience essentially two periods of emotional upheaval—crisis, if you will. The first occurs during a woman's late thirties, when the children all find themselves in school and their mother suddenly finds herself freed from the preschool routine she has followed for years. Says Jim Conway:

> It is not the period of the *empty* nest; it is the period of the *quiet* nest. Yes, there are still children in the home,

when they're not in school. She still has the roles as a
mother, but now there are long periods during the day
when the house is quiet—almost deafeningly so.
There is time to think of what life is all about (Conway 1979, 160).

According to Conway, this reevaluation process for the
woman is also accompanied by an increased sense of aging. She begins to see herself in a "slightly older light,"
(Conway 1979, 161) and the parade of youth-oriented mag-
azines, television shows, and advertisements doesn't help
the situation any. This initial period of "crisis" in a woman's life can, however, have positive results in that at this
time she may take on new vocational and personal challenges, thus filling the void.

The second period of trauma in a woman's life often
occurs (and please be aware that I am speaking in general-
ities here) when she undergoes menopause in her late forties or early fifties. The reality of being unable to bear
children (whether she'd *really* like to have more kids or
not) converges with the actual time of the "empty nest" as
the children leave home, and a crisis of sorts is produced.
This "change of life" can be both a time of physical discom-
fort and emotional tumult.

And to make things even tougher, sandwiched between
her late-thirties blues and menopause, a woman also often
has to deal with a mid-life crisis of a different sort that is
faced by her husband. It is this essentially male trauma
that I feel Solomon, because he is writing about his own
mid-life crisis, mainly addresses in Ecclesiastes. I'd like to
give a brief overview of the subject. Again I'll be borrowing
from Conway's *Men in Mid-Life Crisis*.

I do not claim to be an expert on the mid-life crisis—
merely a victim who has recovered. Nor can these few
pages possibly contain an exhaustive analysis of the problem. The list of suggested readings at the end of this book
will give you some additional sources of information. Rather, what follows are reflections from one who has been
there and who has counseled many who have taken the
same detour.

THE MAN IN CRISIS

Experts agree that just about every man experiences some sort of difficulty as he approaches the middle years. At best, mid-life is a period of questioning in which a man takes stock of his life to date. In this unsettled time he may change jobs, open a new business, take up a special hobby, or escape through an extended vacation. That's *at best*, remember. At worst, the middle-aged man can take the plunge from this period of questioning into the fiery pit of a crisis whose effects can be devastating.

Singer John Denver has performed some songs in recent years that contain lyrics which reflect the mind-set of a man in crisis. Consider these words from Denver's "Gravel on the Ground":

> If our lives could lie before us
> Like a straight and narrow highway
> So that we could see forever
> Long before we took the ride
> We would never look to heaven
> Make a wish or climb a mountain
> 'Cause we'd always know the answer
> To what's on the other side.
>
> But life ain't no easy freeway
> Just some gravel on the ground
> You pay for ev'ry mile you go
> And you spread some dust around
> But we all have destinations
> And the dust will settle down
> This life ain't no easy freeway
> Just some gravel on the ground.

> (Words by Debbie Hupp and Bob Morrison. Copyright 1980 by Music City Music, Inc. All rights reserved. Used by permission.)

Talk about a pessimistic outlook! The lyrics reek of a man with doubts and regrets. The narrator of that song says he wouldn't even make "a wish" unless he knew "the answer to what's on the other side." No, "life ain't no easy freeway," but to the man in the middle of a mid-life crisis it seems more like a dead-end street.

Another song performed by Denver also captures the feeling of an individual in the midst of crisis, an individual, who like the actor Aliterus, has lost his script and lost his way. The following words are the lyrics from "Some Days Are Diamonds (Some Days Are Stone)." They're classic:

> Now the face that I see in my mirror
> More and more is a stranger to me
> More and more I can see there's a danger
> In becoming what I never thought I'd be.
> Some days are diamonds,
> Some days are stone,
> Sometimes the hard times won't leave me alone.
> Sometimes the cold winds blow a chill in my bones,
> Some days are diamonds,
> Some days are stone.

> (Words and music by Dick Feller. Copyright © 1975 by Tree Publishing Company, Inc. International copyright secured. Used by permission. All rights reserved.)

What brings about this depressive period in a man's life when more days seem to be like "stone" than "diamonds," when the face that he sees in the mirror is "a stranger," and when his life appears chock full of hard times that plain won't go away?

WHY NOW?

Before we proceed further, let me say that from my observations the mid-life crisis is a phenomenon far more common in this generation of middle-agers than in previous ones. In the past, when things got rough, most people toughed it out and stuck in there without obvious complaint. Not today. Instead, it seems we modern-day middlescents are shucking our jobs and leaving our wives and families in droves . . . or if we're not actually doing so, we are thinking about it. Why? I have a few thoughts on the matter. These are strictly opinion, but *studied* opinion—the result of observation and reflection. Bear with me while I step on my soap box.

First of all, we are bombarded with the artillery of the media. We're repeatedly ordered to "grab for all the gusto," because we "only go around once in life." And sometimes the straight life seems amazingly devoid of the "gusto" the TV tells us we ought to experience. Second, we make money as never before in this generation, and the pursuit of the dollar consumes so much of our time and energy that burnout at mid-life is often inevitable.

Third, and I think most important, it seems we can't make a move without bumping up against the mentality of the "me" generation. We have basically decided that *we* are the most important creatures around, and if we aren't feeling fulfilled ninety-five percent of the time, then something's got to give. As a generation, we've become so selfish that we've ceased to be servants! God has actually designed us to be servants and givers. When we stop being such, we pay the price. Eugene H. Peterson puts it quite well when he writes in *Run with the Horses:*

> Birds have feet and can walk. Birds have talons and can grasp a branch securely. They can walk; they can cling. But *flying* is their characteristic action, and not until they fly are they living at their best, gracefully and beautifully.
>
> Giving is what we do best. It is the air into which we were born. It is the action that was designed into us before our birth. *Giving* is the way the world is. God gives himself. He also gives away everything that is. He makes no exceptions for any of us. We are given away to our families, to our neighbors, to our friends, to our enemies—to the nations. Our life is for others. That is the way creation works (Peterson 1983, 43).

We are created to be givers, not takers, and when the scales tip too far in the wrong direction, we court trouble. At mid-life, excessive self-concern paves the way for the crisis.

THE BAD GUYS

Regardless of the reasons why the mid-life crisis affects people's lives so frequently these days, the fact is that it is a very common occurrence. What, then, causes this trauma and makes it so devastating to its victims? Jim Conway suggests that a man in mid-life suddenly finds himself confronting four enemies. This "enemy horde," as Conway calls it, wreaks havoc on a man's emotions. I'd like to summarize the author's thoughts on the matter from chapter 6 of *Men in Mid-Life Crisis*.

To begin with, the first foe of which a man becomes aware is his own body. I can assure you that what he says it true. After all, by mid-life, a man starts to slow down. The print gets smaller on the page. Never enough light in the room, is there? Mid-life is when a fellow begins to play doubles instead of singles in tennis and prefers ping-pong to racquetball. He doesn't have the same old zip any more. The pretty girls begin to say "Sir," and they don't even bother to give him a second look. His body clock simply begins to wind down at middlescence.

The second enemy is a man's work. He begins to feel trapped. He starts to wonder why he ever craved a company vice presidency in the first place. As the saying goes, he discovers he's climbed the corporate ladder only to find that it is leaning against the wrong wall. Or, if he hasn't reached the top of his profession, he realizes he never will. That's depressing, and work becomes a grind. Always it's the same song, second verse, a little bit louder, and a whole lot worse.

The third mid-life enemy is a man's wife and family— the bloodsuckers! They demand dollars for cars, homes, vacations, braces, and college. Every month the fat paycheck our middle-aged hero earns is quickly translated into mortgage payments, dental bills, and tuition fees. Many middlescent men long to escape the responsibility, and some take the plunge and follow through on their desires.

And the fourth enemy is God Himself. In Conway's words:

> The mid-life man pictures God leaning over the banister of Heaven, grinning fiendishly and pointing a long, bony finger as he says, "You despicable, disgraceful Christian! You are the worst possible example of a mature man. You are selfish. You are filled with lust. You are lazy. You are so disgusting that I want to spew you out of my mouth!" (Conway 1979, 67).

To the man in the midst of a crisis, it seems nobody, least of all the Lord, is really pleased with him. Only a few months ago a fellow I know who was in the middle of this kind of despair phoned me. He had been having hassles with his wife, children, and business partners, and he simply broke down. "I wish I could make somebody happy just once," he confided tearfully. His self-image was practically non-existent, and he figured God was as dissatisfied with him as everyone else was.

To the man in crisis, God becomes not only an enemy but an "*unfair* enemy" (Conway 1979, 67). And, in the end, it is often God whom the middle-aged man blames for his predicament.

WHEN AND WHOM DOES IT HIT?

By now you may be wondering at what point a person should expect to undergo the time of reevaluation that is characteristic of mid-life. Although a man may have this experience anywhere from age twenty-five to age seventy-five, it seems to occur most commonly as he approaches his forties or fifties. I was running with a young fellow the other day who said, "I had a heckuva time at twenty-eight.

Depression, doubts . . . I didn't see any purpose in what I was doing." After hearing him, I thought, "My goodness, isn't it amazing that someone could hit those kinds of snags so early in life?" Yet even though the crisis can occur sooner for some people than for others, most of those whom I've counseled have not encountered difficulty until their forties. Pastor, psychotherapist, and marriage counselor John Sterner suggests that mid-life trauma "happens from age 35 to 55, but most often at 40" (Sterner 1985, 31).

At times the crisis erupts suddenly with little, if any, advance warning. In other instances, it escalates in intensity over a period of years . . . much like a slow-burning ember which is fanned gradually into a fire. Sterner describes each type of crisis in his book, *Growing through Mid-Life Crises: Thoughts from Solomon and Others.* In the words of one of Sterner's clients, "I woke up one day and thought, 'What difference does it make if I go to work or go to Bermuda or just stay in bed all day?' " "Of course I went to work," the client went on to say, "but the meaning, the pizzazz was all gone." Suddenly. Just like that. Yet Sterner's own mid-life crisis took place, as he puts it, "during a slowly building crescendo toward 40, when the crisis peaked" (Sterner 1985, 31-32).

THIRTEEN TO AVOID

Regardless of how or when it becomes evident, some form of middlescent quandary does occur in the life of virtually every man. For which individuals is this trouble likely to expand into a full-blown crisis? Who is most vulnerable? From my own research, readings, counseling sessions with mid-life men, and study of Ecclesiastes, I've come up with thirteen observations. When a majority of these ingredients join together, the stage is set for problems. Here they are, the unlucky thirteen:

  1. The recognition of the approach of old age, and an increasing desire to avoid it;

2. A sense of boredom after twenty to twenty-five years of marriage;
3. A severe feeling of sadness and loss over the fact that the children are grown and about to leave home;
4. A decline in physical health—the heart palpitates occasionally and the body lugs around extra pounds;
5. Job security threatened by younger workers or computer replacements;
6. Failure—especially the recognition that there are unrealized personal and professional goals which may never be met;
7. Success—(ironically) which has proved unfulfilling, not "all it was cracked up to be";
8. A consuming thirst to get rich;
9. A perceived need for new challenges, experiences, and opportunities;
10. A desire to search for real meaning and purpose in life, coupled with a feeling of futility concerning present activities;
11. Weariness regarding hassles and responsibilities;
12. A fierce longing to escape gnawing problems and instead start over in life, making a new beginning;
13. The absence of an intense desire to walk with God and to know Him more intimately.

When several of these thirteen circumstances exist simultaneously, even in varying degrees, then a very real crisis may occur in the life of a man. When that happens, a man's life becomes a lot like our old van which, with one hundred thousand miles on its axles, blew up one day when the fuel pump became clogged. I was stopped at a traffic light; the signal changed and I pressed on the accelerator . . . there was a hesitation . . . then BLAM! Out shot the muffler, off popped the radiator hoses, and the van's engine became a steaming mass of metal. It was crippled, and unfortunately so are a lot of men whose lives have become clogged with the various problems of mid-life.

Solomon reaches middle age and finds himself literally boiling in an emotional, physical, and spiritual pressure cooker. Like other men in crisis, his perceptions about life have changed. I'd like to briefly discuss these new attitudes here; they'll be covered in more detail in future chapters as we dive into Ecclesiastes.

A MID-LIFE VIEW

Solomon, like many other mid-lifers experiencing difficulty, has indeed begun to view life in specific ways. For one thing, he has started considering life selfishly rather than socially, thinking chiefly of himself rather than of others. He feels sorry for himself, and places his own interests far above those of anybody else. Second, like many middlescents in trauma, he views life as apart from God rather than controlled by Him. He feels the Lord to be an aloof, disinterested, mildly dissatisfied party who takes no personal interest in the affairs of men. And finally, he sees life as bordered solely by the grave. He does not even harbor a secret hope of eternal life. To his way of thinking, all will someday be ashes to ashes and dust to dust . . . and nothing more. Such is the view from the pit, and it is this pessimistic outlook to which Solomon offers practical solutions in Ecclesiastes, as we'll see.

FAILURE TO PREPARE

Why should we bother to study the mid-life crisis? There are many reasons. Evidently the Lord thinks it an important enough topic, since He devotes an entire book of Scripture to the subject. That's reason enough for us to do our homework. Yet there is more to encourage us to study.

Allow me to tell you a little story to illustrate my point. I enjoy running a great deal. In fact, I have participated in four marathons; two I finished and two I was not able to complete. Let me tell you, the two marathons I finished were far more enjoyable than the two I did not finish! You see, because of prior commitments and unforeseen events, I did not have the time to adequately and intensely train for the two races in which I failed to cross the finish line. Believe me, it was no fun at all to stand at the end of the course and watch the other runners come in. And to top it all off, after one of those unsuccessful runs, somebody gave me a T-shirt with the words: "Failure To Prepare Is Preparation for Failure" plastered across the front. That really ministered to my need, I tell you! That T-shirt, coupled with the words "You were running well," from Galatians 5:7 (NASB), which kept ringing in my ears, nearly did me in!

But it's true, isn't it? Failure to prepare *is* the best preparation for failure that I know. That's something we need to think about as we encounter middle age. A mid-life crisis of some sort will affect people we know and love, maybe even ourselves. We can't ignore the problem. We've got to be ready to meet it head-on. We've got to make preparation, and God gives us some excellent instructions in His Word.

NOT ALL BAD

The crisis is not necessarily a totally negative event, either. Many positive results can emerge from the ashes left after the flames of trauma. The potential for significant personal growth is there.

Gail Sheehy, in her book *Passages,* says that out of times of crisis can come times of tremendous growth. She gives the illustration of the lobster as an example. Sheehy observes that when the lobster gets ready to expand or grow, it sheds its shell. Vulnerable for a period of time, it regrows another shell, goes on for a time, becomes vulnerable again, and then grows once again. In essence she means that an individual may progress, even flourish, as he or she undergoes the difficulties of each passage in life (Sheehy 1980, 29).

I certainly agree with her opinion. A fellow I know in Houston, Texas, told me not too long ago: "My mid-life crisis occurred last year, and through it I came to know Jesus Christ in a personal way." I tell you, that knowledge made whatever trouble my friend went through completely worthwhile. Coming to a saving relationship with Jesus Christ is personal growth of the highest order. God uses all circumstances of our lives for His glory when we properly respond to them and to Him. Solomon himself says in Ecclesiastes 3:11 that God makes "every thing beautiful in its time" (KJV). In this case, "every thing" can even include the life of a fellow like Solomon, a man scarred by crisis.

2

A Man in Crisis

In Ecclesiastes, Solomon is the "Teacher" who writes the book when he is in the midst of all of the things that are breaking in upon him in mid-life. His story is the tale of a man who is experiencing the sheer futility of trying to find significance in life. As I see it, he is conducting a desperate search for truth.

Most scholars disagree, noting that Solomon wrote Ecclesiastes as a bitter, angry, defeated old man. The book has been considered the utter embodiment of pessimism. It has been seen as the confused, perplexing ramblings of an elderly king with an affliction like Alzheimer's disease who had forgotten everything he once knew about godliness and contentment. But Ecclesiastes is not a book of mere nonsense. It is not just a collection of disconnected verses thrown together. Rather, it is the story of a man facing a crisis of immense proportions.

Exactly who was this man? Before we talk about his personal trauma, let's take a brief look at Solomon and a quick glance at part of the history of his nation, Israel.

THE KINGDOM

Around 930 B.C. the kingdom of Israel divided in two, splitting into Judah in the south and Israel in the north. Before that division, the country had been governed by three kings. The first of these was Saul.

You see, it seems the Israelites had experienced a little identity crisis somewhere along the way. They began comparing themselves to other nations and decided something was missing at the Hebrew "White House": a king. They said to the prophet of that time, "Samuel, we want to be like everybody else. We want a king." And so a man with the physique of an NBA power forward and the looks of a movie star was anointed and installed as the new monarch. He was tall and handsome, towering "head and shoulders" above everyone else, and his name was Saul. He was by no means a fit choice, and he ended up a suicide victim on the field of battle against the Philistines. (See 1 Samuel 8–31.)

God then took David, a man after His own heart, and enthroned him. David took the kingdom militarily and materially and expanded it to its greatest point. He was, after all, God's man. Following David's death at age seventy, his eldest living son by Bathsheba, Solomon, took the reins of power. Solomon was not much more than a boy—around eighteen years old—at the time he assumed the throne. The kingdom was at its wealthiest and largest. Solomon was to become the richest man on earth in his day, amassing all the fame, money, power, and women that he could ever desire. He had it all, and it's at this pinnacle of worldly success that we find him as the book of Ecclesiastes opens.

Solomon was a man with supernatural wisdom, yet he was also a man who could make some foolish mistakes. He left behind a written record in three volumes. Although his father, David, was a gifted musician and poet, Solomon was primarily an author—his reckonings and recollections appear in his works: Song of Solomon, Proverbs, and Ecclesiastes. And now, with this brief background, let me explain some reasons why I think he was undergoing a crisis at mid-life when he penned the book we're about to study.

In Crisis?

J. Vernon McGee points out that there are three key words and phrases which stand out from the text of Ecclesiastes. The first of these is the word "vanity," also translated as "meaningless," which appears thirty-seven times. The second is the phrase, "under the sun," which makes its appearance twenty-nine times. The last phrase of special significance is "I said in my heart," or "I thought in my heart," and Solomon uses those words with great frequency also (McGee 1977, 10).

"Meaningless . . . under the sun . . . I said in my heart"—those are the buzz words of a man in crisis. When Solomon says them, he reveals that he is in real trouble. It's as if he is saying, "It's meaningless, all this stuff I'm doing! It's under the sun—it doesn't count for anything lasting and eternal." And when he exclaims, "I said in my heart," we sense that he has conjured up moments of wisdom concerning what *he* thinks ought to be done in a situation. He isn't looking for insights from God; he's merely trying to wing it on his own. He is set on doing things his way, and in his "creativity" he forgets the Creator.

SOLOMON'S OUTLOOK

At mid-life Solomon becomes afraid that he's going to miss out on something in life if he sits idly by. To his way of thinking, he's running out of time. The focus of his energy is on finding answers to questions that confound him, and yet his chosen frame of reference prevents him from looking to God for the solutions.

Remember when I said in chapter one that men facing crises in mid-life begin to perceive life differently than before? I also mentioned that in Ecclesiastes, Solomon is in that boat. His outlook has changed, particularly in three specific areas. For one thing, *like other men in crisis, Solomon has started to view life selfishly rather than socially.* He has forgotten about the kingdom and has begun thinking only of himself. To him, everything else is "meaningless," as he so often tells us.

Number two, *Solomon sees life as apart from God rather than controlled by Him.* He doesn't allow the Lord to direct his path. Instead, he views life as independent of the need for divine direction. Rather than hearing him ask God for guidance, we repeatedly hear him utter the words, "I said in my heart" throughout the book of Ecclesiastes. Get it? It's "*I* said in *my* heart" that Solomon continually mouths; it's never anything like: "*God* spoke to me and revealed *His* will."

And third, *Solomon sees the grave as the end: everything is "under the sun."* There is nothing above . . . no heaven, no eternal judgment or justice . . . nothing. He is hung up on life here and now. His lack of hope makes him miserable, too. As the apostle Paul warns us in 1 Corinthians 15:19: "If only for this life we have hope in Christ, we are to be pitied more than all men."

So in Ecclesiastes Solomon is a man who is searching. And he shines the searchlight from out of the hole of his own prejudice and depression. He tries to find genuine meaning and purpose as he undergoes the period of self-doubt and questioning that tends to confront us all at mid-life.

THE PLAN

And what does a man do when he tries to find direction and purpose in his life? He usually tries many different things, doesn't he? In middlescence, time seems to be slipping away, so he starts doing a lot of testing, and in Ecclesiastes we see Solomon making a number of experiments. He searches for meaning through religion; he tries women, wine, and materialism; he hunts for an answer through wisdom, morality, and many other vehicles. He desperately wants to discover the solution to the trauma he is facing so that he can tackle the last half of life. He's got some decisions to make.

He's in the same position that Tom Landry sometimes finds himself in. Actually, the example I'm about to give could apply to any football coach; I just happen to be a Dallas Cowboys fan. When the Cowboys go into a ball game, they have a game plan for the particular team they're playing. Let's say that it is half-time and the score is 21–0 in favor of the other team. Landry has a choice. He's got to either stay with the game plan (with perhaps a few minor adjustments) or scrap it, sketch a new one, and go for broke.

That's exactly what can happen to a man in mid-life. He may feel as though he's been nailed to the wall—it's 21 to nothing—and he, like Solomon, has got a decision to make about his life. Just what is that momentous decision? Our fellow can either scrap the game plan or stay with it, hang in there, and watch it eventually produce because he believes in what he's ultimately doing and where he's ultimately going. The choice is there. And we're going to watch as Solomon tries frantically to scrap the original game plan of his life.

FOUNDATIONS OF SAND

Just why Solomon's mid-life difficulties have expanded into a full-blown crisis is easy to understand, too. James Dobson, in his book *Straight Talk to Men and Their Wives*, puts it so well when he describes the kind of man I think Solomon has become at the time he writes Ecclesiastes. Says Dobson:

> I feel the need to stress what I consider to be *the* fundamental cause of a mid-life crisis. It results from what the Bible refers to as "building your house upon the sand." It is possible to be a follower of Jesus Christ and accept His forgiveness from Sin, yet still be deeply influenced by the values and attitudes of one's surrounding culture. Thus, a young Christian husband and father may become a workaholic, a hoarder of money, a status-seeker, a worshiper of youth, and a lover of pleasure. These tendencies may not reflect his conscious choices and desires; they merely represent the stamp of society's godless values on his life and times.
>
> Despite his unchristian attitudes, the man may appear to "have it all together" in his first fifteen years as an adult, especially if he is successful in early busi-

ness pursuits. But he is in considerable danger. Whenever we build our lives on values and principles that contradict the time-honored wisdom of God's Word, we are laying a foundation on the sand. Sooner or later, the storms will howl and the structure we have laboriously constructed will collapse with a mighty crash (Dobson 1980, 180-181).

That's where Solomon is—he's built his house on the sand and at mid-life he discovers that he is waist-deep in the grit. He has to dig his way out, and we're going to witness his scramble to escape.

Eggs in the Wrong Basket

I recall an article published a few years ago in the *Dallas Insider*, a seminary newspaper. It was shortly after President Carter had announced the United States boycott of the 1980 Summer Olympics that were held in Moscow. Two American athletes, Jeff Wells and John Lodgwick, were interviewed.

Jeff and John were good friends. Both Christians, they had attended Dallas Theological Seminary together and had gone to the Northwest following graduation. Olympic hopefuls, they'd been in training for years in anticipation of being able to compete for the gold in the marathon. When Carter announced the boycott, their Olympic aspirations were immediately crushed.

But they weren't bitter. In fact, Jeff and John were among the few athletes to officially support the President's decision. Sure, they were disappointed as their years of commitment and training suddenly appeared to have been for nothing. I'm sure they had questions about the fairness of it all. Yet they didn't complain. In fact, John commented during the interview that Jeff and he had recognized the futility of putting all of their "eggs" in a basket that could not last.

If we go through a severe, shattering, mid-life crisis, it may be because we have done just that. We have put all of our eggs in a basket that is doomed to deteriorate. Our overcommitted lifestyle, misplaced values, neglect of God, and lack of knowledge about His ways finally catch up with us, as we are tested for unworthy goals. As Dobson writes in *Straight Talk to Men and Their Wives*:

> Stated succinctly, a mid-life crisis is more likely to be severe for those whose values reflect the temporal perspective of this world. A man does not mourn the loss of his youth, for example, if he honestly believes that his life is merely a preparation for a better one to follow. And God does not become the enemy of a man who has walked and talked with Him in daily communion and love. And the relationship between a man and his wife is less strained in the mid-life years if they have protected and maintained their friendship since they were newlyweds. In short, a mid-life crisis represents a day of reckoning for a lifetime of wrong values, unworthy goals, and ungodly attitudes (Dobson 1980, 181).

It was Fred Allen who said, "We sow our wild oats, and then we pray for a crop failure." How true that is! The apostle Paul cautions in Galatians 6:7: "Do not be deceived: God cannot be mocked. A man reaps what he sows." As we search for significance, we may well sow some seeds which harvested will spell trouble for us and for those we love. We may do permanent damage to relationships which are already tender. That's why I believe that in the book of Ecclesiastes God provides us with a biblical example of a man in the throes of a crisis at mid-life. Through the practical application of His Word, it is possible to avoid making those mistakes which destroy lives.

Friends, the chickens will come home to roost, whether we like it or not. It's time now to examine ourselves, to test ourselves for errant values and wrong goals. We'll observe as Solomon does just that in Ecclesiastes. And let's remember that despite our mistakes, God is faithful to freely forgive and to help us forge ahead in His will. It is never too late.

3

Is That All There Is?

Ecclesiastes 1:1-18

One middle-aged man bewailed his fate by complaining, "When I was a kid, I had to do what my parents told me to do. Now that I'm older, I'm supposed to tune in to my kids, to listen to the younger generation. So I want to know, when am I going to get to do what I want to do?" I can sympathize with him—sometimes it seems as if our generation of current middlescents has never really had a chance. We've never really gotten to sing with Frank Sinatra, "I did it *my* way," because somewhere along the line after we learned to respect our elders, it became fashionable to seek wisdom in youth. Talk about unfair!

And yet I saw a wonderful response emblazoned across the chest of a gray-headed guy the other day. T-shirts continue to be so popular. "Body bumper stickers," a friend of mine calls them. I get a kick out of reading their slogans, and the one to which I'm referring was particularly great. A paunchy, middle-aged man sported a shirt with the following message: "I'm getting revenge. I'm going to live long enough to be a problem to my kids!"

That's one way to handle the frustration, I thought. But you know, even that poses some difficulties. There is a basic problem in living such a long life. I'm not talking about the usual woes of arthritis, poor circulation, and senility. Those are bad enough. What I'm suggesting is that the longer one lives, the more futile and mundane life begins to seem. With longevity comes the awareness that life is essentially cyclical. And the monotony of it all can be unnerving.

CYCLE UPON CYCLE

Life indeed consists of cycles. I know a lady, for example, who flatly refuses to discard good clothing that has gone out of style. She also refuses to wear it while it is outdated, mind you, but she figures that fashion trends will come around eventually to what they've been before, if she just waits long enough. She's made an astute observation about human nature: what has been will be again. (Fortunately, she has lots of closet space, too!)

And she's right. According to my wife, shoes with spiked heels and pointy toes were nowhere to be seen after the fifties, and yet the teenaged niece of a friend of mine unwrapped three pairs of spiked-heel, pointy-toed shoes this past Christmas morning. What's more amazing is that she liked them and she wears them! Anyone who shops for a teenager knows how remarkable it is when any gift of clothing is worn outside the house by its recipient.

Think about the business world. A man may spend the better portion of his adult life working for a corporation. Retirement comes, and after a farewell reception, the presentation of a gold watch, and the payment of certain benefits, it's on to Social Security, pension installments, and maybe a Florida condo for our retiree while another employee takes his place in the company. Business continues as usual. Our man isn't really missed, and soon he is only vaguely remembered.

James Dobson gives a similar example as he tells of the feelings of futility which engulfed him when one of his colleagues on the faculty of the USC School of Medicine died unexpectedly. Dobson, with over two hundred of his peers, was called upon to hear a five-minute eulogy and participate in a one-minute period of silence in honor of the deceased. Then it was simply business as usual. Dobson recalls his feelings at the time:

> I was thinking, "Lord, is this what it all comes down to? We sweat and worry and labor to achieve a place in life, to impress our fellow men with our compe-

tence. We take ourselves so seriously, overreacting to the insignificant events of each passing day. Then finally even for the brightest among us, all these experiences fade into history and our lives are summarized with a five-minute eulogy and sixty seconds of silence. It hardly seems worth the effort, Lord" (Dobson 1980, 202).

Life goes on. Sometimes it does seem "hardly worth the effort" as the seasons roll by in what appears to be endless repetition. We eat, work, and sleep. Eventually somebody else takes our place. The monotony of it all can be intolerable. It is, however, a poignant reality to the man at midlife who has viewed the continual overlapping of forty-odd years of activities.

I believe that in the first chapter of Ecclesiastes, Solomon lets us know that he is facing those very feelings of frustration at the apparent futility of life. These attitudes form the foundation of his mid-life crisis. Let's take a look at what he tells us in Ecclesiastes 1:1-18. It is my conviction that God, in Scripture, gives us the answers to such problems. By considering the Lord's Word as it is given, we find His solutions to the dilemmas that plague us. Therefore, we'll be taking a verse-by-verse approach to the study of Ecclesiastes, dealing with God's Word "as is," and remembering, along the way, the apostle Paul's words to Timothy: "All Scripture is God-breathed and is useful for teaching, correcting, and training in righteousness, so that the man of God may be thoroughly equipped for every good work" (2 Timothy 3:16-17).

AN EXPERT OPINION?—ECCLESIASTES 1:1-2

The words of the Teacher, son of David, king in Jerusalem:
"Meaningless! Meaningless!"
    says the Teacher.
"Utterly meaningless!
    Everything is meaningless."

When we open to the book of Ecclesiastes, we read, as verse 1 says, "The words of the Teacher, son of David, king of Jerusalem." Who is speaking? Verse 1 gives us three clues.

First, we have his title. He is the "Teacher," which may also be translated as "Preacher" or, in Hebrew—"Koheleth." He is the communicator. Second, our narrator is the "son of David." Not only is he related to royalty, but he is even in the messianic line. From him, and from his father David, Jesus Christ is descended. Third, his position is that of "king in Jerusalem," a post he is qualified to fill. All of these clues point to one personality: Solomon, son of David and successor to his throne over all Israel. And so we see beyond doubt that it is Solomon who is the "Teacher," and it is Solomon who imparts his wisdom in the book.

Should we listen to him? Does he know what he's talking about? Is he in a position to speak to us with relevance? You'd better believe it!

A friend of mine belongs to a local quarterback club. Each week during football season the club invites professional and collegiate coaches and players to give talks on the subject of the game. The members do not invite politicians, bankers, accountants, math professors or anyone who is not connected with the NCAA or the NFL to address their meetings. They want to hear from experts—people who are knowledgeable because of their backgrounds and experiences.

Solomon is like those coaches and players in that he is in a position to know what he's talking about in Ecclesiastes. He's had more privileges than most of us will ever imagine. He's at the top of the ladder as far as power, finances, and prestige are concerned. If he were alive today, he'd be greeted at each airport by throngs of people. The press coverage he'd receive if he visited the United States would rival that accorded to Prince Charles and Lady Diana. He'd be the subject of special reports, editorial commentaries, and interviews aired on the national news. All of that would occur because, to our way of thinking, Solomon, as Ecclesiastes opens, has got everything. When a man like that finds life unsatisfying and troublesome, it makes us stop and listen to what he has to say.

His message comes through loud and clear in verse 2. "Meaningless! Meaningless! . . . Utterly meaningless! Everything is meaningless," he cries. My secretary's son was cutting up in church one day, much to her embarrassment. When they were in the car after the service, she demanded to know why he had misbehaved so. The twelve-year-old genius simply replied, "Meaningless, meaningless, utterly meaningless, everything was meaningless, Mom!" That pretty succinctly told me what he thought of my preaching! My sermon was to him irrelevant, purposeless, not worth his attention. And that's precisely what life has become to Solomon in his middle years.

In some texts the word "meaningless" is translated "vanity" (KJV, NASB). Either way, the connotation is of sheer emptiness, utter futility. There's no content. Human existence to Solomon is like cotton candy, disappearing when our lips touch it. It's like the soap bubbles we blew as kids. We'd fill the air with iridescent spheres that seemed so solid, until at the slightest touch of a finger, they'd pop.

"Meaningless, meaningless," Solomon repeatedly utters the words. Without a relationship to God through the person of Jesus Christ, this is an accurate portrait of life. The Lord is the ultimate source of all meaning and purpose. As the philosopher Pascal pointed out, there is a "God-shaped vacuum" within us all. We need to live in harmony with the Creator, yet too often we deny His *sovereignty,* the "supreme rulership" of our lives which is His prerogative to exercise (Unger 1966, 1041). Perhaps we'll get by with the denial while young, but to the man in middlescence who, like Solomon, has failed to make peace with his Lord, life is marked by an inescapable barrenness.

Life under the Sun—Ecclesiastes 1:3-7

> What does man gain from all his labor
>   at which he toils under the sun?
> Generations come and generations go,

> but the earth remains forever.
> The sun rises and the sun sets,
>   and hurries back to where it rises.
> The wind blows to the south
>   and turns to the north;
> round and round it goes,
>   ever returning on its course.
> All streams flow into the sea,
>   yet the sea is never full.
> To the place the streams come from,
>   there they return again.

   Thus the Teacher continues his lament, and in his words
we detect the ingredients that have provoked his mid-life
trauma. In verse 3 he poses the question, "What does man
gain from all his labor at which he toils under the sun?" In
other words, Solomon wants to know. "What is the profit in
all I'm doing? What good is it really going to do me? What
is truly meaningful in all of my toil?" Like many men in
mid-life, he sees no purpose in the activities he has undertaken. What's more, he recognizes them as being only "under the sun."
   Solomon reveals that he views life as solely temporal, not
eternal, never *above* the sun. Such an existence is sterile; it
is mere vanity. Our earthly lives are summarized with five-
minute eulogies and moments of silent prayer, then business continues as usual without us. Ultimately the glory of
our accomplishments dwindles, even for the most brilliant
and heroic among us. How ironically appropriate to us all
were the words of General Chuck Yeager on the occasion of
his retirement: "I spent my life flying and there wasn't
even a pigeon in the air when I said good-by" (Yeager 1985,
317). There is no permanent gain under the sun, and in the
first chapter of Ecclesiastes Solomon acknowledges that
depressing reality.
   It's too bad he hadn't heard the story Jesus tells in Luke
12:13-21. The parable concerns a foolish rich man who,
after his servants haul in a bumper crop, plans to build
larger barns, store all his grains and goods, sit back and

relax. The wealthy fool boasts, "I'll say to myself, 'You have plenty of good things laid up for many years. Take life easy; eat, drink and be merry' " (Luke 12:19). He forgets his mortality, but there is a day of reckoning. As Christ says in Luke 12:20: "But God said to him, 'You fool! This very night your life will be demanded from you. Then who will get what you have prepared for yourself?'" The Lord goes on to say, "This is how it will be with anyone who stores up things for himself but is not rich toward God" (Luke 12:21).

So we have it in a nutshell—true wealth belongs to the person who is "rich toward God." Solomon, from his self-centered vantage point, has failed as yet to grasp that truth. He goes on to express the hollowness of life in the succeeding verses of the first chapter of Ecclesiastes.

"Generations come and generations go, but the earth remains forever," he mournfully states. He's right. We live our threescore and ten; we work, and generations come and go. The earth "remains the same"; it just stays here while new people arrive on the scene and others pass away.

And what gain is there, ultimately? We dig trenches; we erect buildings; we build dams and lakes; we plant forests. But in the long run the earth doesn't change much. Man never really wins the battle—certainly not in Solomon's day and not in our modern high-tech times, either. If you don't agree with me, think about how many man-made structures have been swept away in floods, flattened by earthquakes, or ripped to shreds by tornadoes. Man will never fully subdue his planet. At mid-life Solomon is confronted with that realization.

The futility of it all gets to him, as the day to day struggles of life appear increasingly pointless and dreary. We can understand Solomon's feelings. Much of our existence is just plain boring. The other day as I was cutting the grass, I thought to myself that life is a lot like mowing the lawn. We no sooner get done with it than we have to start planning to do it again. There is such repetition. My wife figures life is a lot like doing the laundry, especially when our children were living at home and there was a steady supply of dirty blue jeans, socks, and T-shirts stuffed in the hamper or tossed on bedroom floors. The washing and ironing were constant. The tasks which demand so much of our time frustrate us because they seem trivial and endless.

A NATURAL CONSPIRACY

In addition to the annoyance Solomon feels at the humdrum sameness of day-to-day living, he is also bothered by the fact that even nature operates on a schedule of near drudgery. This natural grind serves only to remind him of the human condition. In verse 5 he observes, "The sun rises and the sun sets, and hurries back to where it rises." The twenty-four-hour timetable is both dull and unwavering. He continues, "The wind blows to the south and turns to the north; round and round it goes, ever returning on its course" (1:6). Just as the wind blows, so life is like a giant merry-go-round or a treadmill. We enter and we exit, and in between we spend the hours going round in circles or literally running in place.

In his despair Solomon gives us one more illustration from nature. He says in verse 7, "All streams flow into the sea, yet the sea is never full. To the place the streams come from, there they return again." Cycle after cycle after cycle—nothing is ever really accomplished. The sea is never filled; the streams never fully emptied. And as he turns his thoughts from nature to man himself, Solomon's conclusions also remain the same.

THERE'S NEVER ENOUGH—ECCLESIASTES 1:8-11

> All things are wearisome,
>   more than one can say.
> The eye never has enough of seeing,
>   or the ear its fill of hearing.
> What has been will be again;
>   what has been done will be done again;
>   there is nothing new under the sun.
> Is there anything of which one can say,

"Look! This is something new"?
It was here already, long ago;
   it was here before our time.
There is no remembrance of men of old,
   and even those who are yet to come
will not be remembered
   by those who follow.

With resignation, Solomon says in verse 8, "All things are wearisome, more than one can say. The eye never has enough of seeing, or the ear its fill of hearing." He hits the nail on the head. There is never enough, is there? Eye and ear are never satisfied by what is seen and what is heard. Kids open Christmas presents and within a week or two begin to look forward to their birthdays. People go on "the trip of a lifetime"—summer after summer after summer. The music of the Rolling Stones has never been among my favorites, but I think down deep we can all empathize a bit with Mick Jagger when he sings, "I can't get no satisfaction!" By nature we are never completely content . . . and Solomon has seen few exceptions to this rule.

He takes things a step further in the next verse, too. It's no wonder we're never satisfied, because the whole of life is wrapped up in the infinitely dull, cyclical routine of which we've already spoken. As Solomon observes, "What has been will be again, what has been done will be done again; there is nothing new under the sun" (1:9). I told you earlier about my friend who saves her outdated clothes for future use. To tell the truth, I've got a couple of suits hanging in the back of the closet that just may come out of the mothballs when the styles change. Several months ago, I got a big kick out of watching some kids play with hula-hoops. They didn't realize that their parents had bellied up to the same toys back in the fifties. There really never is anything totally new, is there? Much of what we think of as new and fresh is really just recycled—over and over again.

No wonder life begins to seem monotonous, especially to a fellow like Solomon who is past halftime in his life and is watching the clock tick away the third quarter. "What has been will be again." It's a tiresome reality, no matter who we are, if our focus is merely earthward.

That reminds me of something. I get teased a lot about the fact that I like to run, and even more about the fact that I do most of my running on a track. When a person gets hit by a car as I did, he runs on a track, and he buys himself a lap counter. If I've got to run around that track forty times in order to get my ten miles in, I run around the track forty times. It's safe enough, but it sure can be boring. I've found that during many of those runs I repeatedly focus on the same spots on the track—a pebble here, a chip in the concrete rim there. I never see anything new because I never break out of my tight little orbit.

Solomon is like that, and I think many other people experiencing mid-life trauma are, too. They're stuck in tight little monotonous orbits—round and round they go until the futility of it all becomes unbearable. They haven't broken out of their constricting circles to discover the immensity of a God out there who loves them and wants a relationship with them. It's so easy to let ourselves become wrapped up in material things and pressures and demands, and forget the One who put us on the planet in the first place. It's often the man who has done just that—confined himself to an endless round of activity in a taut little circular lifestyle—who finds that his mid-life difficulties escalate into a shattering crisis. If during the process of living, he has neglected to build a relationship with the heavenly Father, then he has created an environment for severe problems. He's in danger. Solomon is a prime example of a candidate for such trouble.

The king continues his lament in verse 10: "Is there anything of which one can say, 'Look, This is something new'? It was here already, long ago; it was here before our time." Then he moves on to tell us of something else that bothers him deeply.

THREE TROUBLE SPOTS

Solomon has already told us about two frustrations he has encountered in middlescence. First, he recognizes that there is really no gain in life: water, wind, and sun are unchanging; man never makes a permanent dent in the universe; nothing is ever truly accomplished by his futile efforts. Second, Solomon is also annoyed by the fact that there is never anything completely new under the sun. He reveals his third source of irritation in Ecclesiastes 1:11: "There is no remembrance of men of old, and even those who are yet to come will not be remembered by those who follow." Get it? There's no gain, there's nothing new, and nobody's going to remember us anyway. Don't forget those ideas—they explain why Solomon has decided that life is basically meaningless. He goes on to illustrate his opinions in the verses that follow.

SEEKING THE ANSWERS—ECCLESIASTES 1:12-18

> I, the Teacher, was king over Israel in Jerusalem. I devoted myself to study and to explore by wisdom all that is done under heaven. What a heavy burden God has laid on men! I have seen all the things that are done under the sun; all of them are meaningless, a chasing after the wind.
>
> What is twisted cannot be straightened;
>   what is lacking cannot be counted.
>
> I thought to myself, "Look, I have grown and increased in wisdom more than anyone who has ruled over Jerusalem before me; I have experienced much of wisdom and knowledge." Then I applied myself to the understanding of wisdom, and also of madness and folly, but I learned that this, too, is a chasing after the wind.
>
> For with much wisdom comes much sorrow;
>   the more knowledge, the more grief.

In the midst of his quandary, Solomon lets us know that he hasn't simply sat around moping and bemoaning his lot. He has instead been seeking answers to the bewilderment he feels. He says in verses 12 and 13: "I, the Teacher, was king over Israel in Jerusalem. I devoted myself to study and to explore by wisdom all that is done under heaven. What a heavy burden God has laid on men!" After proclaiming his title again as the "Teacher . . . king over Israel" who resides in Jerusalem, Solomon admits that he has devoted himself to the study of what has gone on under the sun. He hasn't been idle—he's been searching for truth—but his conclusion reflect only pessimism and discouragement.

"What a heavy burden God has laid on men!" he cries plaintively. Isn't that tragic? I tell you, Solomon at mid-life does not have things together with the Lord. He's shouldering the "heavy burden" of his existence all by himself, and that's why it wears him down.

In contrast, Jesus Christ says in Matthew 11:28-30:

> Come to me, all you who are weary and burdened, and I will give you rest. Take my yoke upon you and learn from me, for I am gentle and humble in heart, and you will find rest for your souls. For my yoke is easy and my burden is light.

The apostle Peter, referring to God, instructs us in 1 Peter 5:7: "Cast all your anxiety on him because he cares for you." And Paul, who had been through so much persecution—including flogging, stoning, shipwreck, and imprisonment—could still proclaim in 2 Corinthians 4:17: "For our light and momentary troubles are achieving for us an eternal glory that far outweighs them all." It's light trouble and heavy glory for the man who has a solid relationship with the Lord, but as we see, Solomon in Ecclesiastes 1 isn't taking advantage of that truth.

THE FOLLY OF "WISDOM"

In verse 14 Solomon summarizes his thoughts with a critical statement. He says, "I have seen all the things that are done under the sun; all of them are meaningless, a chasing after the wind." He hasn't found anything under the sun to be purposeful and lasting. The sum total of man's life is merely a "chasing after the wind." It's nothing meaningful, nothing we can get our hands on. Instead, as he continues in verse 15, "What is twisted cannot be straightened; what is lacking cannot be counted." Man's efforts are completely and utterly futile.

Solomon is a man who, as he tells us, has "grown and increased in wisdom more than anyone who has ruled over Jerusalem before," and has "experienced much of wisdom and knowledge" (1:16). Even he cannot make sense out of the human condition. As he says in verse 17, wisdom, madness, and folly are merely "a chasing after the wind." And we read the final statement reflecting his cynicism in verse 18: "For with much wisdom comes much sorrow; the more knowledge, the more grief." His search for truth has done no more than bring him great heartache; with "more knowledge" has come only "more grief."

We don't exactly see in Solomon a portrait of a happy, joyous believer, do we? No, he's just a man at the mid-point trying to sort out the mysteries of life and encountering tremendous troubles in the process.

Is That It?

Solomon simply wants to know the answer to the question, "Is that all there is?" When a man like that—a man with more wisdom, money, and power than any of us will probably ever have—poses a question like this, we'd better sit up and listen. Dismayed and discouraged, he finds himself unable to see any gain resulting from his labor. There appears to be nothing under the sun that is unique and refreshing. And he is further plagued by the worry that his accomplishments won't be remembered anyway.

Solomon's outlook reflects the inevitable reaction to what has been—in critical years at least—a godless life. He mourns the meaninglessness of his existence and he's got a point because, unfortunately, his empire has been built on sand. After several decades, its foundations have begun to crumble.

"Is that all there is?" It's an unavoidable question if one spends forty-plus years, as I believe Solomon has, operating without constant assistance from God. His neglect has set the stage for the epic mid-life crisis which we'll continue to examine as we study the book of Ecclesiastes.

LESSONS

But first, let me present some lessons from Solomon's experiences in the first chapter of Ecclesiastes that we can apply to our own lives.

Lesson number one: *everything is meaningless without God.* When we fail to take Him into account, anything that we do lacks genuine purpose. It's what's above the sun that counts. Solomon's gaze is cemented on only what is under the sun, and he comes up a loser.

Lesson number two: *a man receives no gain for his labor when it is for selfish ends.* Rather, the Lord would love for us to have the attitude of Paul, who writes in Philippians 1:21: "For to me, to live is Christ and to die is gain." God would be so pleased if we could also say, as Paul does in Philippians 3:8: "What is more, I consider everything a loss compared to the surpassing greatness of knowing Christ Jesus my Lord, for whose sake I have lost all things." Man and God have two different ideas about achievement, but only the Lord's concept offers permanent gain and glory.

Lesson three: *there is nothing new under the sun, but coming to know the Son makes all things new.* As 2 Corinthians 5:17 states: "Therefore, if anyone is in Christ, he is a new creation; the old has gone, the new has come!" We can say amen to that one, can't we?

Number four: *though man does not remember us, God never forgets.* Solomon is right when he says in Ecclesiastes 1:11 that "even those who are yet to come will not be remembered by those who follow." Man's memory is short; God's is everlasting. To Him, our lives are computer printouts and He's got each of ours on file in a slot in eternity. We'll see it all on video when we get there—from the day of our new birth to the day of our death. In the words of Paul in 2 Corinthians 5:10: "For we must all appear before the judgment seat of Christ, that each one may receive what is due him for the things done while in the body, whether good or bad." Man forgets—God doesn't.

The final lesson: *if we do not have a relationship with Jesus Christ, then our lives are simply one gigantic frustration filled with futility.* Only Christ gives meaning and purpose to human existence since, as Colossians 1:16 states, "For by him [Christ] all things were created: things in heaven and on earth, visible and invisible, whether thrones or powers or rulers or authorities; all things were created by him and for him." We are created by Him and for Him, and to deny that is to make the greatest mistake possible.

Look Out . . . And Up!

I am certain that some of us can identify to an extent with the difficulties described by Solomon in the first chapter of Ecclesiastes. Maybe the foundation for a mid-life crisis has already been laid in our lives. Possibly we are racing out of control, desperately looking for an exit ramp as life becomes increasingly futile. Wherever we are, there is an answer to the problem.

What is it? The hymnist, Clara Scott, put it so well when she wrote:

> Open my eyes, that I may see
> Glimpses of truth Thou hast for me;
> Place in my hands the wonderful key
> That shall unclasp and set me free.
> Silently now I wait for Thee,
> Ready, my God, Thy will to see;
> Open my eyes, illumine me, Spirit divine!

We must open our eyes to Christ, and get them off ourselves. With Peter, we're going to sink in the waves the minute we start looking only at our circumstances. (See Matthew 14:22-32.) Instead, let's concentrate on the Lord, letting His Spirit renew and refresh us. The key to getting through the trouble spots is found by "fixing our eyes on

Jesus, the author and perfecter of faith" (Hebrews 12:2 NASB). At mid-life—as always—the only favorable option is to run with patience and prayer the course that is set before us, keeping our focus on Christ, drawing every ounce of our strength from Him whose grace and power are totally adequate.

Questions for Personal or Group Study

1. What key question is asked in verse 3?

2. In what ways is nature used in verses 4-11 to illustrate the futility of man's existence?

3. What word in verse 8 conveys an attitude which contributes to the mid-life crisis?

4. Why doesn't Solomon view his own life as making a vital contribution in the course of human affairs? Refer to verses 9-11 for your answer.

5. What are Solomon's conclusions about life, as seen in verses 12-14?

6. In your own words, paraphrase Solomon's reflections in verses 16-18.

7. In your opinion, is there any answer to a meaningless existence? Please explain.

8. How can what Solomon writes in Ecclesiastes 1:1-18 apply to your own life? What lessons may be learned?

4

The Success Syndrome

Ecclesiastes 2:1-26

While I was writing the last chapter, a network news show featured a special report on the mid-life crisis. Curiously enough, the title chosen by the network for its feature was the same one I had already selected for the chapter: "Is That All There Is?" The man in crisis today wrestles with the same question that Solomon did centuries ago. And no matter who you are, it's entirely possible that you'll be struck with the intense desire to search for meaning and purpose at the mid-point of life also.

A friend of mine who had read the biography of the late Erroll Flynn told me that the actor had been in the habit of having everything he owned decorated with question marks. Question marks adorned his limousines, tailored shirts, bathrobes, and abounded throughout his house. I wonder if using those question marks was Flynn's way of expressing his search for significance in life. Like many men, maybe he was simply asking, "Is that all there is?"

Once we voice that question, the next step is to begin looking for an answer. Solomon begins to do that in the first chapter of Ecclesiastes. Remember, he tries wisdom and finds that "with much wisdom comes much sorrow"; in fact, "the more knowledge" one has, "the more grief" that occurs (Ecclesiastes 1:18).

So what's next? In Ecclesiastes 2, Solomon does what many mid-life men attempt. He tries to find meaning through pleasure. He hopes a little hedonism will satisfy. Maybe wine and women will give his life the gusto it lacks.

In his pleasure-seeking Solomon fully embraces a philosophy similar to what Jim Conway calls the "One More Time" stage. As Conway puts it, suddenly it's "one more time with one more woman . . . the newness, the excitement of a new touch, a new face" (Conway 1979, 148) that may become tremendously appealing to the middlescent man. And as a result far too many men and women, Christians included, join the ranks of those involved in extramarital affairs.

John Denver's song "Seasons of the Heart" expresses this dangerous mid-life mentality quite well. Consider the lyrics reprinted here:

> Of course we have our differences
> You shouldn't be surprised
> It's as natural as changes
> In the seasons and the skies
> Sometimes we grow together
> Sometimes we drift apart
> A wiser man than I might know
> The seasons of the heart
> And I'm walking here beside you
> In the early evening chill
> A thing we've always loved to do
> I know we always will
> We have so much in common
> So many things we share
> That I can't believe my heart
> When it implies that you're not there
> Love is why I came here in the first place
> Love is now the reason I must go
> Love is all I hoped to find here
> Love is still the only dream I know.
>
> So I don't know how to tell you
> It's difficult to say
> I never in my wildest dreams
> Imagined it this way
> But sometimes I just don't know you
> There's a stranger in our home

When I'm lying right beside you
Is when I'm most alone
And I think my heart is broken
There's an emptiness inside
So many things I've longed for
Have so often been denied
Still I wouldn't try to change you
There's no one that's to blame
It's just some things that mean so much
And we just don't feel the same

Love is why I came here in the first place
Love is now the reason I must go
Love is all I hoped to find here
Love is still the only dream I know
True love is still the only dream I know.

In Denver's song we see the portrait of a man disenchanted with his home. His wife is a "stranger" to him; in fact he "can't believe his heart" when it implies that his woman isn't there. And the chorus is a classic: "Love is why I came here in the first place. Love is now the reason I must go." Is it *love* that's going to make him call it quits with wife number one and launch an all-out search for satisfaction in some other female? I don't think so. Love is commitment to care forever, but the narrator of the song says with selfish egotism that it's the reason he must leave. His conclusions are morally offensive, but there's another problem with his idea as well.

Once we have indulged in pleasure until we bulge, once we've filled our cup of fun to the rim, we encounter a difficulty. We find we're still not satisfied. Even the new lady in our life doesn't permanently placate the longing we feel. There's still something missing. After we've eaten the finest foods and sipped the most expensive wines, we still wind up with a big, fat zero as far as life goes. Something is lacking. So what do we do then? We do what Solomon does in Ecclesiastes 2, and what many mid-life men attempt to do. We try to find meaning through work, maybe even throwing ourselves into a series of elaborate projects. To quote Jim Conway, the man in crisis seeks the following:

> One more success in business . . . a success so big that everyone around me notices how great I really am— how important I am—how absolutely indispensable I am. One more big success before I step off into the oblivion of mid-life and old age . . . (Conway 1979, 148).

The man in middlescent trauma may become even more of a workaholic than he might have been previously. But the trouble with pouring ourselves into projects is that we'll come up empty in the end. Workaholism does as little as hedonism to bring about lasting satisfaction in life. Let's look now at Scripture and watch Solomon make that discovery.

Recall that at mid-life Solomon is upset by three nagging facts: he sees no gain in life, there's never anything new under the sun, and no one is going to remember his futile actions anyway (1:9-11). From that foundation of desperation, he's going to begin to search for a phenomenon I call the "Success Syndrome." He'll try to escape the drudgery of the everyday and make it big personally and professionally. And the "Success Syndrome" demands that he dally with the "Three W's": work, wine, and women.

LOOKING FOR FUN —ECCLESIASTES 2:1-3

> I thought in my heart, "Come now, I will test you with pleasure to find out what is good." But that also proved to be meaningless. "Laughter," I said, "is foolish. And what does pleasure accomplish?" I tried cheering myself with wine, and embracing folly—my mind still guiding me with wisdom. I wanted to see what was worthwhile for men to do under heaven during the few days of their lives.

In his quest for meaning and purpose, Solomon plunges into the arms of pleasure for a season. He tells us in Ecclesiastes 2:1: "I thought in my heart, 'Come now, I will test you with pleasure to find out what is good.' But that also proved to be meaningless." He starts looking for fun all right, but he looks in all the wrong places.

Jim Conway says of the mid-life search for self-gratification: "This new god is called indulgence. It is the god of pleasure, luxury, gusto, comfort, ease, sensuality— the god of hedonism" (Conway 1979, 129). The man in mid-life may become like the New Testament character Demas, one-time companion of the apostle Paul, who forsakes the ministry because he falls in love with the evils of the present world (2 Timothy 4:10). Tired of a life of giving and sacrifice, the middlescent man decides instead to spend some of the money he earns on wine, women, lust, or leisure. He begins to worship a god of self rather than the God who has sacrificed so much for him. Ultimately this pleasure-seeking proves "meaningless," as Solomon tells us in verse 1.

The Teacher continues: " 'Laughter,' I said, 'is foolish. And what does pleasure accomplish?' " (Ecclesiastes 2:2). Laughter may be therapeutic in some cases, but Solomon sees that too much of it is nothing more than sheer empty-headed silliness. He then voices the question, "And what does pleasure accomplish?"

Well, what *does* it accomplish? Not much, in the end. When all is said and done, there is an empty feeling in the pit of the stomach. We still aren't fulfilled; we still aren't happy. Pleasure for the sake of pleasure cannot satisfy.

For one thing, there's never enough to go around. A quart of indulgence spilled out today will have to be a gallon tomorrow if the same effect is to be produced. A potato chip commercial assures us that we "can't eat just one" of that brand of chip. The same is true of pleasure. We begin to want "one more time for the old times"—one more experience, one more sexual encounter, one more drinking spree. That fact makes us appreciate the character of Moses, of whom it is said in Hebrews 11:25: "He chose to be mistreated along with the people of God rather than to enjoy the pleasures of sin for a short time."

Solomon continues in Ecclesiastes 2:3: "I tried cheering myself with wine, and embracing folly—my mind still guiding me with wisdom." What happens when a fellow takes off on his little pleasure kick? He feels a need to see if satisfaction can be found in a bottle, so he tries some Chablis or Burgundy. He becomes a connoisseur of fine wines and liquors. Maybe he even joins a wine-of-the-week club so he can purchase select vintages at discounted prices. I'm not criticizing the use of alcohol, just its *abuse* (see Ephesians 5:18). There are enormous numbers of alcoholics in our society today; many I've known have sought solace in drinking during mid-life trauma. These folks have tried to find meaning in a bottle, have tried to escape life by drowning in the spirits, but they've found it doesn't work. Solomon discovers that also.

Fortunately for him, he manages to stay levelheaded during the process. As he tells us, during the investigation his mind still guides him "with wisdom" as he imbibes. He exercises disciplined restraint, not allowing himself to become addicted to drink while he conducts his experiment. Solomon keeps himself in check, but this is often not the case with many people who drink to excess.

But not only does Solomon try cheering himself with wine, he also takes a shot at "embracing folly" (2:3). What does that mean? It means he succumbs to the lure of the "other woman" and leaves behind him the lady who had been the greatest love of his life, his wife Shulamith. Later, in Proverbs 5, Solomon would write a scathing condemnation of adultery, closing the chapter with this warning: "The evil deeds of a wicked man ensnare him; the cords of his sin hold him fast. He will die for lack of discipline, led astray by his own great folly" (5:21-22; see also Proverbs 6 and 7).

It *is* folly for a man to seek satisfaction with a mistress. But, according to Jim Conway, "Of all the solutions that the man in mid-life may try, the affair is perhaps the most common—at least, one of the most talked about" (Conway 1979, 98). Solomon engages in a series of lustful physical affairs—his sexual appetite, like that of his father David, taking him far afield of the marriage bed. His life seems empty. He's not getting any younger. Like many mid-life men who become enmeshed in extramarital sex, he feels an intense desire to rekindle the sparks of youth, once again proving that his masculinity, his virility, are still intact. Maybe he's looking for the understanding, appreciation, and attention he feels is missing from his marriage.

Solomon adds some of the new women in his life to his harem. Others are merely "one-night stands." It's interesting that he would label his escapades acts of "embracing folly," because the ultimate foolishness of it all is that each relationship into which he enters is a temporary set-up, a momentary seduction going nowhere, offering no hope of permanence, no lasting fulfillment.

Solomon is lucky in a sense. He experiments with wine without becoming hopelessly ensnared by the bottle. As the king he seduces the women of his choice without fear of reprisal. But what he does is dangerous and immoral, and his research does not bring him happiness. He reaches for a light, but winds up still in the darkness.

And yet there is a reason prompting his investigation. He lets us know this purpose in verse 3 with an utterly depressing statement: "I wanted to see what was worthwhile for men to do under heaven during the few days of their lives." Isn't that pathetic? Man's life under heaven measures merely a "few days," then the clock runs out. Quoting many a stewardess, "Our ground time here will be brief." This sad but true conclusion slaps many men in the face at mid-life. As the New Testament writer James, in chapter 4, verse 14, of his book, says: "What is your life? You are a mist that appears for a little while and then vanishes." That's all we are—on earth at least. No wonder Solomon undertakes his great search for meaning.

THE WORK ETHIC—ECCLESIASTES 2:4-9

> I undertook great projects: I built houses for myself and planted vineyards. I made gardens and parks and

planted all kinds of fruit trees in them. I made reservoirs to water groves of flourishing trees. I bought male and female slaves and had other slaves who were born in my house. I also owned more herds and flocks than anyone in Jerusalem before me. I amassed silver and gold for myself, and the treasure of kings and provinces. I acquired men and women singers, and a harem as well—the delights of the heart of man. I became greater by far than anyone in Jerusalem before me. In all this my wisdom stayed with me.

Solomon continues his quest. Pleasure has proved essentially empty, so he turns to work in an attempt to find purpose. In so doing, he fully embroils himself in the "Success Syndrome" of which I spoke earlier. He tries frantically to make himself even more materially successful than before, a feat that hardly seems possible considering he is the richest man alive at the time he writes Ecclesiastes.

REAL SUCCESS

But before we talk further of his attempt, let's get a few things straight. I am not criticizing the idea of being successful professionally. God wants us to be successful; He may even want us to be materially prosperous. He promises to take care of our needs (see Philippians 4:19). Some—not all—of us He will make wealthy. We find that among the most prominent biblical characters are men like Joseph, Jacob, and Abraham, who were extremely rich.

The key to dealing with worldly success is found in Matthew 6:33: "But seek ye first the kingdom of God, and his righteousness, and all these things shall be added unto you" (KJV). It's placing the Lord first in every area of our lives that assures fulfillment. We live in a day when the market is flooded with books on money management, motivation, goals, and positive thinking. Many of us are doubling our activities in a vain search for material success because we've lost our way spiritually. We try to become millionaires by age thirty-five and, along the way, we often experience spiritual bankruptcy. We feel guilty, we fear failure, we desire to escape our circumstances, and we're willing to settle for worldly goals instead of godly ones, so we permit the poison of workaholism to seep into our lives. That's precisely what has happened to Solomon as he pens chapter 2 of Ecclesiastes.

BACK TO WORK

The king pours his energies into significant, constructive projects to use up his time, building monuments to himself to ensure a measure of immortality. We see in Ecclesiastes 2 that Solomon's accomplishments are indeed many.

He tells us in verses 4-6: "I undertook great projects: I built houses for myself and planted vineyards." Building a mansion is his first project. Anyone who has been involved in designing and constructing a new home knows that the whole process can severely strain a relationship. What some people will do just to acquire a fatter monthly mortgage note and some extra square footage is amazing. Wives and husbands drive each other crazy and sometimes take the architect and contractors to the mental ward with them.

Besides that, Solomon's new house must satisfy a thousand women! 1 Kings 11:3 tells us that Solomon "had seven hundred wives of royal birth and three hundred concubines." Upon hearing that, a friend of mine exclaimed, "Good grief, I'm having enough trouble trying to keep one female happy!"

In erecting his structure, Solomon isn't merely concerned with maintaining the neighborhood status quo, either. He is actually a trendsetter—the main mover and shaker in Jerusalem. The palace he builds is by far the fanciest place in town. It's got to be magnificent—after all, Solomon is in charge of constructing the temple in Jerusalem! His own home must be the epitome of luxury—enclosing millions of square feet and carrying an enormous price tag.

After he finishes dabbling in the home building business, Solomon next turns to another project; he takes up farming. He plants vineyards, hoping this enterprise will give him the fulfillment he lacks. Then he gets into landscaping, making "gardens and parks" and planting "all kinds of fruit trees in them" (Ecclesiastes 2:3). The king becomes a Hebrew version of Lady Bird Johnson, beautifying the countryside with trees and shrubs wherever he can find a bare spot. It's a consuming task, and it generates even more work because as Ecclesiastes 2:6 says, Solomon also has to create "reservoirs to water groves of flourishing trees." He enlists the aid of the "Israeli Corps of Engineers"; they come in with a federal grant and erect some dams and lakes so all the new vegetation won't dry up and blow away.

Naturally, all this new foliage has to be maintained, so Solomon acquires some additional hired help. As he tells us in verse 7, he buys many male and female slaves, and their number is increased by other slaves who are born in his house. He becomes the head of a giant corporation, an employer of thousands. Continuing his search for satisfaction, Solomon delves into ranching, increasing his holdings until he owns "more herds and flocks than anyone in Jerusalem" 2:7). He's a cattle baron with enough livestock to cover the renowned King Ranch in Texas. He owns enough horses to play polo until he's too old to ride. And that's not all.

Solomon also begins to play around in the precious metals and commodities markets, amassing for himself gold, silver, and "the treasure of kings and provinces" (2:8). He is successful in all of his ventures, gathering great wealth for himself and probably delivering hefty commissions to his brokers.

Like many other rich people, he becomes a patron of the arts, too; verse 8 tells us that Solomon acquires "men and women singers." He hits the society pages with his sponsorship of operas and musicals by the score, counting on entertainment to lighten his heart with merry medicine. Having earlier tasted of pleasure, he decides not to forsake the more earthy delights either, and he expands his harem to include a bevy of additional beauties (2:8).

In short, Solomon undertakes eight major projects: building a huge new home, planting lush vineyards, creating beautiful parks, engineering dams and lakes, increasing his number of slaves, entering the ranching business, engaging in the silver and gold market, and becoming the patron of both musicians and desirable women. But as the old saying goes, "The opera ain't over till the fat lady sings." And she's still a long way from warbling in Ecclesiastes 2, because Solomon is still a long way from happiness, despite each massive accomplishment.

In verse 9 he says, "I became greater by far than anyone in Jerusalem before me. In all this my wisdom stayed with me." From his words we know that Solomon reaches the pinnacle of earthly success, scaling the ladder until he stands on a rung higher than anyone else in Jerusalem. He manages to hold on to his wisdom, not to mention his sanity, in the process. But he is not yet content.

THE "GOTTA HAVES"

Solomon in Ecclesiastes 2 reminds me of many people I know, more than a few of them at the mid-point of their lives. The house they have isn't big enough, so they have to build a bigger one. The car they drive has covered too many miles and isn't the latest model, so they trade it in on a newer one. The boat they own isn't big enough to go in the ocean, so they've got to buy a larger one. The ranch they've purchased needs a few more acres, so they add the land next to it. The recreational vehicle they bought for last summer's trip was too cramped, so they exchange it for a more spacious one.

These folks are tyrannized by the "gotta haves"—"gotta have this" and "gotta have that"! Unfortunately, all some people live for is a brand new toy to keep them entertained and to cover the guilt and emptiness in their lives. Ironically, even the expansive projects Solomon undertakes cannot fill the void he experiences at mid-life.

MUCH VENTURED, NOTHING GAINED—ECCLESIASTES 2:10-11

> I denied myself nothing my eyes desired;
>   I refused my heart no pleasure.
> My heart took delight in all my work,
>   and this was the reward for all my labor.
> Yet when I surveyed all that my hands had
>   done
>   and what I had toiled to achieve,
> everything was meaningless, a chasing after the
>   wind;
>   nothing was gained under the sun.

Solomon's discontent is hard for most of us to understand because he owns every type of material possession we could want. He's got one or more of everything in his garage! He has it all. He states in verse 2: "I denied myself nothing my eyes desired: I refused my heart no pleasure." Two members—the eye and the heart—Solomon had satisfied fully. If he saw something he wanted, he bought it. If he felt something he desired would bring him pleasure, he acquired it. If a certain project appealed to him, he set about accomplishing it. Money was no object—Solomon gave no thought to financing arrangements, interest rates, and capital expenditures. He simply procured and produced.

He summarizes the experience by saying, "My heart took delight in all my work, and this was the reward for all my labor" (2:10). He receives personal satisfaction in having done so much. That is his reward, but is it enough?

Not for Solomon. He tells us in verse 11: "Yet when I surveyed all that my hands had done and what I had toiled to achieve, everything was meaningless, a chasing after the wind; nothing was gained under the sun." Each immense and elaborate attempt at success proves shallow at the end. As Solomon tells us using his three pet phrases, it is all "meaningless, a chasing after the wind," in which ultimately "nothing" is gained.

Charles Bridges, in his book on Ecclesiastes, points out

the following: "Let nothing of earth be our rest—God never intended so poor a portion for His redeemed ones" (Bridges 1960, 36). How accurate are his words! God does not intend for us to be satisfied merely with what this world has to offer. Much, much more awaits us in eternity. As 1 Corinthians 2:9 says: "No eye has seen, no ear has heard, no mind has conceived what God has prepared for those who love him." Solomon does not and cannot find permanent happiness and peace with earthly pleasures and projects. It doesn't work that way—even for those of us who achieve much.

Consider author Ernest Hemingway—few Americans have led as fascinating a life as he. He was an infantryman and ambulance driver in World War I, a war correspondent in the Spanish Civil War and World War II. In peacetime, he was an avid sportsman, hunting big game in Africa and fishing off the coasts of Key West and Cuba. He traveled extensively. His novels hit the bestseller lists time after time. In winning the Pulitzer in 1953 and the Nobel Prize for Literature in 1954, he established a place for himself as one of the greatest American authors of all time. By most standards, he had it all, but it must not have been enough. Discouraged and despondent, he blew his brains out in a cabin in Idaho in 1961.

What this world has to offer pales beside the hope of eternity in Jesus Christ. By themselves, scintillating pleasures and enormous ventures can bring us no lasting peace.

WHERE WISE MEN AND FOOLS TREAD—ECCLESIASTES 2:12-16

> Then I turned my thoughts to consider wisdom,
>   and also madness and folly.
> What more can the king's successor do
>   than what has already been done?
> I saw that wisdom is better than folly,
>   just as light is better than darkness.
> The wise man has eyes in his head,
>   while the fool walks in the darkness;
> but I came to realize

that the same fate overtakes them both.
Then I thought in my heart,
"The fate of the fool will overtake me also.
What then do I gain by being wise?"
I said in my heart,
    "This too is meaningless."
For the wise man, like the fool, will not be long
    remembered;
    in days to come both will be forgotten.
Like the fool, the wise man too must die!

After we've tasted of nearly every conceivable earthly delight and we've busied ourselves with works of the greatest magnitude, what else is there to do? Not much. So Solomon starts to reflect, turning his thoughts "to consider wisdom, and also madness and folly" (2:12). He thinks about all that he has done, all that he has accomplished, and he reaches the inevitable conclusion: "What more can the king's successor do than what has already been done?" (2:12). In other words, he figures, "I've done it all! What could the next king do that could possibly surpass all that I have achieved? Nobody's going to break my records—they'll stand forever."

He's right, too. As far as wordly accomplishments go, he'll certainly be guaranteed a spot in the record books, but these conclusions don't give him an ounce of comfort. Instead, they bring him an even greater awareness of the futility of life. He even begins to consider the value of the wisdom God has given him.

Solomon observes in verse 13: "I saw that wisdom is better than folly, just as light is better than darkness." He's willing to concede that it's undoubtedly superior to be smart than stupid. No one wants to be a fool, right? Arthur Bloch, in his humorous book *Murphy's Law and Other Reasons Why Things Go Wrong!*, aptly covers our feelings on the subject when he offers this maxim: "A fool in a high station is like a man on the top of a high mountain; everything appears small to him and he appears small to everybody" (Bloch 1977, 60). Being a fool is never in style. But

Solomon is also painfully aware that, in the end, one's intelligence doesn't make a whole lot of difference.

And why not? Solomon continues in verse 14: "The wise man has eyes in his head, while the fool walks in darkness; but I came to realize that the same fate overtakes them both." He comes to the awareness that a wise man and a fool are both going to die. They'll both be six feet under some day, and they're both going to leave everything they've got to somebody who isn't going to appreciate it. Solomon realizes that no matter what our IQ is, our lives are simply ventures in frustration that end only in death.

He personalizes things in verse 15: "Then I thought in my heart, 'The fate of the fool will overtake me also. What then do I gain by being wise?'" Solomon faces the fact that in the end it doesn't matter how many degrees he has after his name—the result will be the same. All men eventually wind up with a tiny plot of land marked by a headstone. This knowledge is particularly frustrating to a fellow starting to confront the final half of life. Solomon is disturbed, and in the last part of verse 15, he voices his feelings with the familiar words, "This too is meaningless."

The king wraps up his lament with one last reflection, mourning the fact that the "wise man, like the fool, will not be long remembered"; indeed, "in days to come both will be forgotten" (2:16). It's the same old story. We work, strive, and sweat to achieve a measure of success and in the end we discover that we've used the wrong set of tools. What we've built won't last, and what we are will be forgotten. The Nobel Prize winner will meet the same fate as the man who cannot spell his own name. As Solomon reiterates in verse 16: "Like the fool, the wise man too must die!"

It's depressing, isn't it? It's discouraging to think that death will claim us all, that even the shiniest stars among us will share the same destiny as village idiots. Solomon's despair at this circumstance illustrates the fact that, in middle age, he cannot see beyond the grave. He's living his life with blinders on; in fact, he's positively blindfolded when it comes to thinking in eternal terms.

Nothing of this world *will* last, but the man who clearly sees past his own funeral service is the one who may well avoid a severe crisis at mid-life. Such a man is truly wise. Hebrews 9:27-28 states:

> Just as man is destined to die once, and after that to face judgment, so Christ was sacrificed once to take away the sins of many people; and he will appear a second time, not to bear sin, but to bring salvation to those who are waiting for him.

If the Lord doesn't return in our lifetime, we will all die, and much of what we've done will die with us. For the famous, a brief eulogy will be given on the nightly news; maybe some film clips will be shown. For most people, it'll be simply a short obituary in the daily newspaper, then services and interment.

But death will be a beginning for those of us who have received Jesus Christ as Savior—that's the hope we can cling to when our present life seems "meaningless." Instead of spending the second chapter of Ecclesiastes mourning the vanity of his earthly existence, a better recourse would be for Solomon to bow before God and seek a proper relationship with Him. It's hope beyond the grave that he so desperately needs at the mid-point of his life.

HATING LIFE—ECCLESIASTES 2:17-20

> So I hated life, because the work that is done under the sun was grievous to me. All of it is meaningless, a chasing after the wind. I hated all the things I had toiled for under the sun, because I must leave them to one who comes after me. And who knows if he will be a wise man or a fool? Yet he will have control over all the work into which I have poured my effort and skill under the sun. This too is meaningless. So my heart began to despair over all my toilsome labor under the sun.

Crushed by the apparent futility of life, does Solomon fall to his knees and beg mercy and forgiveness of the heavenly Father? Does he implore God to show him the meaning and purpose of life? To put it briefly: no! Instead, he lashes out bitterly with these words: "So I hated life, because the work that is done under the sun was grievous to me. All of it is meaningless, a chasing after the wind" (2:17). How about that? A man who has said, done, and seen it all decides he despises living! He hates his very existence, even after all the pleasures and projects.

Solomon's attitude isn't uncommon. Whether or not we're at the mid-point, life can be a gigantic hassle. Mark Twain wrote so many sage pieces of advice, but when it came to pondering the human existence, all he could say was, "Life is just one darn thing after another." I think Charlie Jones, in his book *Life Is Tremendous,* offers some worthwhile counsel when it comes to coping with each "darn thing" life tosses our way. Let's take a quick look at his words—he's a terrific motivator:

> Do you know what I like? I like to relax; I like to *talk* about work. I like vacations, conventions, commissions, salary increases, long luncheons. What do I get? Headaches, heartbreaks, turndowns!
>
> But do you know what I've been learning? If I don't get excited about what I don't like to do, I don't get much that I do like to be excited about.
>
> I've been learning that life is not doing what you like to do. Real life is doing what you *ought* to do (Jones 1968, 23).

"Oh, I hated life!" Solomon cries. I think he needs a dose of Charlie Jones to lift him out of the pits. And not only does our hero Solomon detest life, but he also hates what he has worked so hard to acquire. He says in verse 18: "I hated all the things I had toiled for under the sun, because I must leave them to the one who comes after me." He doesn't enjoy his new house. He'd like to slaughter his livestock and auction off his farm and ranch land. He'd like to drain the lakes and plow up the gardens and parks. He hates what he has labored so long and hard to produce.

Solomon is like many of us. In the words of American humorist Will Rogers: "Too many people spend money they haven't earned, to buy things they don't want, to impress people they don't like" (Tan 1984, 826). Solomon has expended huge sums of capital and immense energy on megaprojects. He's built things he neither needs nor, in the end, wants. Not only that, but the gnawing problem remains that he'll have to leave it all to the one who follows, a successor he can't control.

He continues his complaints about his heir in verse 19: "And who knows whether he will be a wise man or a fool? Yet he will have control over all the work into which I have poured my effort and skill under the sun. This too is meaningless." Solomon rails at the injustice of the situation. Whoever is next in line for the throne will inherit whatever he has constructed, right down to the park benches and barbwire fences. How much Solomon resembles a twentieth century man who has spent his life slaving for earthly goods, for success, for a corporate presidency. He arrives at mid-life and knows it hasn't been worth all the effort. He's bitter! He's angry!

Solomon, in sheer desperation, utters the words of verse 20: "So my heart began to despair over all my toilsome labor under the sun." Why is he so desperate? Why do his achievements seem completely hollow and empty? I wondered at Solomon's excessive self-pity, and then I found the answer by reading a little book: *Man's Problems—God's Answers*, by Dr. J. Dwight Pentecost. Pentecost gives an illustration that settles the issue. He writes of an ox and a lion, and I'd like to paraphrase his example here.

You see, God created within the animal kingdom the ox and the lion. The ox feeds on grass; the lion is nourished by meat. We can feed meat to an ox all day, and he'll starve to death. We can give a lion nothing but grass to eat, and he'll die. And according to Dr. Pentecost, man was created by God to be a spiritual being. A spiritual being can never be satisfied with material things. Just as the lion cannot be nourished by grass and an ox cannot be sustained by meat, so man cannot be fully satisfied by what is material. He can only be completely edified by spiritual meat (Pentecost 1979, 189). We're never content with the substitutes—they're like uncooked soy beans instead of medium-rare steak.

WHAT DO YOU GET FOR ALL YOUR TROUBLE?—ECCLESIASTES 2:21-23

> For a man may do his work with wisdom, knowledge and skill, and then he must leave all he owns to someone who has not worked for it. This too is meaningless and a great misfortune. What does a man get for all the toil and anxious striving with which he labors under the sun? All his days his work is pain and grief; even at night his mind does not rest. This too is meaningless.

Solomon continues in verse 21: "For a man may do his work with wisdom, knowledge and skill, and then he must leave all he owns to someone who has not worked for it. This too is meaningless, and a great misfortune." The situation with his future heir keeps bothering him. Life just isn't fair. A person performs his job well. Maybe he spends years in medical or dental school, acquiring much knowledge. Or with an MBA under his belt, he becomes skilled in corporate negotiations and he climbs the career ladder. Perhaps he masters statistics or marketing strategies. In other words, whatever he does, he does thoroughly and efficiently. Of course he makes plenty of money. What a pity that all he has acquired will pass on to someone who hasn't had to work for it, who hasn't had to gain the knowledge and skills he has mastered.

At mid-life, Solomon simply asks the question, "What is the use of leaving a bunch of things to people who won't care about them anyway?" Some parents feel they've done their duty if they give a houseful of furniture, a new car, and a substantial trust fund to their grown children. Folks, if you're in that category, you're making a big mistake if you leave your kids little to work for. They won't appreciate what they receive if it costs them nothing. Giving everything to an ungrateful child is indeed, as Solomon says, "a great misfortune." And yet, that's all he can look forward to doing at this stage in his life—it's a penalty attached to his immense success.

Several years ago a well-known comedian was burned severely, bursting into a human torch when he was accidentally set aflame. I recall listening to an interview during which he said of his experience, "As I was burning, I found I called on God, not BankAmericard." Under fire, this man showed phenomenal insight. There are just a lot of things that American Express, MasterCard, Visa, and BankAmericard can't get for us in this world, and the most important of these is spiritual peace. Only God can handle that. Psalm 73:26 states: "My flesh and my heart may fail, but God is the strength of my heart and my portion forever."

Solomon next asks himself the question, "What does a man get for all the toil and anxious striving for which he labors under the sun?" (2:22). I'm reminded of that Hal David/Burt Bacharach song, "I'll Never Fall in Love Again," from the Broadway musical *Promises, Promises.* An excerpt from David's lyrics follows:

What do you get when you fall in love
A guy with a pin to burst your bubble
That's what you get for all your trouble
I'll never fall in love again
I'll never fall in love again

What do you get when you kiss a guy
You get enough germs to catch pneumonia
After you do, he'll never phone you
I'll never fall in love again

Don't tell me what it's all about
'Cause I've been there and I'm glad I'm out

Out of those chains, those chains that bind you
That is why I'm here to remind you

What do you get when you fall in love
You only get lies and pain and sorrow
So for at least until tomorrow
I'll never fall in love again
I'll never fall in love again.

This poor girl—what does she get for all her trouble? Heartaches, lies, pain, and sorrow. No wonder she'll never fall in love again! It's hardly worth the effort. At mid-life, that's the way Solomon feels about his work.

Well, what do we get for all our trouble, all our "anxious striving," all our labor "under the sun"? Not enough, in the end. Solomon says of man in verse 23, "All his days his work is pain and grief; even at night his mind does not rest. This too is meaningless." Addicted to his work, Solomon has poured himself into vast projects and probably neglected his family in the process. Machine-like in his busyness, he has not developed deep relationships with others, sacrificing instead for the corporation and the almighty dollar. He's been the type of fellow who brings his work home, talks to clients and coworkers on the phone in the den, goes to bed thinking about the office. He can't even sleep at night with all the worry. This workaholism ultimately brings him only "pain and grief." Eventually, it all proves "meaningless."

WHAT'S THE ANSWER?—ECCLESIASTES 2:24-26

A man can do nothing better than to eat and drink and find satisfaction in his work. This too, I see, is from the hand of God, for without him, who can eat or find enjoyment? To the man who pleases him, God gives wisdom, knowledge and happiness, but to the sinner he gives the task of gathering and storing up wealth to hand it over to the one who pleases God. This too is meaningless, a chasing after the wind.

What is the answer then? When it's all said and done, what will bring lasting fulfillment? Solomon gives some valuable insights in verses 24-25: "A man can do nothing better that to eat and drink and find satisfaction in his work. This too, I see, is from the hand of God, for without him, who can eat or find enjoyment?" A man who enjoys the simple pleasures of life, and who finds satisfaction in what he does for a living, pleases God. And to the man who does His will, the Lord gives much, according to Solomon in verse 26:

> To the man who pleases him, God gives wisdom, knowledge and happiness, but to the sinner he gives the task of gathering and storing up wealth to hand it over to the one who pleases God. This too is meaningless, a chasing after the wind.

Becoming a workaholic, devoted solely to the job and nothing else, is a surefire way to determine personal failure. The man who pleases God is the one with his priorities straight. Read in the Bible about the lives of men like Abraham and Joseph. They amassed tremendous material wealth, but only because they adhered to the rules laid out in Joshua 1:8: "Do not let this Book of the Law depart from your mouth; meditate on it day and night, so that you may be careful to do everything written in it. Then you will be prosperous and successful."

It's the man who humbly, with a broken and contrite spirit, comes before God who will have a successful life. Bound by His unfailing cords of love, the man who recognizes that the Lord is the true source of happiness and fulfillment and places his trust in Him, will find peace in a reservoir of spiritual wealth. That man will learn to find meaning and purpose in life because God is the One in whose orbit he operates . . . and breaking out of that control means getting lost in space.

LESSONS

There's a great deal that we can learn from Solomon's plight in Ecclesiastes 2. Let's apply God's Word to our lives and look briefly at some lessons from the text we've considered.

Lesson number one: *the pursuit of pleasure will only leave us thirsty.* We'll want "one more time for the old times" over and over again.

Lesson two: *cheering oneself with wine and folly will simply end in futility.*

Lesson three: *there is no valid purpose in becoming a workaholic.* We won't be happy.

Number four: *possessions and pleasures don't bring lasting satisfaction either.*

Five: *frustration occurs when we have to leave everything we have acquired to others who won't appreciate it.*

Six: *man will only find satisfaction in his work when he does it for the glory of God.* Solomon lets us know that whatever is only "under the sun" is "meaningless, a chasing after the wind." God designed life and work for us to enjoy, and for us to glorify Him in the process.

And lesson seven: *a man shows what he is by what he does with what he has.* Ephesians 6:7 contains the exhortation: "Serve wholeheartedly, as if you were serving the Lord, not men." This admonition is given to slaves. How much easier it should be for us, as free men, to do our work with the proper attitude, remembering that it is Christ who employs us, in the long run! Let's never forget that, especially at mid-life. Focusing on Jesus Christ is the answer, even to the pressure-packed busyness of work-a-day life.

TOO BUSY TO ENJOY IT

I was talking to one of my buddies the other day. He's making money hand over fist in his business. He and his wife have purchased a new home and a new car. They've put a down payment on a lake cottage. Despite all the activity, my friend said to me, "I'm so busy acquiring it that I don't have time to enjoy it."

Does that statement describe you? Maybe at mid-life (or before or after) you find yourself engrossed in building empires rather than developing relationships. You're chiefly concerned with capital gains and you refuse to submit to the Savior's reins. If so, it's time to get your priorities realigned so that you won't "be weighed in the scales and found wanting," as was Belshazzar (Daniel 6:27). And balancing the scales from God's perspective means that more weight must be given to the spiritual than the material.

If you're searching for meaning through work, pleasure, drugs, sex, alcohol, or some other worldly means, you're going to come up empty. Like Solomon, everything you do will seem a meaningless chasing after the wind. You'll be "shooting the breeze," when you could be scaling the summits of God's grace. Think about it. Satisfaction with life, even mid-life, comes from pursuing reality, and it is God who must ultimately become real in our lives if we are to be happy.

Questions for Personal or Group Study

1. With what pleasurable pursuits does Solomon experiment in Ecclesiastes 2? Do they satisfy him?

2. What great projects does Solomon undertake in verses 4-8?

3. According to verse 11, what are the results of all his efforts?

4. What is Solomon's verdict regarding wisdom and folly in verse 15?

5. Why does Solomon actually begin to hate life, according to verses 17-19?

6. What does a man get for all his toil and anxious striving, according to verse 23? Do you agree? Why or why not?

7. What role does God play in our search for satisfaction in work? Refer to verses 24-26 when considering your answer.

8. In what ways can you apply what Solomon learns in Ecclesiastes 2 to your own life?

Whatever Will Be Will Be

Ecclesiastes 3:1-22

I remember arriving a few years ago at the home in Alexandria, Louisiana, of the couple who was hosting our Bible study series there. My subject that evening was to be chapter 3 of Ecclesiastes. I rang the doorbell and, after a few minutes, the wife answered it, looking exhausted and harried. "You won't believe this," she sputtered. "Both kids have got the flu, the dog is in heat, the dishwasher is overflowing, and we're expecting forty for Bible study. I'm ready for a mid-life crisis!"

I felt so sorry for her! But I don't think she had really reached the point of mid-life crisis in her life, at least not on that specific evening. Instead, she was overwhelmed by circumstances beyond her control. She couldn't cure the children, put the dog on ice, or fix the dishwasher. And she certainly couldn't phone forty people and hope to reach them all before time for the study. They were going to descend upon her house within the hour and she couldn't do a thing about it.

We made it through the evening. The kids suffered in silence, and as far as I know our forty-member class did not contract the flu; the dog was locked in the garage; no one noticed the broken dishwasher. Things had gone haywire, though, and the situations beyond her control caused that wife a lot of grief.

That's kind of what happens to men in mid-life crises, too. There is just an awful lot in this life that we cannot control, and that can be frustrating to us. It can cause us to want to try to fight against situations that God has placed in our lives, especially if we are weary and sick of the frustration. Solomon, in chapter 3 of Ecclesiastes, confronts the awesome desire to buck the Lord's plan.

We've seen him undergo so much. Remember that the stage for Solomon's mid-life crisis is set in chapter 1 of his book when he comes to the realization that there is no gain in what he is doing, that there is nothing new under the sun, and that nobody will remember him anyway when it's all said and done. Those beliefs form the foundation of his trauma.

Then, in Ecclesiastes chapter 2, we see Solomon caught up in the "Success Syndrome." He tries throwing himself into pleasure and projects—wine, women, and work—and he comes up empty-handed. In fact, he's even more upset than before because he realizes that he'll have to leave the management of all his corporations, lands, and offices to a successor who might turn out to be a small-minded incompetent. The whole idea makes him sicker than ever.

And as we come to the third chapter of Ecclesiastes, we'll view Solomon bumping up against another problem. When we understand a bit more about men in crisis, then I believe that the words of Ecclesiastes 3 will come alive for us. We'll be amazed at how relevant God's Word really is in the situation.

TWO STONE WALLS

Often men have trouble emerging from mid-life crises because of two factors—two "stone walls" which they keep ramming into and can't seem to scale. The first is stubbornness, and the second is selfishness.

Stubbornness—I think the epitome of stubbornness was old Harry Truman. I don't mean Harry S. Truman the President, but Harry Truman the crusty innkeeper who owned a lodge at Spirit Lake on Mount St. Helens. Harry refused to believe that the mountain would blow up. He wouldn't listen to warnings and leave his home for safety. And on

May 18, 1980, he was buried under forty feet of mud and hot lava and steam when the volcano erupted.

Men in the midst of mid-life crises can be just as bullheaded as old Harry. Their reasoning goes something like this: "I'm too proud to admit that I'm going the wrong way. I don't need any help. Just leave me alone. The problem isn't mine, anyway—why don't you talk to my wife, kids, boss, in-laws, etc.? They're the ones causing me problems."

In my experiences as a pastor, I have seen plenty of women lining up at my door wanting counsel in their marriages, but their husbands wouldn't darken that door for love nor money because they're just too stubborn. They think it's the woman's problem, not the man's! They're too proud to admit that they've got needs and that someone could actually tell them something that could be of help. That's just plain stubbornness, and we see a lot of it in a fellow in the middle of a crisis. Such pigheadedness is like going swimming with concrete blocks tied around the ankles—it's nearly impossible to surface, much less gasp for air, and it's very easy to drown.

The second problem often characterizing a man in crisis is selfishness. A friend slipped me a little poem the other day which fits wonderfully here. It's called "The Tea Party," and the poet, whomever he or she is, surely captures the essence of self-centeredness:

> I had a little party
> One afternoon at three;
> 'Twas very small, three guests in all,
> Just I, myself, and me.
> Myself ate up the sandwiches,
> While I drank up the tea,
> 'Twas also I who ate the pie
> And passed the cake to me.

Talk about egotistical—and yet a man floundering in mid-life trauma is often just as bad, making a habit of thinking only of himself, or as the poet puts it: "I, myself and me." He's tired of giving and he wants to receive and enjoy. He longs to be the sole guest at a tea party of his own making.

My wife, Pearl, is an expert at gently popping the bubble when I start acting selfish. I recall a week when I was completely exhausted from traveling and teaching classes, and I was facing the difficult task of having to conduct the funeral of a three-year-old boy the next day. I called Pearl on a Thursday evening and in my most pitiful monotone mumbled a few remarks like: "Honey, you know, I have poured myself into this week; it's the third week of the tour. I'm weary, and I don't have a word to say at that funeral tomorrow."

She hasn't lived with my selfishness for thirty-two years and learned nothing! Pearl's soft-spoken reply sliced into my self-centeredness like a saber saw into pine. She said simply, "Why don't you start thinking about where that family is coming from and what their needs are, rather than your own problems? Then, when it's all over, you can go get your rest." When she speaks, I'd better sit up and listen, and I did.

The problem is that it's easy to start thinking selfishly, especially if we become weary of good works. We begin to feel that we're being used and that nobody appreciates us. If *we* don't look out for ourselves, then who will? That sort of philosophy plagues many mid-lifers, and a whole lot of men flatly refuse to seek counsel.

QUE SERA, SERA—WHATEVER WILL BE, WILL BE

Why do people, especially those in mid-life crisis, react to their situations with stubbornness and selfishness? The chorus to a song that was popular some years ago sums it up well: "Que sera, sera—Whatever will be, will be. The future's not ours to see; Que sera sera." As I said earlier, God controls our lives, and there's really not much we can do about it because He is sovereign. The future is *not* ours to see, nor is it ours to manipulate outside of His will. Thousands of years ago He set the giant clock of the universe in motion. The winds and tides obey Him. Every millisecond of our lives is etched in granite and resting in His hands. In a very real sense, as far as our existence goes, "whatever will be, will be."

Out of Control?

The reality that his life is beyond his control may hit a man in mid-life hard, like a heavyweight boxer's punch to the belly. Not only does God dictate the movement of the years, but our middle-aged fellow's family, friends, and career may seem to function independently, too. His wife may begin to try her wings and return to school or the work force. His kids are probably typical teenagers who increasingly flaunt their independence. Situations at work occur over which our hero has no say; younger employees join the company and challenge his position. His boss fires, hires, transfers people, and generally operates without his consent. Even his buddies, his close friends, prove that they are beyond his dominion. Some of them change jobs or marriage partners and move away. One or two of them contract cancer or heart disease, and may even die. More than ever before, the mid-life man comes to the terrible realization that his world is humming along nicely without him and that he can do little to govern events.

Frustrated by this out-of-control state of affairs, the mid-lifer may begin to resent God's sovereignty. With characteristic selfishness and stubbornness, he may start trying to fight the system God has laid out. In fact, one of the main reasons a severe mid-life crisis occurs in the life of an individual is because he's attempting to combat something that God has permitted in his life.

The fellow in crisis is increasingly dissatisfied with the circumstances in which the Lord has placed him. Maybe he decides to leave his wife and kids. Perhaps he tires of submitting to the authority of his employer and hands in his resignation at work. Whatever it is that bothers him, there is a sense of gnawing unhappiness in his life. This unhappiness is really rebellion, resistance to God's will.

That is the position in which we find Solomon in Ecclesiastes 3, in a standoff with God. And the rub is that no matter how we resist, the Lord isn't going to budge till we break (see Psalm 51:17).

LEAVE IT TO HIM

We're lucky that God does maintain His command over our lives. It is more than important that we submit to His system—it is essential! In Isaiah 55:8-9 the Lord declares: "For my thoughts are not your thoughts, neither are your ways my ways. . . . As the heavens are higher than the earth, so are my ways higher than your ways and my thoughts than your thoughts." God's way of doing things is always the best. One of the most tragic pictures of human unhappiness is found in the book of Judges. Why? It's because, as Judges 21:25 says, "everyone did as he saw fit." In other words, nobody bothered to seek God's counsel. Instead, each did as he pleased.

Saul of Tarsus found himself doing as he pleased, and as he journeyed to Damascus to help wipe out Christians, the Lord struck him down on the road with these words recorded in Acts 9:4-5: "Saul, Saul, why persecutest thou me? . . . I am Jesus whom thou persecutest; it is hard for thee to kick against the goads" (KJV). In other words: "Isn't it awful lonely, Saul, kicking against the goads, trying to fight My will?" Saul was converted; he became the apostle Paul, and the rest is history.

Struggling with God is lonely for Solomon, too. At the beginning of chapter 3, he is a tired man. He has been looking for answers; he has fought; he has indulged; he has worked himself to the point of exhaustion; his marriage, or rather, marriages, are in trouble; his job is a hassle; his kingdom is crumbling; he can find no meaning and purpose in life. Everything he tries seems to fail. He's been living as though the grave were the end, and he is desperately unhappy. With that, let's begin to look at Ecclesiastes 3.

A Moment of Surrender—Ecclesiastes 3:1

> There is a time for everything,
> and a season for every activity under heaven.

With resignation and a sense of surrender, Solomon makes a surprisingly truthful observation. In verse 1 he says, "There is a time for everything, and a season for every activity under heaven." In his *head* he realizes that God has his life planned out. If only Solomon could admit in his *heart* that the Lord holds the recipe for happiness and that every activity under heaven has the potential to be an ingredient in that formula, he'd see a way out of his misery.

Time Enough

There is a time and season for everything, according to God. With Satan, it's just the opposite. Satan isn't concerned with proper timing. Look at how he tempted Jesus in Matthew, chapter 4. He urged Christ to turn stones into bread so that Jesus might eat. Eating is a good thing, a pleasant activity, but it wasn't the right time. The Father was going to take care of the Son in His own way, and Satan's suggestions were out of line. Later in that same passage, the devil begged Jesus to cast Himself off a tower, saying:

> If you are the Son of God . . . throw yourself down. For it is written: "He will command his angels concerning you, and they will lift you up in their hands, so that you will not strike your foot against a stone" (Matthew 4:6).

Trusting in the Lord's protection is a good idea, but the way Satan wanted Jesus to go about it was wrong. He wanted Him to tempt God, to actually dare Him. There is a time for everything, and this was not it. It wasn't the moment for Christ to fall into God's protective arms. Satan's formula is to take a good idea, a wholesome activity, and pervert it so that it becomes a wicked—and potentially dangerous—practice.

Many times in our own lives doing even good things at the wrong time can rob us of joy. We pick the flower bud before it's had a chance to bloom. I think nowhere does that become more apparent than in the days of courtship. Sexual attraction is high, and many of us bear the marks of guilt in our marriages because of actions we took before the marriage vows. A little discipline, the proper timing, would have made all the difference. Instead, we feel defiled.

It's very important for us rather to do as Proverbs 3:5-6 instructs:

> Trust in the LORD with all your heart
> and lean not on your own understanding;
> in all your ways acknowledge him,
> and he will make your paths straight.

It's the leaning "unto your own understanding" that gets us in trouble. The prodigal son had that problem. He went off into the far country, spent his bucks, lived the high life. When he ran out of cash he stubbornly continued to work for a farmer. And then as the little phrase in Luke 15:17 says, "he came to his senses," quit slopping hogs, and went home to his dad.

WHERE ARE YOU COMING FROM?

Many times men slip into shattering crises in mid-life because they are in "far countries" in terms of their marriage, work, and lifestyle. Like Solomon, life is bondage to them, not fun. If you are in that position and really desire to find out what's gone wrong, then you've got to examine yourself. Have you tried to resist God's authority somewhere? Have you refused to submit to Him? Have you become involved in situations contrary to what is said in His Word? If so, like the prodigal son, your life will literally reek of misery.

If you're not in a "far country" in terms of your conduct, then maybe something else is off-base. Perhaps you are resisting a situation God has placed in your life; you're letting the drudgery of the job weigh you down; you're growing tired of your spouse; you're sick of the demands placed on you by your kids. What you've forgotten (or maybe never known) is that every tear, every moment of laughter, every sorrow, every difficulty comes along with some purpose in mind—His mind, that is. As Joni Eareckson says in *A Step Further: "Wow! Sometimes as Christians we're just not given any choice in the matter. If we care at all, we have to handle things God's way"* (Eareckson 1978, 29-30, italics in original). And she certainly has a lot to let God handle since she is a quadraplegic and is expected to remain so for the rest of her life.

To everything there is a God-ordained season, and we are simply not equipped to manipulate all the events of our lives to our liking. When difficulties arise, we can respond in one of two ways. We can resist like Jacob and say, "All these things are against me" (Genesis 42:36 NASB), or we can submit like Joseph and state, "You meant evil against me, but God meant it for good" (Genesis 50:20 NASB). We can be like Jeremiah and complain, "Why did I ever come forth from the womb/To look on trouble and sorrow" (Jeremiah 14:18 NASB). Or, we can continue to trust as Job did, saying, "Though He slay me, I will hope in Him" (Job 13:15 NASB). Surrender or struggle: that's our choice. Chuck Swindoll sums up what our response to trouble should be in his book, *Three Steps Forward, Two Steps Back*. Says Swindoll:

> You can't carry yourself through the storms; it's too much for you. When will we come to the realization that the blizzards in our lives are allowed by God? Those threatening storms are designed to slow us down, to make us climb up into His arms, to force us to depend on Him.
>
> Maybe it's time to say, "Lord, I love You. Thank You. Through Your strength I will not be moved. I will stop

running, stop striving. I will not fear. I will hold on to You. I will count on You to build that tent around me and protect me from the blast. Thank You for giving me, in love, this blizzard of stress. Thank You that I can't even see the distance or the goal. I admit my weakness. I need Your strength (Swindoll 1980, 46-47).

Smack in the middle of a "blizzard of stress" is where Solomon finds himself as Ecclesiastes 3 opens. In verses 2 through 8 he goes on to give examples of fourteen contrasting experiences of life which illustrate just exactly how "there is a time for everything, and a season for every activity under heaven." Let's examine what he says.

A TIME FOR ALL—ECCLESIASTES 3:2-8

> a time to be born and a time to die,
> a time to plant and a time to uproot,
> a time to kill and a time to heal,
> a time to tear down and a time to build,
> a time to weep and a time to laugh,
> a time to mourn and a time to dance,
> a time to scatter stones and a time to gather them,
> a time to embrace and a time to refrain,
> a time to search and a time to give up,
> a time to keep and a time to throw away,
> a time to tear and a time to mend,
> a time to be silent and a time to speak,
> a time to love and a time to hate,
> a time for war and a time for peace.

In verses 2-8, Solomon muses, mentioning twenty-eight experiences which encompass nearly the whole of life. In so doing, he proves that there *is* a time for everything in God's plan. But as we discuss his reflections, we need to remember also that Solomon's viewpoint is that of a man in mid-life; some of what he speaks he says with a sense of frustration, an awareness that he bumps into the Lord's sovereign cycle no matter where he turns.

First, Solomon says, there is a "time to be born and a time to die" (3:2). How does that relate to the mid-life crisis? In middle age, we're sitting down at halftime reflecting on how we've lived, and we realize that our deathday is now closer than our birthday. Each day we live marches us twenty-four hours nearer the moment of our demise. We may get a little shaky inside as it becomes all too clear that our time truly is in somebody else's hands.

Only Jesus Christ has known with certainty the moment of His death. Not until after He triumphantly entered Jerusalem for the last time, did He tell the disciples that the hour was near for Him to be glorified (see John 12:27). Within a week He would be hanging on a cross, suffering an agonizing death just so He might pay the penalty for the sins of all who believe (see Romans 5:8).

Jesus knew His death date beforehand, but we never do. Even terminally-ill patients are not able to mark specifically the hour of their passing. We all know that death will come, but we're never really prepared for it, are we? Our time is truly in God's hands. That's what Solomon is trying to say in Ecclesiastes 3:2.

In the second half of verse 2, he continues his observations, mentioning that there is "a time to plant and a time to uproot." We plant gardens in the spring and then we tear them up in the fall—except for me. I plant my garden each spring; the sun burns it up in June, so I pull it up then! There's also a time to settle down, to "plant" roots in our lives. People change careers; they move and "uproot" too. To do some of this uprooting frequently becomes the desire of many men in mid-life. Job changes are common then. Moves are often made. I think of the story depicted on ABC's *20/20* news show of a successful Washington lawyer who reached a crisis stage in middlescence, packed up his wife and kids, and resettled them all in England. The problem is that an awful lot of middle-aged men are tempted to uproot themselves, split from the family, and plant themselves in a new lifestyle which has a minimum of responsibility and few binding relationships. There's the danger.

DESTRUCTION AND CONSTRUCTION

Solomon goes on in verse 3 to present two more contrasts, saying that there is "a time to kill and a time to heal, a time to tear down and a time to build." There is "a time to kill," isn't there? A few years ago I was driving along the back roads to Camden, Arkansas, to give a Bible study class, and two beautiful deer pranced right out onto the road. Hunting season was a few weeks away and I figured they'd be long gone by then, because that is the time to kill. If we shoot a buck before opening day, we run the risk of penalty. If we're caught, we'll be fined and our rifles confiscated. We won't even have any venison for the pot, either, because the game warden will seize the deer we've illegally shot. We'd better not kill anything until it's time to do so!

There's also "a time to heal." If we're sick, we go to the doctor, maybe even to the hospital. There's "a time to tear down and a time to build." A building becomes outdated and we tear it down. We rake the ground, lay a new foundation, and erect a modern structure which scrapes the sky.

JOY AND SADNESS

There is also, as Solomon states in verse 4, "a time to weep and a time to laugh, a time to mourn and a time to dance." When is there a time to weep and mourn? The Bible teaches us that there are three times when it is proper to cry: one, when a loved one has died; two, over our own sin and selfishness; and three, over the lost condition of those people around us who do not know Jesus Christ as Lord and Savior. Psalm 126:5 says, "Those who sow in tears will reap with songs of joy." Someday God is going to wipe away all the tears from the eyes of those who know Him. We will mourn no more. (See John 11:30, Psalm 39, Matthew 23:37, and Revelation 21:4.)

There is a time to cry and mourn, but there's also "a time to laugh" and "a time to dance." Why do we laugh? There is a little saying that, in a moment of spiritual victory, "joy is the evidence of the King in residence." When the Spirit of

God is flowing in our lives, there is an inextinguishable joy which is ours. That's the "time to laugh," and the "time to dance" as well. Take the example of David. Filled with God's Spirit he danced gleefully in the streets of Jerusalem on the day that the Ark of the Covenant was brought back home (see 2 Samuel 6).

LABOR, LOVE, LOOKING, AND LOSING

Solomon goes on to say that there is "a time to scatter stones and a time to gather them, a time to embrace and a time to refrain" (3:5). When do we "scatter stones"? We do this scattering when we're getting ready to make a road; we scrape and smooth the ground. Then we gather the stones again, add others, and use the gravel to pave the new street. We scatter stones when we dig holes; we gather them when we fill what we have dug. It's hard work, this scattering and gathering.

There is much more to life than just this sort of labor, however. In Solomon's words there's also "a time to embrace and a time to refrain." The apostle Paul gives us some instruction on how that principle applies to a marriage relationship. He says in 1 Corinthians 7:5: "Stop depriving one another, except by agreement for a time that you may devote yourselves to prayer and come together again lest Satan tempt you because of your lack of self-control" (NASB). The Lord knows us well, doesn't He? He provides us with pleasure, and expects us to keep it within proper bounds. Even so, as we've seen in Ecclesiastes 2, passionate extramarital pursuits often characterize mid-life.

Solomon goes on in Ecclesiastes 3:6 to proclaim that there is "a time to search and a time to give up, a time to keep and a time to throw away." King Saul went looking for his father's donkeys. Finally he heard from Samuel, the man of God, that the beasts had been found. Saul gave up the search (see 1 Samuel 9). There were ninety and nine safe in the fold, but the Lord went out to look for the one lost sheep. When He was successful, He gave up the search, but He wasn't content until He had all one hundred in the fold (see Luke 15:3-7). There's a time to search and a time to give up.

There's also "a time to keep and a time to throw away." No matter how we dread it, once in awhile we've got to clean out the closets, call Goodwill or the Salvation Army, and get rid of some of the junk we've accumulated. Husbands can be constant complainers about the unworn clothes hanging in their wives' closets, and that's ironic. Most women I've talked to claim that *they* are the ones who set household items out by the curb so the stuff can be hauled away, and then their husbands trot out to curbside and "rescue" all their priceless little treasures, carting them right back into the house or garage. No matter how we might resist, there simply has to be a time to keep and a time to throw away.

SAVING, SPEAKING . . . AND HANDLING SIN

There's additionally, as Solomon states in verse 7, "a time to tear and a time to mend, a time to speak and a time to be silent." If there's a tiny hole in the knee of some jeans, then it can be patched. A rip in the seam of a T-shirt can be stitched, but if the shirt is full of holes it would be more practical to tear it into rags and use it to wash the car. And there's always a "time to mend" in terms of human relationships, too. Many mid-life men mistakenly decide that healing broken or hurting relationships with their friends, wives, and families is not worth the trouble. Tragically, it may seem easier to make a clean break, tear themselves away from the supposed problem people, and begin anew.

Solomon continues in verse 7 with his wisdom, reminding us that there is a "time to be silent and a time to speak." Sometimes it's right for us to speak up, but it's easy to spout off before we stop and think. Most of us are tremendously gifted at cramming our big feet into our equally big mouths. James cautions us against speaking inadvertently, saying that "the tongue also is a fire, a world of evil among the parts of the body" (James 3:6). His is a broiling denunciation of any manner of gossip in which we might engage.

Tongues out of control pose a terrific threat where any group of people hopes for oneness of spirit.

And finally, in verse 8 Solomon concludes his observations of life with one last parallel, saying that there is "a time to love and a time to hate, a time for war and a time for peace." We're supposed to love the sinner, but hate the sin, aren't we? And what of war and peace? In his book *Real Peace*, former President Richard Nixon writes the following:

> Paradoxically, though war is obsolete we live in a world that is perpetually at war. . . . Since World War II there have been 140 wars, resulting in the deaths of over ten million people. . . . Because of the realities of human nature, perfect peace is achieved in two places only: in the grave and at the typewriter. Perfect peace flourishes—in print. It is the stuff of poetry and high-minded newspaper editorials, molded out of pretty thoughts and pretty words (Nixon, 1984, 3-4).

Nixon makes an insightful observation: man's sinful nature is geared for conflict. Matthew 24:6 states, "You will hear of wars and rumors of wars, but see to it that you are not alarmed. Such things must happen, but the end is still to come." Periods of war will explode our peacetimes until the Lord establishes a new heaven and earth for eternity (see Revelation 21). That's just how it will be.

WHAT ELSE?

Solomon has clearly shown us that there is a time for everything, hasn't he? Why has he spilled so many words in his effort to sum up life? I think he's trying to tell us something extra. In Solomon's way of thinking, there is a time for each activity, *no matter what*. Regardless of man's attempts to regulate his universe, it is God's sovereign purpose that he encounters time after time after time. And so the fact that there is a proper hour for each action is really God's idea, the Lord's way of running things. Man has to cope with the cycle of life as best he can, and at mid-life Solomon is plainly frustrated by the whole process. How can I justify that claim? Let's look at what Solomon says in the next few verses of the third chapter of Ecclesiastes, and we'll see.

WHY THE HASSLE?—ECCLESIASTES 3:9-11

> What does the worker gain from his toil? I have seen the burden God has laid on men. He has made everything beautiful in its time. He has also set eternity in the hearts of men; yet they cannot fathom what God has done from beginning to end.

"What does the worker gain from his toil?" asks Solomon in verse 9. Does that sound familiar? He said the same thing back in Ecclesiastes 1:3 while describing the foundation of his problem. To Solomon and to the man in mid-life crisis, God's sovereign holding patterns make life seem futile. There is a time for everything, no matter who or what we are. We'll be born, we'll eat, drink, tear down, mend, fight wars, and eventually die, and there's not a whole lot we can do about it because the Lord controls the outcome. Everything is mapped out in advance. To some of us that truth is reassuring, but to a man facing middle-age trauma it can be an upsetting reality.

Let me explain. Put yourself in Solomon's place. It's likely he's asking these sorts of questions at the mid-point. "If everything is planned out and there's a right moment for each activity, what am I gaining from all this sweat and blood? What's the use of this wearisome struggle? Why bother to fight? Why am I pouring myself into life, if ultimately everything about it is in God's hands anyway?" As he says in Ecclesiastes 3:10, "I have seen the burden God has laid on men."

You see, life has become a "burden" to Solomon. It's a struggle, a tiring and futile fight after which God dictates the final score anyway. His life is only a burden, however, because Solomon refuses to accept God's control. His existence wouldn't be such a hassle if he would acknowledge in his middle-aged heart that the Lord's way is best and that it's good to submit to Him. In fact, the burden of life would become an actual blessing if Solomon at mid-life would only submit to the plan of God in his life. If he would stop "kicking against the goads" of God's restraining hand, he'd find contentment. The same can be said of many middlescent men.

In an all too real sense it's true that in our lives, "Que sera, sera—whatever will be, will be." Things will move along as God dictates. "In his heart a man plans his course, but the Lord determines his steps," says Proverbs 16:9. When we stop fighting God's guidance, we'll find happiness. As Psalm 37:4 says, "Delight yourself in the Lord and he will give you the desires of your heart." When we, with joy and faith, commit our way to the Lord and trust Him to control our path, we'll find that He satisfies us. We'll discover that He is sufficient. Solomon is just barely beginning to recognize that reality in Ecclesiastes 3. We know he's starting to acknowledge the wisdom of God's sovereignty because of what he says in verse 11:

> He has made everything beautiful in its time. He has also set eternity in the hearts of men; yet they cannot fathom what God has done from beginning to end.

That is my very favorite verse in the entire Scripture! The "its time" of which Solomon speaks is really "His time"—God's time. The frustration of a mid-life crisis is that we become upset with the hand we've been dealt by Him. We want change now; in fact, we want it *yesterday!* And we're going to let the world know of our longings.

But it's true, as Solomon says, that man "cannot fathom what God has done from beginning to end." The apostle Paul echoes that in 1 Corinthians 13:12 when he declares: "Now we see but a poor reflection; then we shall see face to face. Now I know in part; then I shall know fully, even as I am fully known." Since we can't hope to understand the Lord's ways fully, we've got to trust that He knows best.

Until we yield to Him, life will continue to be a burden. It won't be a blessing, and it won't be very beautiful.

In His Time

Perched on a lily pad, his skin shiny with slime, the frog sat waiting, watching the large, juicy fly as it buzzed nearby. Eyeballs bulging in anticipation, tongue poised to strike and slurp, the little frog savored the thought of flicking the fly from the air and sucking it down. This was the highlight of his day. . . until the beautiful princess happened by. She planted a kiss on the frog's forehead, and he turned into a handsome prince. As that frog was changed into something radiant, so can God transform our ugly, sinful lives into that which is beautiful. The changes won't be instant. He doesn't use "magic." He acts in His time.

It's necessary to come to the foot of the cross and say, "God, I've been fighting the system. I'm lonely; I'm tired; I'm through. I've come to my senses and I recognize there's no way but Your way." That's surrender. The Lord wants to treat us like the prodigal son was treated by his dad when he returned home. God wants to place rings on our fingers, fresh, clean robes on our backs, and sandals on our feet. He longs to be able to say like the wayward son's father did, "Bring the fattened calf and kill it. Let's have a feast and celebrate. For this son of mine was dead and is alive again; he was lost and is found" (Luke 15:23-24).

God wants all of this for us, so what can we do, especially if we've reached middle-age and we're weary of the treadmill on which we've become trapped? We can get in step with the Lord. We can let His time be our time in all things: in family matters, career choices, friendships, leisure activities, financial decisions, hours of worship and prayer. Life is not some tube of toothpaste that we squish and squeeze until the last bit oozes out. Life to the fullest means surrendering to God's sovereign and eternal purpose, and finding the blessing waiting there. If we allow everything its season and proper moment as He dictates, we'll find satisfaction and happiness.

A Touch of Wisdom—Ecclesiastes 3:12-15

> I know that there is nothing better for men than to be happy and do good while they live. That every man may eat and drink, and find satisfaction in all his toil—this is the gift of God. I know that everything God does will endure forever; nothing can be added to it and nothing taken from it. God does it, so men will revere him.
>
> > Whatever is has already been,
> > and what will be has been before;
> > and God will call the past to account.

The next few verses of Ecclesiastes 3 show that Solomon is beginning to realize that everything in his life adds up to zero unless he includes God in the equation. In verse 12 he admits, "I know that there is nothing better for men than to be happy and do good while they live." He's getting smart, isn't he? Instead of struggle and strife, the appropriate alternative is surrender to the Sovereign.

Solomon goes on: "That every man may eat and drink, and find satisfaction in all his toil—this is the gift of God." We'll find satisfaction. We'll find fulfillment. They're gifts from God as we submit to His plan. Eating, drinking, working, and enjoying the lot that the Lord has given us—those are the keys to satisfaction.

Solomon levels a third shot of wisdom at us in verse 14: "I know that everything God does will endure forever; nothing can be added to it and nothing taken from it. God does it, so men will revere him." When the Lord's hand is in something, it will be lasting. It will be of substance. It won't break down, spring a leak, or blow a gasket. Without the Maker, man's feeble efforts to run his own life are doomed from the start.

The Danger of Trying to Untangle Yourself

That makes me think of some of our salmon fishing trips in recent years. I love that sport. When we take a group of men to the Northwest for their first try at salmon, I always make a point of giving them specific instructions on how to use the special rods and reels needed. No matter how much I explain and explain, after the first cast with a star drag reel, somebody will get tangled up, his line a gigantic snarled mess. And it never fails—before bringing me his tangled rig, that fellow will try to smooth things out himself. The result? Usually the line is in worse shape when I finally get to it because the guy trying to do the unraveling didn't even know where to begin.

That's similar to what we frequently do in our own lives, too. When we encounter problems, when we face situations which make us uneasy, when we start to become unhappy with circumstances in our lives, we try to work things out ourselves. Just like those fishermen, we get our lives tied up in backlashes and granny knots, and we try to unsnarl the confusion on our own. It doesn't work, either. It's not until we can say, "God—here, take it! Please fix it!" that we'll see results.

Too often for our own good, we prefer to attempt to work things out ourselves, without consulting the Lord for help. Flying solo in mid-life can be especially damaging because the man in his middle years is responsible for many people. He probably holds an integral position in his company; he has responsibilities in the community; his family depends on him. When he faces problems and starts to question the worth of keeping on in the lifestyle God has designed for him, then disaster is imminent, especially if he insists on attempting to resolve his troubles by himself.

I'm reminded of a friend of mine, a frustrated mechanic. If he takes the car to the shop to get it fixed and it still seems just a tad off, he starts messing with the carburetor and the points. Pretty soon the car sits there and it won't start at all any more. What does my pal do? He blames the mechanic for the problem, even though he's been tinkering with the motor himself. You know, he's got four cars in his driveway, a lawn mower and tractor in his garage, and none of them work! We mustn't let our lives get like those broken pieces of machinery. Rather than going it alone, we ought to let an expert, the heavenly Father, handle our hassles and smooth out our rough spots.

Proverbs 16:3 says: "Commit your works to the Lord,/ And your plans will be established" (NASB). We're not master repairmen when it comes to fixing our own lives. Only God has that classification. In Ecclesiastes 3, Solomon begins to realize the truth of that statement. He also starts to recognize some of his own mistakes.

FORCED TO "FESS UP"

He says in verse 15: "Whatever is has already been, and what will be has been before; and God will call the past to account." Fed up with the life God has given him, Solomon has been bucking the power structure by trying to find fulfillment on his own. He's getting a little shaky about his efforts, too. He realizes that "God will call the past to account," that he'll have to answer to the Lord for some of the actions he's taken. He'll be held accountable for all of the years that he has lived chiefly for himself.

As Christians we'll all face that day of reckoning. If we've accepted Jesus Christ as Savior, we'll end up in heaven someday, but not without being forced to acknowledge how often we've failed in this life. In Romans 14:12 we read, "So then, each of us will give an account of himself to God." (See also 2 Corinthians 5:10.) While we won't lose our salvation, we'll be forced to witness a virtual parade of our mistakes. That's reason enough to iron out the wrinkles in our relationship with God here and now, isn't it?

MORE OF JUDGMENT—ECCLESIASTES 3:16-17

> And I saw something else under the sun:
>   In the place of judgment—
>   wickedness was there,
>   in the place of justice—wickedness
>   was there.
>   I thought in my heart,
>   "God will bring to judgment
>   both the righteous and the wicked,
>   for there will be a time for every activity,
>   a time for every deed."

The Lord is perfectly just and totally merciful. He lays out His requirements for us in His Word. By accepting the sacrifice of Christ on the cross, we insure ourselves an eternity with Him, even though we'll become aware of just how willful and sinful we have been. There is a sharp contrast between the systems of justice of God and men. Solomon points this out in Ecclesiastes 3:16: "And I saw something else under the sun: In the place of judgment— wickedness was there, in the place of justice—wickedness was there."

He means that in this world there are evil men in the courts who finagle the law to their own purposes. That was true in Solomon's time, and it's still true today. By the time we reach our middle years, we've seen so many episodes of injustice that the last youthful sparks of idealism are squashed. That's right where Solomon is in Ecclesiastes 3:16.

In verse 17 he continues his observations and gives us a key message which lets us know that he is still caught up in the vain attempt to fight God's sovereignty. Says Solomon, "I thought in my heart, 'God will bring to judgment both the righteous and the wicked, for there will be a time for every activity, a time for every deed' " (3:17). The righteous will be judged before the judgment seat of Christ, as we've mentioned earlier. The wicked—those who have not been made righteous through faith in the finished work of Christ on the cross—will stand before the great white throne and be judged eternally (see Revelation 20:11-15). Why? As Solomon states, "There will be a time for every activity, a time for every deed."

Even in the face of death and judgment, God is in control. What Solomon is saying is essentially this: "I am locked into the sovereign purpose of God and I will never be free from it. One day I will have to give an account of my relationship to that sovereign purpose. There's no escape." The supreme selfishness in which he has wallowed for years has caught up with Solomon at mid-life. His wrong priorities and mixed-up lifestyle have set him apart from God's ideal. And the fact that he will eventually be accountable for his behavior bothers him greatly.

ONLY ANOTHER ANIMAL?—ECCLESIASTES 3:18-21

> I also thought, "As for men, God tests them so that
> they may see that they are like the animals. Man's fate
> is like that of the animals; the same fate awaits them
> both: As one dies, so dies the other. All have the same
> breath; man has no advantage over the animal. Every-
> thing is meaningless. All go to the same place; all
> come from dust, and to dust all return. Who knows if
> the spirit of man rises upward and if the spirit of the
> animal goes down into the earth?"

Solomon in Ecclesiastes 3 reveals that he feels a bit guilty.
He transmits a few sparks of wisdom as he admits some of
his mistakes. Even so, he is still in the midst of crisis, still
depressed, still pessimistic about life. Just look at what he
says in verse 18: "I also thought, 'As for men, God tests
them so that they may see that they are like the animals.' "
That idea bothers us, doesn't it? Solomon approaches the
end of the chapter and decides to wrap things up by saying
that men are exactly like the animals and that God wants
us to share that conclusion, so He tests us. Is Solomon
right?

Let's consider what a test does to us. When we are under
stress, we discover just how selfish we really are, don't we?
If we're under the gun it's easy to think in terms of Number
One. "How am *I* going to get out of this mess?" we ask.
"Who can help *me*?" Those are our concerns—selfishness
supreme. We *are* just like the animals in that sense.

If you don't think the animal world is a world of self-
centeredness, consider these examples. Lion cubs don't take
turns when it comes to mealtime. They claw and push and
shove each other away in their desire to get some milk
from Mama Cat. Fish zip to the surface of the aquarium as
soon as the food is sprinkled in. We used to have a little
neon tetra that could gobble fish food faster than any other
aquatic creature in the tank. That fish had no scruples
about consuming the last morsel! We're like that. When
things fall apart, we think of ourselves first and foremost.

We forget everyone else, figuring we really aren't responsible for those people anyway.

That's precisely the message of John Denver's song, "Seasons of the Heart," mentioned earlier. A little stress hits the marriage, and as the lyrics so graphically tell: "Love is the reason I came here in the first place. Love is now the reason I must go." When we emit that kind of a selfish response, how different are we from the animals, really?

Solomon draws another parallel between man and beast in verse 19: "Man's fate is like that of the animals; the same fate awaits them both: As one dies, so dies the other. All have the same breath; man has no advantage over the animal. Everything is meaningless." Remember we said that in the midst of his mid-life crisis, Solomon, like many other men, views life as bounded only by the grave? It's ashes to ashes and dust to dust and nothing more, to his way of thinking. A billionaire will end up with the same reward as his pedigreed pet, so what's the use of trying?

I believe that Solomon speaks the words of verse 19 and those of verses 20 and 21 because he is in the grip of a severe depression which will become more evident in later chapters. Consider the comparisons he draws between men and animals in Ecclesiastes 3:20-21: "All go to the same place; all come from dust, and to dust all return. Who knows if the spirit of man rises upward and if the spirit of the animal goes down into the earth?" Are those rational statements? I don't think so.

When a man feels hemmed in by his problems, when he feels crowded by circumstances, when he's compelled to take a long, hard, revealing look at himself, he often reacts by making some brash statements that he doesn't really mean. Solomon is being forced to realize that he is engaged in a losing battle with God; there's no way he can avoid the Lord's sovereign purpose. In retaliation and frustration, he spits out a few wild, senseless comments. Could he really feel that "man has no advantage over the animal"? I'd say at the very least even Solomon would have to admit that his plush palace is a lot more comfortable than the foul caves which house the wolves and bears. He's not being rational, and his remarks betray his dejection.

Solomon resembles the fellow who wails, "Oh, I can't go on! I am finished. I've had it! I'm quitting! I don't care if they fire me—I'm through!" Many of us have made similar statements, but most of the time we don't really mean them.

Recall, if you will, that in Ecclesiastes 2:16 Solomon says, "For the wise man, like the fool, will not be long remembered; in days to come both will be forgotten." These sentiments are repeated at the end of chapter 3, and they mirror sharply the attitudes of many men in mid-life crisis. Basically, the philosophy is this: Look, there might not be any life after death, so I'd better grab for all the gusto I can because this is all I've got. I've got one chance for happiness, and I am going to reach for it. The family can get along without me. I just want to put myself first for once in my life, before it's too late.

That kind of thinking enshrouds the man in crisis. The grave is the end, he figures. That's not what the Bible says. Jesus closes the beatitudes by telling His audience, "Rejoice and be glad, because great is your reward in heaven" (Matthew 5:12). Beyond physical death, there is eternity.

Solomon hasn't reached the point of accepting that, however. He's still stuck in the middle of an enormous pessimism. Yet there is a glimmer of hope that we'll see when we read his final statement in chapter 3.

MERELY A GLIMMER—ECCLESIASTES 3:22

So I saw that there is nothing better for a man than to enjoy his work, because that is his lot. For who can bring him to see what will happen after him?

In verse 22 Solomon reveals that he is begrudgingly getting his act together, at least partly. He admits that "there is nothing better for a man than to enjoy his work. . . . For who can bring him to see what will happen after him?" In other words, it's good for man to do his best to be content with the circumstances God has permitted. The future is not ours to see, and struggle in the face of that reality is pointless.

Solomon has not solved all of his mid-life problems by any means. He still has some tremendous hurdles to overcome. Even so, by the end of Ecclesiastes 3, he is at least willing to admit that surrender to God's sovereign purpose in his life is probably his best bet for happiness. He admits the truth, but is he willing to act on that opinion? We'll see.

LESSONS

For the present, let's look at some of the lessons we can learn from this chapter of Ecclesiastes.

Lesson number one: *there is a time for everything and a season for every activity.* As he did with Christ, Satan will always tempt us with the right thing at the wrong time. We must be careful.

Lesson two: *a man in mid-life crisis is often found rebelling against God's eternal purpose.* Maybe he longs to escape from the family responsibilities the Lord has designed for him. Whatever the circumstance, the fellow in crisis fails to synchronize himself with God's plan.

Lesson three: *God sees the total picture of our lives and is working all the details together for good, whether we believe it or not.* Even seemingly senseless situations have eternal purposes. As Joni Eareckson writes of her attempts to discern the Lord's reasons for permitting her paralysis:

> There's nothing like seeing our difficulties from God's perspective. But what a mistake to think that I would ever be able to complete the *whole* puzzle of suffering. For wisdom is more than just seeing our problems through God's eyes—it's also trusting Him even when the pieces don't seem to fit (Eareckson 1978, 172).

Number four: *cooperating with God's plan brings joy and fulfillment.* Solomon grudgingly comes to that conclusion as chapter 3 ends. The seventeenth century French churchman Fenelon said it this way: "And you will be better off both physically and spiritually when you quietly place everything in God's hands" (Fenelon 1973, 36).

Lesson five: *the Lord will bring to judgment both the wicked and the righteous.* We shall be held responsible for our actions, reaping eventually what we sow.

And finally, number six: *suffering reveals the stubborn or submissive heart.* If our hearts are stubborn, like Solomon we'll become bitter and resentful under pressure. If our hearts are submissive, we'll learn from what the Lord has given us. We'll make adversity a climbing block toward something better in the future.

Where to Go from Here

If you are unhappy with your life the way it is, you have some choices. First, if you have not accepted Jesus Christ as Savior, now is the time to do so. Read the Bible. Discover the resources available through the risen Lord. And ask Him to come into your life and take over. Your problems will not magically disappear, but you will find the strength to cope and eventually to triumph.

What if you are already a believer? Then take a reading on your relationship with God. Are you staying in the Word? Are you talking to the Lord in prayer? Are you being sensitive to that still, small voice within that is saying, "This is the way; walk in it" (Isaiah 30:21)? Are you letting God order your steps? Whatever the problem—midlife trauma or some other difficulty—the solution won't come until after you surrender to His sovereignty.

Questions for Personal or Group Study

1. Do you agree with Solomon when he says in Ecclesiastes 3:1 that there is "a time for everything, and a season for every activity under heaven"?

2. What fourteen contrasting experiences does Solomon use to summarize life (refer to verses 2-8)?

3. What is Solomon's opinion of God's design for man's life (refer to verse 10)? Do you agree? Why or why not?

4. What does Solomon admit that God has done, according to verse 11? Do you think that God's action in this instance has any significance for your own life? Explain.

5. What is God going to do eventually, according to verse 15?

6. Do you feel that Solomon's conclusion about man's justice in verse 16 is accurate? Why or why not?

7. Do you agree with Solomon when he states in verses 18-21 that man is just like the animals? Explain your opinion.

8. What lesson(s), if any, have you learned from this study?

Caught in the Corporate Squeeze

Ecclesiastes 4:1–5:7

Erma Bombeck once called mid-life the "metallic age"—silver in the hair, gold in the mouth, and lead in the britches! And she's right! When we reach our forties and fifties the "bridge over troubled waters" might turn out to be something we wear in our mouths!

Mid-life can be a time of "troubled waters" in another sense, too, in that for many it is the time of trial, the time of what Rutherford called the hammer, the file, and the furnace. We are pounded, scraped, and burned by the hammer, file, and furnace of trial. Especially at middlescence, life seems to become just plain rough.

We expect some of the difficulties. We know our parents are getting older; we recognize that tough decisions will eventually have to be made concerning their welfare. We expect that our own middle age will prove to be the time we have to say to our folks: "Mom (or Dad), you can't live alone any more. It's not safe." Difficult choices are put before us: whether our parents will move in with us, buy or lease a senior citizens' apartment, or enter a nursing home. We anticipate those types of trials, although we certainly don't welcome them.

Trouble spots on the home front don't come as total surprises for us either. By the time we hit middle age, most of us have one or two (or, in my case, five) teenagers around the home. No teenager is easy to live with one hundred percent of the time. All adolescents test their limits and we expect some rebellion, even from the most obedient of kids.

What we don't usually expect at mid-life is trouble on the job. It sneaks up on us, especially if we've been faithful workaholics, routinely putting in sixty-hour work weeks over a twenty-year haul. And yet difficulties at work happen quite often as we hit middle age. Gordon MacDonald states in *Living at High Noon*:

> It is a mid-life experience to suddenly come to the conclusion (or discovery) that our vocations, in one way or another, have "gotten us" or that they are just about to get us. My more dignified term for "being gotten" is *vocational entrapment* (MacDonald 1985, 118).

MacDonald goes on to explain that vocational entrapment happens as a man realizes that he is unable to extricate himself from a job and pursue an alternative career route. He is ensnared by what he has come to detest, resenting the job yet forced to continue because of financial, societal, or self expectations.

Feeling trapped is unpleasant. It can happen to anybody—no matter how far up the company ladder he has been able to scramble. If a man has arrived at the top level, he may discover that the view was not worth the climb. If he has been scratching his way upward but hasn't reached the summit at mid-life, he is forced to admit to himself that he may never get there. Either way our man is disappointed. Once a source of tremendous challenge—maybe even the focal point of his entire existence—the job can become meaningless, a pointless hassle, to the middle-aged man.

A feeling of career futility plagues Solomon as he begins to write chapter 4 of Ecclesiastes. By placing what he says in the context of the modern business world, we'll gain some fresh insights into God's Word. I think you'll agree that much of what Solomon writes in chapters 4 and 5 of his book sheds light on life in the corporate squeeze.

CAUGHT IN THE CORPORATE SQUEEZE

When chapter 4 opens, Solomon resembles the man who has spent his life slaving for the corporation. You know the type of fellow I mean—perhaps you're one of them. You've done everything for the company. When your button has been pushed, you've performed, despite the fact that you've felt dehumanized in the process. When you've verbalized your frustration, it's been met with the reply, "If you can't handle it, we'll get somebody else who can. If you don't do what we want you to do and move when and where we want you to move, we'll get someone who will." You've even seen the ax fall on people without any explanation whatsoever.

That's the world's attitude: everything for the sake of the corporation and its profit margin. The corporate treadmill can make anyone fit for a mid-life crisis. In fact, the three wrong perspectives which mark Solomon and other men in crisis are really natural outgrowths of a life lived for the company.

Let me explain. Remember I said earlier that men in crisis view life selfishly rather than socially, apart from God rather than controlled by Him, and as bounded only by the grave. How well this coincides with life in the job jungle! It's "dog eat dog" out there, isn't it? Talk about living life selfishly rather than socially! It really isn't normal in the business world to look out for another person's interests. "Look out for number one," that's what we hear. That's why salesmen unload shoddy merchandise, supervisors pass on good ideas without giving credit to the subordinates who thought them up, and anyone who makes a miscalculation tries to blame the mistake on somebody else. Pass the buck before it's too late, people think. Do it to them before they do it to you!

And isn't life viewed as apart from God in corporate America? I'm not saying that businessmen are never Christians; in fact, many businesses are run on solid biblical principles. But, by and large, the job jungle is a secular maze, not a sacred garden. It's life without a whole lot of attention to God. The typical thought pattern is that if an employee has a personal problem or a need for God or "religion," he ought to take care of that on Sunday, and leave it home on Monday—the Lord belongs in the church, not in the office.

A man running on the corporate treadmill is seen as heading only for the grave. There's no hereafter, only the here-and-now. For many a man the philosophy of "eat, drink, and be merry for tomorrow we die" provides an excuse for regular stops at the local bar and binges at conventions. It means he can cheat on his income taxes, his expense reports, and his wife, because there's no day of reckoning.

With the secular nature of the world of work, is it any wonder that so many men approach middlescence ripe for a crisis? Like Solomon, we're living the nightmare. And waking up can be very hard to do.

A Look Back

We've learned much about Solomon so far. We know he's unhappy in Ecclesiastes 1; there we see him protest against the meaninglessness of life. In chapter 2, he explores the pursuit of pleasure—wining and womanizing to his heart's discontent. He then pours his energies into massive projects only to discover that he's still not fulfilled. In Ecclesiastes 3, he expresses his discovery of an outside restraining force which constantly confronts him. He finds himself bumping up against God's eternal purpose no matter where he turns. In quiet desperation he wants things his own way, but God's sovereignty prevents him. And, at the end of that third chapter, he admits that his frustration is further compounded by the fact that he'll have to give an account of his actions someday.

When our relationship with the Lord disintegrates like that, when things fall apart on the vertical, the decay naturally extends to our horizontal relationships also. That's what happens to Solomon in this next chapter of Ecclesiastes.

BIG DOGS AND PUPS—ECCLESIASTES 4:1

> Again I looked and saw all the oppression that was
> taking place under the sun:
>> I saw the tears of the oppressed—
>> and they have no comforter;
>> power was on the side of their oppressors—
>> and they have no comforter.

Solomon's focus changes as chapter 4 opens. In chapter 3 he repeatedly knocked his head against the wall of God's sovereign purpose. In Ecclesiastes 4, he shifts gears—he turns from fighting against God to fighting man. He opens the chapter by telling us that he has seen "all the oppression that was taking place under the sun" (4:1). Things are bad for the underdogs—as Solomon says, "I saw the tears of the oppressed—and they have no comforter" (4:1); not only that, but "power was on the side of their oppressors—and they have no comforter" (4:1).

Wait a minute! Solomon is one of the big shots, isn't he? He's one of the men with all of the power. How can he sympathize with "the tears of the oppressed"? How can he understand life at the other end of the spectrum? I think I can explain that. Let's consider a moment just who Solomon is. In many ways, what he undergoes is not all that different from what a modern-day, middle-aged business executive might experience.

After all, Solomon is president of a major "corporation"—king of the land. At first glance, we might think of him as only one of the oppressors, the big men unmercifully yanking the strings of people's lives. But I think he also experienced his share of difficulty—oppression, if you will. Don't you think he ever had a Watergate-like scandal in his administration? Didn't some of his trusted subordinates ever misappropriate funds? Didn't employees he depended upon ever resign unexpectedly? Didn't he ever have to deal with people who were more interested in lobbying for their own interests than in doing the job for the sake of the kingdom? Sure he did!

Solomon can identify with "the tears of the oppressed." He's been there. His is a high-level competitive spirit living in a world of dog-eat-dog. He's shared the same feelings that overcome the fellow who walks in the door at work and hears his boss say, "Don't bother to take off your coat." He understands the emotions which overwhelm the man who has just been told some trite phrase like: "Reorganization has made it necessary for us to terminate your position."

No, he hasn't been fired, but as king he has faced the day-to-day criticism, disappointment, and heartache which come with the job. People have double-crossed him; he's been betrayed; so-called friends have sold out to his enemies; and even his job security isn't absolute. He faces daily the threat of losing his throne or his life if his subjects get tired of having "God's anointed" in the palace. The irony of it is that at mid-life Solomon begins to see himself more as one of the oppressed than as one of the oppressors. The view at the top of the heap only shows him that the scenery isn't much to look at.

THE TEARS OF THE OPPRESSED

How can Solomon's feelings relate to us? He reminds me of several men I have known—business executives, men in mid-level and upper management positions, who have allowed the focus of their lives to center upon their careers. And they've shed the "tears of the oppressed" as they've been edged gracefully aside or shoved viciously off the crosspieces of the corporate ladder. I can think of nothing more oppressive than for a man at mid-life to be kicked out the back door of the place where he has worked. The feelings of discouragement, loss, and isolation which Solomon wearily expresses in Ecclesiastes 4 are very similar to those experienced by a man who has lost his job or received a demotion at work.

Think about what happens when we're fired or forced to step down from a position. First, we begin to feel extremely lonely. It seems like we have been cut off from the rest of the world. I remember one evening not too long ago when I was teaching a class which met at a bank in a town in Arkansas. One of the men attending that night had been released from the same bank that very afternoon. Sitting in a Bible study in the community room of the bank from which he had just been fired was extremely painful for him. He experienced a traumatic sense of isolation and loneliness which none of the rest of us could identify with so directly. We feel completely alone when we lose a job.

Second, we feel left out. Everything we've worked for is suddenly gone, wiped out, snatched from our hands. We're no longer a part of the team. In my friend's case, the accounts he had handled were no longer his concern; the loans he had authorized were no longer his responsibility. Even the secretary he had hired had been assigned to someone else. It was worse than being a benched third baseman—he was made a free agent in the middle of the season, and no organization seemed to care about picking up his option.

Third, when we face a job loss, our self-image is dealt a tremendous blow. It's as if we aren't significant. What we've done hasn't been important enough for them to keep us around. We don't count. We feel just like a wife who has been replaced in her husband's affections by another woman.

Finally, fourth, we are deeply wounded emotionally. Our hearts ache because of the misunderstanding that has taken place. We feel rotten. When the going has become rough, the people we've trusted—the ones who have signed our paychecks—haven't stuck by us. We've been betrayed, and it hurts. I know. I've been there.

Back in 1967 I came to Texas from a wonderful ministry in the Northwest. I was happy and fulfilled helping to staff a ski lodge and a summer camp, and writing Bible study curriculum for counselors and campers. I was involved in a major conference center. Life was great. Then I was asked to come to Texas to help develop a new camp. I accepted the job. The challenges were exciting, the opportunities apparently unlimited.

My family and I worked to build that conference center. My wife even did all the cooking and the camp grew to be a large operation by 1972. But as the camp grew, so did some differences of opinion; the board of directors and I got to the point where we did not see eye-to-eye on some important issues. I realized that I was no longer a part of something that I had helped to bring into existence. Reality hit with an enormous thud when I was given three months' severance pay and told to leave.

I felt betrayed. I felt like someone had backhanded me in the face, kicked my shins while my head was turned, and then counted me out. I figured I'd better get myself a job selling insurance so that I could put my kids through college. I felt like one of the "oppressed" of whom Solomon speaks—like a man with leprosy shoved outside the gates.

No Comforter?

But Solomon maintains in verse 1 that the oppressed have no "comforter," and there he is wrong. My friend from Arkansas found great solace in laying out his situation before the Lord in prayer. I spent much time reading the Word and talking with God in the months after leaving that Texas conference center. To repair my damaged morale, the Lord used such verses as James 1:2-3: "Consider it pure joy, my brothers, whenever you face trials of many kinds, because you know that the testing of your faith develops perseverance." I can remember reading 1 Peter 4:12-13 also:

> Dear friends, do not be surprised at the painful trial you are suffering, as though something strange were happening to you. But rejoice that you participate in the sufferings of Christ, so that you may be overjoyed when his glory is revealed.

And 2 Corinthians 1:3-4 is a terrific source of encouragement when the hammers, files, and furnaces of life eat away at us:

> Praise be to the God and Father of our Lord Jesus Christ, the Father of compassion, and the God of all

comfort, who comforts us in all our troubles, so that we can comfort those in any trouble with the comfort we ourselves have received from God.

There *is* a Comforter: God the Father, the Spirit, and the Son. He bandages our wounds and makes us whole again. Even after we've been kicked out the company back door, He picks up the pieces.

Would you like to know the rest of the story? Within a week of his being fired, a job opened in a nearby town for my banker friend. He sold his house after it was on the market for only a day. I told him as he stopped in to say goodbye, "You've got a new missionfield." And he did. He trusted, and God took care of him.

As for me, that heart-wrenching job loss turned out better than I could have ever imagined. Six weeks after my dismissal, an attorney friend presented me with the papers for a non-profit organization he had set up. That was the start of Don Anderson Ministries, and I've been traveling and teaching ever since. It's one of the greatest things that has ever happened in my life. I would have missed so much blessing had I not gone through that trauma of years ago.

The Lord took our circumstances and created something beyond anything we had dared hope. That's the way He works when we submit to His authority in our lives. I think that the words of Job 23:10 speak to us all: "But he [God] knows the way that I take; when he has tested me, I will come forth as gold."

STILL A REBEL—ECCLESIASTES 4:2-3

> And I declared that the dead,
>   who had already died,
> are happier than the living,
>   who are still alive.
> But better than both
>   is he who has not yet been,
> who has not seen the evil
>   that is done under the sun.

In chapter 4 of Ecclesiastes, Solomon hasn't yet reached that point of surrender to the Lord. All he can see is the oppression, the hurt, the tears wrought by the power-crazy world in which he lives; he's tired of seeing the weak crushed by the mighty; he can find no comfort because he refuses to turn to the Comforter.

So Solomon continues in verse 2 with another lament: "And I declared that the dead, who had already died, are happier than the living, who are still alive." He says bitterly that it is better to be dead than to be alive, and we can sense that his every syllable drips with misery and resentment.

When we meet opposition on both the vertical and horizontal levels, it does get rather lonely. It's tough to have God and the boss both on our backs. Solomon is on the edge of that kind of despair; he feels utterly alone. When we place ourselves in that position—at odds with the Maker and with men, too—it's easy to develop a consuming desire to call it quits. Suicide becomes a viable option when we find ourselves fighting both God and man. No wonder Solomon muses that the "dead . . . are happier than the living" (4:2).

He takes his despondent reflections a step further in the next verse. "But better than both," he says in verse 3, "is he who has not yet been, who has not seen the evil that is done under the sun." Being born is just the beginning of our problems. We were better off before we ever entered the womb. What an utterly pessimistic outlook!

And why, according to our hero, are those who have never been born better off than those who are living and oppressed or those who have died? It's simple: the unborn have never been forced to witness "the evil that is done under the sun" (4:3). At mid-life Solomon has seen a lot of that kind of wickedness. Like all of us, he has suffered and has seen suffering. And we know also from his cynical comments that he hasn't come close to finding the answer to the despair he feels.

WHAT HE IS MISSING

What is the answer? Solomon has got to get his eyes off his circumstances and onto the Lord. That's the only solution guaranteed to work. "Through It All," that beautiful song recorded a few years ago by Andrae Crouch, tells it better than I ever could:

> I've had many tears and sorrows;
> I've had questions for tomorrow;
> There've been times I didn't know right from wrong;
> But in ev'ry situation God gave blessed consolation
> That my trials come to only make me strong.

> I've been to lots of places;
> And I've seen a lot of faces;
> There've been times I felt so all alone;
> But in my lonely hours, yes, those precious lonely hours,
> Jesus let me know that I was His own.

> I thank God for the mountains,
> And I thank Him for the valleys;
> I thank Him for the storms He brought me through;
> For if I'd never had a problem,
> I wouldn't know that He could solve them,
> I'd never know what faith in God could do.

> Through it all,
> Through it all,
> Oh I've learned to trust in Jesus,
> I've learned to trust in God.
> Through it all,
> Through it all,
> Oh I've learned to depend upon His Word.

> (Words and music by Andrae Crouch. Copyright 1971 by Manna Music, Inc. International copyright secured. All rights reserved. Used by permission.)

That song will always be special to me. A dear fellow whom I'd had the privilege of leading to the Lord was out with a group of friends waterskiing one day. The innertube on which he was lying was being pulled rapidly along behind a boat, when suddenly the pilot veered sharply. That quick, unexpected turn threw my friend off of his innertube, and he became like a fifty-cent piece, skipping along the shore of the lake. He died instantly as he hit a tree. He was only twenty-two years old.

His wife, pregnant with their second child, suffered through the agony of losing her husband. Four weeks after his funeral, I asked her if she would sing for the church. She replied, "Yes, but I will only sing one song: 'Through It All.' " What a testimony and witness that was as this beautiful girl, in the midst of her pain, raised her voice to the Lord in praise.

We can learn a great deal from that young woman. Hers was a proper response in the midst of trial. If we're being steamrolled by problems, we should do likewise. Does that mean that we get a grin on our faces and say, "Oh, good, I lost my job!"? No, but it does mean that we, like that young wife, should place our trust and confidence in the Lord. We can search for signs that His sovereign hand is at work, realizing that God controls each heartbeat, and that tremendous blessing can come from even the most adverse circumstances.

Solomon in Ecclesiastes could be so different. He could solve his problems, bury his crisis, if he would simply search for the Lord's hand in the middle of the adversity. Instead he insists on wallowing in suspicion and self-pity. He nurtures the feeling that God is against him and, in his defensive mood, the word "surrender" isn't part of his vocabulary.

THE COMBAT CONTINUES—ECCLESIASTES 4:4-6

> And I saw that all labor and all achievement spring from man's envy of his neighbor. This too is meaningless, a chasing after the wind.
> The fool folds his hands
>   and ruins himself.
> Better one handful with tranquility
>   than two handfuls with toil
>   and chasing after the wind.

Things aren't the way Solomon wants them. Rather than submitting to his situation, he continues to struggle. He makes a statement in verse 4 which further vents his frustration. He says: "And I saw that all labor and all achievement spring from man's envy of his neighbor. This too is meaningless, a chasing after the wind."

Solomon not only views the oppression of the corporate power structure, but he sees the competition seething between people who are clawing their way up the ladder. "All labor and all achievement" are the result of man's desire to keep up with the Joneses. People have tennis courts built, swimming pools dug, yards professionally landscaped, and interiors redecorated in an effort to maintain the suburban status quo. We've got to admit that what Solomon points out is true today. The longing to be ahead of others materialistically is a driving force in our society.

But as believers, we can be different. The challenge to the Christian is to allow God to take all of that inborn drive and channel it, not into competition, but into doing something significant for Him. Paul says in Philippians 3:14: "I press on toward the goal to win the prize for which God has called me heavenward in Christ Jesus."

In Ecclesiastes 4, Solomon is still stuck in reflecting on the envy and strife of the world. And look at what he says in verse 5: "The fool folds his hands and ruins himself." In other words, some people just give up! They grow tired of fighting God and hassling with man, and they fold their arms in exasperation, hopelessness, and despair. They don't surrender *to* God, but *in spite* of Him.

GIVING UP, IN SPITE OF GOD

One of my good friends in Tyler is a physician. He converted an old meat market into office spaces, and his practice is located in half of the building. The offices of Don Anderson Ministries are housed in the other half; we have together what we affectionately call, "the body and soul clinic." I get to see plenty of sick and dying people who have folded their arms on life and have simply given up.

Lots of folks literally mess up their bodies in one last

giant act of defiance against the way things are, against themselves, against God. They eat too much; they drink too much; they smoke too much. One cannot do that for long without suffering the consequences. As my doctor friend once told me, "People just don't care. You tell them that nutritionally they are what they eat, but that doesn't make any difference. They want you to stick 'em with something or give 'em a pill. Then they blame you for the way they feel and away they go. They're bent on ruining themselves."

One of my best friends died in mid-life from a bleeding ulcer. I loved that man dearly and I know I'll see him in heaven some day but, in all honesty, his lifestyle killed him. He sought release from pressures by drinking too much, puffing on too many cigarettes, and violating practically every nutritional fact known to man.

Our human tendency is to overindulge. Couple that natural bent with mid-life problems and we have a powder keg with a very short fuse. In the midst of rebellion each of us, like Solomon's fool, has the chance to be defiant by giving up on life, folding our arms, and ruining ourselves. We can neglect exercise and decide rather to eat, drink, and smoke ourselves into oblivion. If we're at mid-life, our bodies are beginning to show signs of wear and tear anyway, so why not accelerate the decline? That's the fool's way of coping.

A PEACEFUL ALTERNATIVE

In a flash of wisdom, Solomon gives us a much better alternative in verse 6. "Better one handful with tranquility than two handfuls with toil and chasing after the wind." It's better to have a little bit of peace than a whole lot of meaningless strife and struggle. Keeping up with the Joneses is senseless; folding our arms and giving up on life accomplishes nothing. Instead we need to be content with what the Lord has given us. I think one of the keys to becoming a fulfilled individual lies in being satisfied to live with less—a single handful of peace beats fighting for two handfuls any day. The writer of the book of Hebrews urges us:

Keep your lives free from the love of money and be content with what you have, because God has said,
"Never will I leave you;
never will I forsake you" (Hebrews 13:5).

That is real peace. And we'll only find it when we give up to God, instead of in spite of Him. We'll only find it when we turn over our problems, our desires, our disappointments, to Him. We'll only find it when we focus on loving Him. Isaiah 26:3 says it well: "Thou wilt keep him in perfect peace, whose mind is stayed on thee, because he trusteth in thee" (KJV). We can let our mid-life time of re-evaluation build to crisis stage, or we can hand over our questions, fears, and longings to the Lord. Peace will result after we legitimately say, "Okay God, it's all yours."

ALONE AT THE TOP—ECCLESIASTES 4:7-8

Again I saw something meaningless under the sun:
There was a man all alone; he had
neither son nor brother.
There was no end to his toil, yet
his eyes were not content with his wealth.
"For whom am I toiling," he asked,
"and why am I depriving myself of enjoyment?"
This too is meaningless—a
miserable business!

Solomon continues in verse 7, telling us that he has seen something else "meaningless under the sun." So far in chapter 4 he has discussed oppression: powerful people hurting others, employers mistreating employees. He has also commented on competition and its accompanying "keep up with the Joneses" mentality. Now he informs us of a third tragedy born of the corporate-like treadmill. He paints the verbal portrait of a workaholic who is completely isolated from close personal relationships with others, a "man all alone . . . [with] neither son nor brother. There was no end to his toil, yet his eyes were not content with his wealth" (4:8).

This is one unhappy fellow, and I can think of men exactly like him. They've refused to get their priorities straightened out with the Lord and have continued in their own forms of rebellion. They have emptied themselves into their careers, never taking the time to develop close friendships or forge deep commitments to others. If they've found time to marry, all too often their wives have become tired of being in second place to the job and have divorced them. Their kids have grown up and left home, having managed without too much influence from terribly-busy Dad. They find that their adult children are strangers to them because they haven't taken the time to really get to know them.

What's our man's eventual response? The reality of the emptiness of his life hits him like a ton of bricks. He wonders, as Solomon suggests, "For whom am I toiling . . . and why am I depriving myself of enjoyment?" In other words, "Why am I bothering? Why am I slaving at this job for twelve to fourteen hours each day? The only person who gets anything out of it is me, and I'm too busy to enjoy it." And the fellow wakes up. Hopefully, it's not too late.

Another of John Denver's songs expresses the frustration felt by the workaholic who awakens to realize the hollowness of his life. These words are from "Sleepin' Alone":

> For someone who's got ev'rything, life can still be rough
> If things are what you're lookin' for, there's never quite enough
> And all the tea in China won't make a house a home
> You can be a millionaire and still be sleepin' alone
>
> There might be some one night stands to ease the pain inside
> Or someone you can call around if you've lost all your pride
> Please don't be mistaken, I don't mean to put that down

I know there's times when anything is better than
  sleepin' alone

Sleepin' alone can make a bottle just about your
  dearest friend
Sleepin' alone can make you swear to God this night
  will never end

You know that it's not company you are lookin' for
You know it's not just pleasure, you know it's
  somethin' more
You know it's not the answer if it's not like comin'
  home
If the one who's there doesn't really care, it's worse
  than sleepin' alone.

Sleepin' alone can make a bottle just about your
  dearest friend
Sleepin' alone can make you swear to God this night
  won't ever end

For someone who's got everything, life can still be
  rough
If things are what you're lookin' for, there's never
  quite enough
And all the gold that glitters won't make a house a
  home
You can be a millionaire and still be sleepin' alone
You might be a millionaire and still be sleepin' alone.

As Denver says, "all the gold that glitters won't make a
house a home." Like the man in Ecclesiastes 4:8 who toils
ceaselessly and is never "content with his wealth," the end
result of such striving may be only loneliness and isolation.
If we see any of ourselves in that picture, we'd better ask
the question now, "Is it worth it?"

TWO BY TWO—ECCLESIASTES 4:9-12

> Two are better than one,
>> because they have a good return for their
>> work:
> If one falls down,
>> his friend can help him up.
> But pity the man who falls
>> and has no one to help him up!
> Also, if two lie down together, they will keep
> warm.
> But how can one keep warm alone?
> Though one may be overpowered,
>> two can defend themselves.
> A cord of three strands is not quickly broken.

Solomon evidently feels that there is a better alternative to being alone. He agrees that having company beats being lonely, since he says in verse 9: "Two are better than one, because they have a good return for their work." He's right. Most of the time, more can be accomplished two-by-two instead of in isolation.

Solomon continues in verse 10: "If one falls down, his friend can help him up. But pity the man who falls and has no one to help him up!" It's hard to drag ourselves up off the mat when we've been battered by life. We need some help in times of trouble. God knows that, and so He give us chances to develop friendships, to allow individuals into our lives to share both our triumphs and our trials. Many people find great consolation in the midst of trauma by turning to a friend for comfort. And of course the ultimate Friend that any of us could have is Jesus Christ.

I am reminded of a young man's account of the years he spent at Fayetteville, Arkansas. He was helping to establish a campus ministry at the University of Arkansas. The work was rewarding, but often lonely because Fayetteville was a long way from his close friends and family. In his first months there, he had made many acquaintances, but intense friendships take time, and the young fellow simply hadn't been on campus long enough to establish close bonds. He recalls the special moments he spent each evening walking to and from the dorms in which he was working. He walked alone, but not really, because in those times of isolation he poured his heart out to God—confiding in his Friend—laying his loneliness and fears at the Lord's feet. He found God to be the best friend he had ever had, and so for him those hours of forced isolation became times to treasure.

How different was this young man's response than the way most of us behave in the face of difficulty. Men only reluctantly turn to God or godly friends for counsel and encouragement in crisis. Instead, like highly-bred animals, they often run off and hide by themselves and lick their wounds. The apostle Thomas is a classic example of this "run and hide" attitude.

Do you remember when Christ made His first appearance to the disciples after His resurrection? Two weren't there for the revelation; Judas had already committed suicide, and Thomas was off in the woods somewhere, licking his wounds. His Master was dead, his world had crumbled, and so Thomas isolated himself and cried a lot. By declining to seek solace from his friends, he missed out on the chance to catch his first glimpse of the risen Christ (see John 20:19-30). It's so hard for some of us to share our burdens with others. When things fall apart, we do too, and we generally do our disintegrating alone.

Solomon sees the foolishness in all of that. "But pity the man who falls and has no one to help him up!" he exclaims (4:10). "Also," he says in verse 11, "if two lie down together, they will keep warm. But how will one keep warm alone?" There is a great deal of comfort in confiding in someone else. When we're hurting, we need that sort of comfort. We also need companionship, consolation, and counsel. We need to have someone say, "Hey, I'm for you. I believe in you. I want to help you." God will give us opportunities to establish relationships with other Christians—they are chances to be seized.

There's an old tactical saying that "the best defense is a

good offense." I disagree. I think our best defense against the pitfalls of life lies in developing relationships with God and His people. As Solomon continues in verse 12: "Though one may be overpowered, two can defend themselves. A cord of three strands is not quickly broken." In Proverbs 11:14 he echoes these thoughts with the words: "Where no counsel is, the people fall; but in the multitude of counselors there is safety" (KJV). And there is also encouragement, too.

I will always remember the beautiful time of fellowship which followed the death of that three-year-old boy mentioned in chapter five of this book. Soon after little George had died, his mother, father, grandfather, and I gathered together. There's not much one can say at times like that—the best thing to do is simply to pray. The three of them led in prayer, and it was a magnificent time of encouragement—courtesy of God in the midst of tragedy. I knew that the three of them would look to one another and to the Lord in the months to come, and that the heartache would be eased for each. Indeed, in terms of relationships, a "cord of three strands is not quickly broken" (Ecclesiastes 4:12).

THE BIG DOGS GET IT, TOO—ECCLESIASTES 4:13-16

> Better a poor but wise youth than an old but foolish king who no longer knows how to take warning. The youth may have come from prison to the kingship, or he may have been born in poverty within his kingdom. I saw that all who lived and walked under the sun followed the youth, the king's successor. There was no end to all the people who were before them. But those who came later were not pleased with the successor. This too is meaningless, a chasing after the wind.

It's true that friendships built on solid biblical foundations can be sources of great encouragement. These close personal relationships last; they withstand the test of time; they are not temporary or fleeting in nature.

I guess we might say that our friends will always be our

fans. The reverse isn't true, is it? Our fans won't always be our friends, will they? No, they won't. I recall hearing a statement made by former New York Yankees infielder Bobby Richardson when giving his testimony. Speaking of the public, Richardson said, "They cheer like mad until you fall, and that's how long you last." If we've achieved a measure of success in the public eye—we've been elected to the Senate, we've won an Academy award, we've made it into the starting line-up of the World Series—we'll be popular, for a time. We'll ride the crest of a tremendous wave of public opinion. We'll be the center of national attention, until as Richardson put it, we "fall." Then we'll be forgotten. Who remembers the names of the players who lost the 1980 World Series? No one except a staunch baseball afficionado even remembers the name of the team.

They also cheer like mad until you fall in corporate America. You may be one of the top dogs: your company's vice president of sales in charge of a six-state area. You're considered a marketing genius, as long as sales climb. Let the numbers drop for a couple of quarters, and the cheering stops. It's out the door or down the ladder a few rungs for you. The shouts of acclamation are replaced by something akin to: "The board feels that it is in the best interests of the company for you to resign." And the company then moves some bright, ambitious, young fellow into your slot.

You see, it's not just the little fish Solomon speaks of in the first part of Ecclesiastes 4 who suffer oppression. The big men often quickly and dramatically lose their positions too. Solomon reflects on the ironies of such injustice at the close of chapter 4. He says in verses 13–15:

> Better a poor but wise youth than an old but foolish king who no longer knows how to take warning. The youth may have come from prison to the kingship, or he may have been born in poverty within his kingdom. I saw that all who lived and walked under the sun followed the youth, the king's successor.

We see in those words the picture of a man who has felt the adoration of the crowds and has heard the praises of the masses. But he's been perched so long at the top of the totem pole that he "no longer knows how to take warning" (4:13). Like a corporate executive about to be asked to clean out his desk, the king Solomon tells us about will soon be replaced by a young fellow who has won the hearts of the people because he will listen to them.

The ultimate irony of it all is expressed by Solomon in verse 16 when he states: "There was no end to all the people who were before them. But those who came later were not pleased with the successor." Even the young successor will only momentarily hold the reins of power. Then he too will be cast down and forgotten. Oh yes, they do cheer like mad until you fall.

It's frustrating to devote our lives to attaining the topmost perch, then to be toppled from the nest. How well the contents of chapter 4 of Ecclesiastes portray life in the corporate squeeze of today, when both the chiefs and the Indians get scalped as the hatchets fall. Is it any wonder that Solomon, at mid-life, disgusted with the impermanence of "success," ends chapter 4 with the words: "This too is meaningless, a chasing after the wind" (4:16)?

WHEN THE FLAK IS BURSTING EVERYWHERE—ECCLESIASTES 5:1-3

> Guard your steps when you go to the house of God. Go near to listen rather than to offer the sacrifice of fools, who do not know that they do wrong.
>> Do not be quick with your mouth,
>>> do not be hasty in your heart
>>> to utter anything before God.
>> God is in heaven
>>> and you are on earth,
>>> so let your words be few.
>> As a dream comes when there are many cares,
>>> so the speech of a fool when there are many words.

So far every direction Solomon has taken in his search for meaning and purpose at mid-life has proved to be a wrong turn. His only real hope, as I've mentioned earlier, lies in shifting his focus to the Lord and in allowing God to straighten out those priorities which are misaligned. But even turning to God may present some potential trouble spots, as Solomon goes on to explain in the first part of chapter 5 of Ecclesiastes. It can really be too easy sometimes for a fellow stuck in the mid-life squeeze to look up for an answer. We must be very careful about seeking religion as an escape from stress and failure. Solomon cautions us about this in verses 1 and 2.

As Solomon begins to turn to God for answers to his mid-life trauma, he supplies us with three warnings. First, we are to guard our steps when we go to the house of the Lord. When we go to church, we've got to take the service and message seriously, not lightly; we must listen intently. Second, we must not be quick with our mouths; we must be careful not to say a lot of words that we don't mean. Third, we should not be hasty in our hearts when approaching the Lord; any decisions we make to follow Him must not spring from simple emotion. God doesn't want us to give fancy testimonies, sign pledge cards, or get baptized without careful and prayerful deliberation.

Often men in crisis do turn to a form of religion without bothering to conform to the stipulations Solomon sets forth. They grasp for God as frantically as if He were the last life jacket on a sinking ship. Thankfully, many commitments to Christ, made while undergoing tremendous trauma, are genuine and lasting. However, sometimes people only grab at God as a last straw, a temporary means of escape. Penned in their foxholes by the machine-gun blasts of trial, they make lovely promises to the Lord which they forget as soon as the smoke clears. As a friend of mine told me when we were talking about his war experiences: "When I was flying a B-24 on a bombing mission in World War II, I saw flak bursting all around me for the first time, and I promised a lot of things to God if He'd get me down out of there. God did, and I've forgotten most of what I told Him."

My friend reacted in a moment of panic and fear. He sought God as a temporary emergency exit from trouble, not as a permanent solution to the perplexities of life. It was not until later that he made a genuine, thoughtful decision to serve Jesus Christ. It is with deep understanding of human nature that Solomon warns us about making desperate pleas to God while caught in foxholes. I'm always suspicious when I hear about dramatic conversions experienced by people as they teeter on the brink of disaster. Charting a course for Christ demands careful consideration. In decisions about faith as in all things, we should be "quick to listen, [and] slow to speak" (James 1:19).

Solomon continues his advice in Ecclesiastes 5:3 with these words: "As a dream comes when there are many cares, so the speech of a fool when there are many words." When we are in the middle of an intense struggle it's easy to dream of after-the-battle possibilities. For a man on the corporate treadmill at mid-life, it's tempting to muse about what things might be like. He may wonder what it would be like to be successful, free of pressure, devoid of responsibility. He'd better watch his words, however—making sure that what he utters is not "the speech of a fool."

STAND IN AWE . . . OF GOD—ECCLESIASTES 5:4-6

> When you make a vow to God, do not delay in fulfilling your vow. It is better not to vow than to make a vow and not fulfill it. Do not let your mouth lead you into sin. And do not protest to the temple messenger, "My vow was a mistake." Why should God be angry at what you say and destroy the work of your hands? Much dreaming and many words are meaningless. Therefore stand in awe of God.

We must never take the Lord lightly. Solomon drives home that point in verse 4 by urging us not to delay in fulfilling commitments we make to God. In fact, he says that it "is better not to vow than to make a vow and not fulfill it" (5:5). We must not make sparkling but meaningless promises that will go as flat as carbonated water left open on the counter too long.

And Solomon utters a final warning in verse 7: "Much dreaming and many words are meaningless. Therefore stand in awe of God." If we want to emerge from the fires of crisis, we mustn't delude ourselves with visions of grandeur—they are the stuff that pipe dreams are made of. Rather, we should "stand in awe of God." We must respect Him and realize what He can do in our lives when we seriously, thoughtfully, deliberately commit ourselves to Him. There's hope in the trenches, even in the corporate foxholes, but we've got to be careful how we go about trying to grasp the rescuing hand of God (see Hebrews 2:1, 3).

LESSONS

From the passages we have considered, several lessons can be drawn and applied to our lives. Let's look at a few.

Lesson one: *oppression is a fact of life where there is competition.* There will always be somebody who wants our jobs. We can expect it.

Lesson two: *God hears and comforts the oppressed.* He listens to our prayers. He supplies us with His Word and His Spirit.

Lesson three: *two or three together are better than being alone.* When we're hurting, let's do the unnatural thing and reach out for someone else, allowing them to minister to us.

Number four: *we should accept the counsel of others.* It's good to go beyond simply sharing our troubles. We must listen to the advice that is offered, considering it thoughtfully and prayerfully.

Lesson five: *let's spend time cultivating relationships with members of our family and with our friends.* We don't want to become like the man Solomon mentions in Ecclesiastes 4:8, the workaholic who wakes up to realize that he is "all alone," toiling for no one but himself.

Lesson number six: *we mustn't be overly zealous in our religious endeavors when we are under a great deal of stress.* We should never make empty promises and meaningless vows to God in exchange for His getting us out of difficult circumstances. I'm not saying that we shouldn't seek the Lord, but we should not fall into the trap of thinking of Him as an emergency exit from trial. Making a decision for Christ should involve sober reflection.

BEYOND THE PRESENT

The sickrooms of the terminally ill have been the scenes of the saddest conversations I have ever held. The talk has been tragic when the patients have been unbelievers. Comments like these have poured out from the bitter hearts of cancer victims who do not know God through His Son: "I hate God for letting this happen. If God loves me so much, why is He letting me suffer? If God answers prayers, what about mine? How can I love a God who says no all the time?"

Like Solomon in Ecclesiastes, those patients were focused on life "under the sun." They couldn't see beyond the temporal into the eternal. They didn't have the ability to conceive of a heaven where the temporary pains and sorrows of earthly existence would be replaced by an eternity of peace and joy. Unlike those resentful sufferers, we must realize as the apostle Paul did, that the outward man is perishing, passing away, while the inward man is renewed daily through a relationship with Christ (see 2 Corinthians 4:16).

Such is the way of man. Such is the character of life. We'll fade away as the leaf. We'll be as the dust one day. Yet in the process of passing away, the spirit, the inner man, can be renewed day by day. It is this renewal which gives meaning to our lives, which enables us to keep our priorities straight and traverse even the pitfalls of corporate life without hopelessly losing our balance.

Questions for Personal or Group Study

1. Why does Solomon conclude in Ecclesiastes 4:2-3 that the dead and the unborn are better off than the living? Do you agree?

2. Paraphrase the thoughts Solomon expresses in verse 4 of Ecclesiastes 4. Are his reflections accurate in your opinion? Why or why not?

3. Have you known of any instances where people have, like the fool Solomon speaks of in Ecclesiastes 4:5, folded their arms, given up on life and God, and ruined themselves?

4. Describe the type of individual to whom Solomon refers in verse 8 of chapter 4.

5. Why, according to Ecclesiastes 4:9-12, does Solomon believe that "two are better than one" (4:9)?

6. What type of power struggle does Solomon describe in verses 13-16 of chapter 4? Have you witnessed any similar situations? Explain.

7. What warnings does Solomon give in verses 1-7 of chapter 5?

8. Name one lesson that you have learned from this particular study, and if you wish, explain how you will apply what you have learned.

7

Snared by Materialism

Ecclesiastes 5:8–6:12

So far we have heard Solomon protest at life's meaninglessness and caution us about the emptiness of pleasures and projects in and of themselves. We've seen his vertical relationship with God suffer some bruises as he bumps into the Lord's sovereignty time and time again. We've seen the disintegration extend to his horizontal relationships as he deals with corporate-like oppression. We've listened to his warnings about workaholism and foxhole religious commitments. Now, with fleeting flashes of wisdom, he offers us insights about the seductiveness of possessions.

We all have materialistic leanings. We like to own things, nice things. Some of us are more wrapped up in the material than others, even to the degree that we are possessed by our possessions, rather than the other way around. Materialism presents its own peculiar brand of snare to the mid-life man, and that is the trap which Solomon warns us about in chapter 5 of Ecclesiastes.

THE GREENBACK TRAP

I might have called this chapter, "The Misfortunes of Having a Fortune." You see, money is okay in the life of a person who is thinking of others. Once selfishness sets in, money becomes a snare. It is especially so for men in the middle of mid-life crises who have begun to view life selfishly rather than socially. Money can be a slowly seeping poison in the life of a man who has become tired of respon-

sibility. Sick of shelling out bucks for braces, club member-
ships, groceries, and station wagons, the man in crisis begins to ask, "Hey, what about me? When can I enjoy some
of what I work so hard to earn?" The greed is only made
worse by the fact that he also views life as apart from God
and bounded only by the grave. There is a desperate urge
to get all he can (and *can* all he gets), because death is but a
few decades away. Time is running out.

So materialism is an easy trap, one that is nearly unavoidable to a man like Solomon who is searching in all the
wrong places for answers to the questions which confound
him. Ironically, much of what Solomon has done in his
quest for meaning at mid-life has only compounded his
problems. The projects he has undertaken, the corporate-
like treadmill on which he has run, have generated big
bucks for him. As a natural outgrowth of pursuing earthly
goals, he has accumulated even more wealth. As his bank
account has grown, so has his unhappiness.

Let's look now at the fifth chapter of Ecclesiastes, beginning with verse 8. Solomon, in the grip of despair, manages
to give us some guidelines on dealing with worldly wealth.
He shows moments of great wisdom, as we see the faint
beginnings to the end of his mid-life trauma.

THE ROOT OF MUCH EVIL—ECCLESIASTES 5:8-9

> If you see the poor oppressed in a district, and jus-
> tice and rights denied, do not be surprised at such
> things; for one official is eyed by a higher one, and
> over them both are others higher still. The increase
> from the land is taken by all; the king himself profits
> from the fields.

Solomon's search for meaning at mid-life has indeed
caused money madness. Fiscal prosperity has been the natural outgrowth of his elaborate projects and financial
wheeling and dealing. But his bank balance hasn't brought
him contentment. The bottom line has only generated misery and oppression. Solomon feels no peace, and neither do

those whose lives are affected by his profit margin. Not even blue-chip stocks or a vault full of gold bullion can guarantee happiness.

He tells us in verse 8 that we should "not be surprised" if we see "the poor oppressed in a district, and justice and rights denied." Why? As Solomon explains, "for one official is eyed by a higher one, and over them both are others higher still" (5:8). In other words, the thirst for wealth and the accumulation of riches cause hardship for many. The picture Solomon paints is of government officials scrambling for power while most of the population is bled dry by taxation. Says Solomon, "The increase from the land is taken by all; the king himself profits from the fields" (5:9). Even the king benefits from the labor of the "little guys" (note 1 Kings 12:4). The love of money and the lust for power are catalysts for oppression.

Today we see a parallel to this situation in the modern business community. The goal of most junior executives is to reach the top, get the big job and earn the fat salary. In the process, the struggle for power is constant. Over the years I have taught hundreds of business people's classes. From time to time I have been given the use of company offices for my studies. I have had many opportunities to witness the corporate in-fighting and shake-ups that are by-products of the trip up the ladder. It seems that some firms conduct an unending version of musical chairs: new faces regularly appear as people are forced to leave the game, executives are shifted from position to position, from division to division. And when things start to settle down, the company is sold or reorganized, the rulers of the roost are jostled off their perches, and the cycle begins again. The scramble for prestige, control, and salary ensues once more.

Solomon simply tells us not to be surprised at such oppressive maneuvering. It happens. Money creates the kind of environment which encourages it. And often it is the women and men at the middle or bottom of the ladder who, like the oppressed poor of whom Solomon speaks in verse 8, suffer the most. Job descriptions are changed, positions eliminated, resignations called for, moves required, all at the whim of those in control.

AN ALTERNATIVE TO THE SYSTEM

Money, power, and position can never of themselves bring contentment to one's life. If the focus of a man's existence has been on the achievement of such, then it is not surprising when he suffers a crisis at mid-life as he realizes the emptiness of his goals.

In his book, *Between a Rock and a Hard Place,* Senator Mark Hatfield has a few words to say about the dangers inherent in the struggle for power. As a Christian in public office, he has had countless opportunities to witness the ravages of a power-crazy environment. His frame of reference is the political arena, but I believe that his reflections on the often subtle dangers of power are applicable to most areas of life. Writes Hatfield: "The allurement of power and honor subtly but malignantly grows within the politician, often gaining control of one's whole being before it is discovered" (Hatfield 1976, 17).

Power and position—whether financial, political, or social—hold great appeal for us. The desire to achieve these can exert a pervasive influence in the life of an individual, affecting decisions and directions, even altering ideals and standards. Once power and prestige are attained, they must be maintained. Their lure is self-perpetuating. The more we have, the more we seem to want. Yet whether we're clawing our way to the top of the corporate heap or we're running fast and hard for reelection, we find that prestige, prerogative, and profits alone will not supply us with genuine peace. Strangely enough, real satisfaction results not from scrambling to get to the top, but from stopping along the way to serve others. As Christians, it is in service that we find fulfillment. Says Mark Hatfield:

> Service to others, solely for their own behalf and even entailing deep sacrifice, is the true essence of leadership and the ultimate form of power. There is a power

in servanthood which transcends all notions of power sought after so avidly in the secular political sphere of life (Hatfield 1976, 27).

Hatfield goes on to describe the ultimate standard of servant-leadership as seen in the person of Jesus Christ. He gives the example from John 13 of Christ washing the feet of the disciples as an illustration. It's a beautiful picture. The Lord enters a room where His followers are arguing about who is going to be secretary of state in the kingdom. Their hearts are filled with pride; their feet are dirty. Jesus takes the bucket of water and towel and redefines leadership, authority, and power by beginning to wash the feet of each one present.

Wouldn't it be tremendous if each Washington politico, each executive, began to exercise Christ-centered servanthood? Rather than madly dashing for power and prestige, they would be "washing the feet" of their constituents, customers, employers, and fellow employees. It would be revolutionary! And it could provide each with the meaningful lifestyle sought after by Solomon and so many others who are frustrated and tired of striving for status.

NOTHING BUT TROUBLE—ECCLESIASTES 5:10-12

> Whoever loves money never has money
>   enough;
> whoever loves wealth is never satisfied with his
>   income.
> This too is meaningless.
> As goods increase,
>   so do those who consume them.
> And what benefit are they to the owner
>   except to feast his eyes on them?
> The sleep of a laborer is sweet,
>   whether he eats little or much,
> but the abundance of a rich man
>   permits him no sleep.

Money cannot bring happiness. It cannot satisfy. As Solomon says in Ecclesiastes 5:10: "Whoever loves money never has money enough; whoever has wealth is never satisfied with his income." That statement wouldn't mean much coming from me. I'm not wealthy, nor is it likely that I ever will be. But Solomon is the richest man on earth at the time he writes those words. Surely he has the authority to caution us about the impossibility of finding fulfillment in financial prosperity.

Young men in business tell me of two nagging fears besetting them. First, they are afraid of not being able to make enough money, of not being able to achieve and maintain the standard of living which they desire for themselves and their families. At the same time, they also fear that they will become slaves to the pursuit of money, locked into careers they do not enjoy ("Vocationally trapped," as Gordon MacDonald might say). They fear having too little cash and they dread with equal fervor the idea of being in bondage to the almighty dollar. According to Solomon in Ecclesiastes 5, those concerns are valid. Even billionaires never seem to have enough in the bank.

The apostle Paul gives us warnings about being concerned with padding our portfolios and augmenting our incomes when he writes the following to Timothy:

> But godliness with contentment is great gain. For we brought nothing into the world, and we can take nothing out of it. But if we have food and clothing, we will be content with that. People who want to get rich fall into temptation and a trap and into many foolish and harmful desires that plunge men into ruin and destruction. For the love of money is a root of all kinds of evil. Some people, eager for money, have wandered away from the faith and pierced themselves with many griefs (1 Timothy 6:6-11).

We brought nothing into this world; we can take nothing out of it. As one writer has said, considering the type of world it is, we're lucky to break even! It is both fruitless and dangerous to search for purpose in life by building our bank balances. In Solomon's words, such attempts are "meaningless" (5:10).

Besides, wealth brings with it all kinds of problems. "As goods increase, so do those who consume them," Solomon says in Ecclesiastes 5:11. Isn't that true? With lots of money come lots of "friends." People love to enjoy the prosperity of others. They like to go swimming where they haven't paid for the pool, the pump, or the chlorine. Those who "have not" welcome with outstretched open hands the generosity of those who "have"! As our material possessions increase with our net worth, so do the hangers-on who help us play with our new toys.

And what good to us, really, are all the fancy cars, houses, jewels, stock certificates, and insurable treasures? According to Solomon, who definitely ought to know, possessions are only good for their owner "to feast his eyes on" (5:11). They're pretty to look at, that's all. They give no significance to life. Actually, the things we acquire give us more worry than pleasure.

Solomon continues in verse 12 with these words: "The sleep of a laborer is sweet, whether he eats little or much, but the abundance of a rich man permits him no sleep." Why is the sleep of a laborer "sweet"? Think about it. A laborer works hard, earns a set wage—enough to feed, clothe, and house his family, and not much extra. He returns home each evening, bone-tired and muscle-weary. He sleeps soundly and awakes refreshed, ready for the fields, the road crew, the construction site, once again.

Most of us have experienced those days when the grace of exhaustion has made our eyelids heavy and our sleep easy. An accountant friend of mine, for example, finds immense relaxation in helping another friend work at his ranch. We might not think that a day spent digging trenches, spreading gravel, building deer blinds, and branding cattle would be fun, but it is a means of escape for my friend, the CPA. And at the end of the day, sleep is sweet.

There is another reason why the sleep of a laborer is

pleasant. His job has a definite starting and ending time—
he clocks out each night and leaves the work worries behind. No nagging thoughts and gnawing concerns accompany him to bed. Contrast that with the wealthy mogul:
Solomon says that "the abundance of a rich man permits
him no sleep" (5:12). With hefty checking accounts and
bulging stock portfolios come round-the-clock cares.

A business people's class that I teach is in a financial
district of downtown Dallas. Among those who attend are
corporate officers, brokers, bankers, investors, company executives—men and women whose sense of well-being can
all too easily become dependent on filling their quotas and
expanding their profit margins. One week I taught about
money, prayer, and fasting from the Sermon on the Mount.
The following week the lesson was going to deal with
Jesus' teachings on worry, so I told my roomful of fiscally-
solvent folks that I hoped the stock market would fall fifty
points within the next few days so they'd all want to come
to class and learn how to handle worry.

People can get so agitated about the stock market! If it
shoots up twenty points one day and drops out of sight the
next, so do they! Anxiety levels rise in our ulcer-ridden
society as the economy flip-flops. Some friends of mine
stagger around with knots inside as big as basketballs
when financial trends go from boom to bust. Their emotional security is entwined with the behavior of the economy; their concerns are many and their restful nights few.

AND MORE TROUBLE—ECCLESIASTES 5:13-17

I have seen a grievous evil under the sun:
  wealth hoarded to the harm of its owner,
    or wealth lost through some misfortune,
  so that when he has a son
    there is nothing left for him.
Naked a man comes from his mother's womb,
and as he comes, so he departs.
He takes nothing from his labor
  that he can carry in his hand.

This too is a grievous evil:
As a man comes, so he departs,
　and what does he gain,
　since he toils for the wind?
All his days he eats in darkness,
　with great frustration, affliction and anger.

Money can bring big trouble . . . and still more trouble. Solomon tells us in Ecclesiastes 5:13-14 that he has seen another "grievous evil under the sun: wealth hoarded to the harm of its owner, or wealth lost through some misfortune, so that when he has a son there is nothing left for him."

Wealth is transitory. Stock markets crash, sales fall off, businesses collapse, tax shelters fold, and investments are lost. More than one family fortune has slipped through the fingers of a generation of sons and daughters, dwindling to nothing before the next generation has a chance to touch it. It's altogether easy for wealth to be "lost through some misfortune." But wealth can also be "hoarded to the harm of its owner," as Solomon suggests.

In the October 14, 1980, issue of the *Tyler Morning Telegraph* was an article about Maddalena Borella, who lived in the village of Gorduno, Switzerland. Local children feared the eighty-eight year old Maddalena, and called her a witch. She never washed and never changed her clothes. She slept on a straw mat on the floor of a dirty, dilapidated hut. When she collapsed in the middle of the road one day, doctors said that she was weak because of malnutrition— she had been eating only one meager meal per day. Maddalena was hospitalized, then placed in a home for the aged. She died shortly thereafter.

Officials sealed Maddalena's hut, then began to search for her only relative, a nephew who was living in the United States. Once the nephew was located, the authorities inspected his aunt's tiny home to see what, if anything, was of value. To their amazement, they found a bank savings book showing that Maddalena had $312,000 in an account. They also found a key to a safety deposit box which, when opened, was discovered to hold gold coins worth one and a quarter million dollars!

I'd say that was an instance when wealth was hoarded to the detriment of its owner. Maddalena Borella chose to live in a filthy hovel and starve herself rather than spend some of the precious treasure she secretly stored. It may be that she never understood the value of what she had hidden away. A millionaire, she lived and died no differently than a pauper.

As in the case of Maddalena Borella, wealth that is hoarded is useless at best. It may also be dangerous. I remember hearing of a museum in Deadwood, South Dakota, which displays an inscription scrawled by a harried prospector over a hundred years ago: "I lost my gun, I lost my horse, I am out of food. The Indians are after me, but I've got all the gold I can carry." Lucky man, was he? I'm afraid his bags full of gold dust did little more than slow down his flight and speed up his demise. As the old saying goes about wealth, "You can't take it with you!"

Those are Solomon's sentiments also, as he remarks in Ecclesiastes 5:15: "Naked a man comes from his mother's womb, and as he comes, so he departs. He takes nothing from his labor that he can carry in his hand." Diamond stickpins, cuff links, and rings may be on the clothing, wrists, and fingers of a corpse at a funeral, but they won't follow the deceased to his final destination.

Solomon's words closely parallel those uttered by Job after he receives word that his property, servants, and family have been destroyed. Upon abruptly learning that he is destitute, and childless, Job exclaims, "Naked I came from my mother's womb, and naked I will depart. The Lord gave and the Lord has taken away; may the name of the Lord be praised" (Job 1:21-22). Yet while the first portion of Job's statement resembles what Solomon says in Ecclesiastes 5:15, the similarity ends there. Job closes his remarks by praising God; Solomon, stuck in the grip of a depressive mid-life trauma, cannot bring himself to bless the God who gives and who takes away.

And according to Solomon, there is still another "grievous evil" (5:16) which has made itself known. "As a man comes, so he departs, and what does he gain, since he toils for the wind? All his days he eats in darkness, with great frustration, affliction and anger" (5:16-17). The man who spends his life pursuing financial success toils only for the wind. He is accompanied by "frustration, affliction and anger." Personally, I don't want those kinds of friends for company! How true is the statement I once heard: "Make money your god and it'll plague you like the devil." On the first leg of a lengthy trip out of his mid-life quandary, Solomon makes some most insightful observations.

Words to the Wise—Ecclesiastes 5:18-20

> Then I realized that it is good and proper for a man to eat and drink, and to find satisfaction in his toilsome labor under the sun during the few days of life God has given him—for this is his lot. Moreover, when God gives any man wealth and possessions, and enables him to enjoy them, to accept his lot and be happy in his work—this is a gift of God. He seldom reflects on the days of his life, because God keeps him occupied with gladness of heart.

We are greeted with a few more morsels of wisdom in the final verses of Ecclesiastes 5 as Solomon continues to struggle in the search for solutions to his questions about life. He thinks about the circumstances he has considered and sums up his reflections with these words: "Then I realized that it is good and proper for a man to eat and drink, and to find satisfaction in his toilsome labor under the sun during the few days of life God has given him—for this is his lot" (5:18). A man must eat, drink, enjoy life, and find fulfillment in his work. Why? According to Solomon, it is because life is too short to do otherwise.

Once again, as in Ecclesiastes 2:3, Solomon reminds us that the lives of men measure but a "few days"—an awesome reality to the man in mid-life forced to focus clearly on the downhill stretch of his existence. That's the way things are. God permits this to be the lot of man, according to Solomon. We detect in his words the awareness of the Lord's sovereignty. He has been resisting the system; now we view the first inklings of submission to God's purpose.

You see, what the Lord wants is for Solomon—and each of us, for that matter—to be content with the fruits of our labors, to be satisfied with our circumstances. God isn't pleased when the pursuit of profit is the overwhelming ambition of our lives. In our quest for the almighty dollar we find that, in God's eyes, we're only chasing after small change. We're overlooking the fortune in favor of the frivolous, because life's true wealth is not made of money. That's a principle of which even Christians need to be reminded.

In fact, one of my pet peeves is the abundance of believers today who seem caught up in craving the material. This becomes so apparent on television. Too frequently I'll tune in a program only to hear twenty-five minutes worth of some polished, media-slick preacher begging for money for a project that won't get done without massive economic input. During the last five minutes of the show the viewers are treated to a story about how someone came to know Jesus. Then everyone watching is implored to commit his life to Christ—and also to write a check! Prosperity is promised if we send in a pledge. "Sow your seed of faith with us and God will multiply it!" we are falsely told. It distresses me to see a Christian "servant" begging for bucks!

As Solomon states in so many words, we are to be content in all things. Let's take an imaginary visit to Rome during the days of the apostle Paul. Let's go to the jail, underneath the city. The air would be stale, rank with the smell of the open sewer flowing a hundred yards away. Take a look at the apostle Paul, sitting in the darkness of that prison, and let him be our Bible teacher for the day.

What would Paul tell us about money? Would he outline his needs in detail and beg for contributions? No. Just look at the words he penned to the church at Philippi from the very depths of that prison:

> I am not saying this because I am in need, for I have learned to be content whatever the circumstances. I

know what it is to be in need, and I know what it is to have plenty. I have learned the secret of being content in any and every situation, whether well fed or hungry, whether living in plenty or in want. I can do everything through him who gives me strength (Philippians 4:11-13).

Paul had learned to "be content whatever the circumstances." He would assure us that through Jesus Christ— "him who gives me strength"—he could do all things. It is God who is the source of all that we are and all that we have.

Four Thoughts

In Ecclesiastes 5:19, Solomon reveals that he recognizes the truth mentioned above. He says, "Moreover, when God gives any man wealth and possessions and enables him to enjoy them, to accept his lot and be happy in his work— this is a gift of God." Notice four important phrases. They suggest guidelines to help us handle our money.

First, *God gives any man wealth and possessions.* It is the Lord who is the giver. Any cash or commodity we have comes from Him. We must remember that.

The second phrase is: *enables him to enjoy them.* God enables men to delight in what He has provided. Not all of us do that. One of my close friends told me the other day, "I'm making more money that I've ever made in my whole life, and I don't have a chance to have any fun with it." He's caught up in the stresses and activities of making his company successful, and he is frustrated.

The third phrase, *to accept his lot*, must be the aim of every individual. Submissive surrender to the sovereignty of God is essential. It is nothing to fear. The Lord doesn't want to rob us of pleasure. He wants us to humble ourselves and in brokenness say, "Father, my life is Yours. Handle it Your way!"

In fact, as the fourth phrase suggests, it is a gift of the Lord for a man to *be happy in his work.* That's contentment, made possible for us through surrender to Christ.

Look what Solomon says in verse 20. The man who enjoys his God-given possessions, accepts his lot in life, and is happy in his work, "seldom reflects on the days of his life, because God keeps him occupied with gladness of heart" (5:20). Such a fellow doesn't worry about the middle of life or the end of life; he doesn't mourn the passing of youth or the onset of old age; and he doesn't become hopelessly stuck in the midst of a severe mid-life crisis.

With those words, Solomon isn't describing himself . . . yet. We read the final verses of chapter 5, and it seems he's got his problems licked. That's not the case, however. What we have seen are flashes of wisdom, transient insights, because the verses of Ecclesiastes 6 show us without doubt that Solomon still struggles with questions and uncertainties.

NOT YET AT REST—ECCLESIASTES 6:1-6

> I have seen another evil under the sun, and it weighs heavily on men: God gives a man wealth, possessions and honor, so that he lacks nothing his heart desires, but God does not enable him to enjoy them, and a stranger enjoys them instead. This is meaningless, a grievous evil.
>
> A man may have a hundred children and live many years; yet no matter how long he lives, if he cannot enjoy his prosperity and does not receive proper burial, I say that a stillborn child is better off then he. It comes without meaning, it departs in darkness, and in darkness its name is shrouded. Though it never saw the sun or knew anything, it has more rest than does that man—even if he lives a thousand years twice over but fails to enjoy his prosperity. Do not all go to the same place?

Solomon is bothered by another situation he has encountered as he has tried to find meaning in materialism. He tells us what he has observed is an evil "under the sun," which "weighs heavily on men" (6:1). That evil situation occurs when "God gives a man wealth, possessions and honor, so that he lacks nothing his heart desires, but God does not enable him to enjoy them, and a stranger enjoys them instead" (6:2). Solomon describes a circumstance where a man who has accumulated all that he wants is prevented from making use of his property.

I can't tell you how many times I have run into just that type of situation. The two churches at which I preach weekly are located at lakeside retirement areas. From their congregations I can recall literally hundreds of times when couples have finally retired, built their dream homes . . . and then been struck by tragedy. Maybe a member of the couple has died. Perhaps the husband had a heart attack or the wife developed cancer—and just at the point when both spouses thought they had everything going for them.

Usually the services I've conducted have been those of men who have died. In some of the occasions, the dearly departed had been living for sixty-five or more years as though God didn't exist. He had been focusing on squeezing life for every last ounce it would offer. Retirement time came and he couldn't handle being free of the stress, scheduling, and hectic pace which had accompanied his working days. He folded under the *lack* of pressure, leaving behind all that he had given his energies to accumulate, to be enjoyed by others.

The writer of this poem expresses the irony of the situation well:

> He always said he would retire
> When he made a million clear,
> And so he toiled into the dusk,
> From day to day, from year to year.
> At least he put his ledgers up,
> And laid his stock reports aside,
> And when he started out to live,
> He found he'd already died.   (Tan 1984, 826)

What a sad set of circumstances, as Solomon says in Ecclesiastes 6:2, "meaningless, a grievous evil." From man's perspective, the death of a newly retired person may seem unfair. But with God, there is no such thing as a premature death. The Lord has a perfect plan for each of our lives that already includes the hour in which He will take us from this earth. It's all been scheduled. Our reservations have been confirmed.

In Ecclesiastes 6, Solomon isn't looking at things that way. He isn't glancing beyond the grave, where he would see that the Christian who dies is in a more wonderful place than he could ever be on earth, even with wealth, honor, and possessions galore. For the non-Christian who has never given God His proper place in his life, death marks the end of all opportunities. It brings with it an immeasurable sadness, but no injustice.

Solomon will not yet acknowledge those truths. In verses 3-6 of chapter 6, he compares the man who is never able to enjoy his prosperity to "a stillborn child," arguing that the miscarried infant is "better off" than the man who dies before he can take pleasure in what the Lord has given him (6:3). After all, as Solomon bemoans, "Do not all go to the same place?" (6:6).

What a pessimistic statement! No, "all" do *not* "go to the same place" after death. Those who know God immediately come into His presence (see 2 Corinthians 5:8). Solomon's outlook is limited to life before the grave. His vision is distorted. Why?

There is a simple explanation. Solomon at mid-life finds himself in the quagmire of a deep depression—the first indications of which we saw in Ecclesiastes 3. His irrational statements reflect his confusion. His thoughts are colored by his emotional gloom. Just look at the final six verses of Ecclesiastes 6 and observe his unreasonable assertions, the products of his bleak viewpoint.

IN THE GRIP OF GLOOM—ECCLESIASTES 6:7-12

> All man's efforts are for his mouth,
>   yet his appetite is never satisfied.
> What advantage has a wise man
>   over a fool?

> What does a poor man gain
> > by knowing how to conduct himself before
> > others?
> Better what the eye sees
> > than the roving of the appetite.
> This too is meaningless,
> > a chasing after the wind.
> Whatever exists has already been named,
> > and what man is has been known;
> no man can contend
> > with one who is stronger than he.
> The more the words,
> > the less the meaning
> > and how does that profit anyone?
> For who knows what is good for a man in life, during the few and meaningless days he passes through like a shadow? Who can tell him what will happen under the sun after he is gone?

As a successful Christian pastor, Don Baker seemed like the type of person who would be immune to such feelings. His marriage was solid, his family loving, his work rewarding, his church supportive. Yet into an intense and sunless depression Don Baker fell. He writes of his experience in *Depression: Finding Hope and Meaning in Life's Darkest Shadow.* In that book, he recounts a period during his gloom when he felt convinced that his wife and marriage were the major causes of his problems. To his beloved wife Martha, he directed such venomous remarks as, "I think I'd like to have a divorce. I don't care what happens to you. I don't care what happens to the family. I don't care what happens to the church." Writes Baker about those irrational outbursts: "When I spoke them, they came unexpectedly from somewhere deep in my black world and exploded with powerfully destructive force upon my wife" (Baker 1983, 77).

From the sinkhole of depression can spew forth unbridled the most senseless, angry words. As Don Baker observes: "Depression speaks a totally foreign language at times. As it gropes for meaning, it looks at anything and everything that might be its cause and sometimes draws some very foolish conclusions" (Baker 1983, 81). I firmly believe that much of what Solomon spouts in chapter 6 of Ecclesiastes has its roots in the fact that he is severely depressed. He is about as down and dejected as a man can be. As we look next at Ecclesiastes 7, we'll see him slide farther into a spiritual slump, then offer pieces of wisdom as he inches his way outward and upward. For now, let's examine his closing statements from chapter 6.

"All man's efforts are for his mouth, yet his appetite is never satisfied," he wails in verse 7. That's true enough, and it is reminiscent of the thoughts he has already expressed in Ecclesiastes 1:8. Solomon continues in verse 8: "What advantage has a wise man over a fool? What does a poor man gain by knowing how to conduct himself before others?" It's as if Solomon is bitterly repeating ideas with which we thought he had already come to grips. In chapter 2 he had considered wisdom and folly—now he reiterates his opinion, lashing out in his despair.

He goes on in Ecclesiastes 7:9: "Better what the eye sees than the roving of the appetite," and he once again uses his pet phrase to sum up this portion of his despondent reflections: "This too is meaningless, a chasing after the wind."

With his next words, Solomon hearkens back to chapter 1, where he had complained about the cyclical nature of life. He states in verse 10: "Whatever exists has already been named, and what man is has been known; no man can contend with one who is stronger than he." At mid-life Solomon contends with a depression that is far stronger than he.

His statement in verse 11 expresses his cynicism: "The more the words, the less the meaning, and how does that profit anyone?" Ironically Solomon depicts himself here. As he mouths his illogical outbursts, he is repeating concepts he has previously mentioned. He is meandering back and forth. "With more words" does come "less meaning," as his statements seem more like wild ravings than thoughtful reflections.

And Solomon closes the chapter with a final plaintive, desperate question. "For who knows what is good for a man in life, during the few and meaningless days he passes through like a shadow? Who can tell him what will happen under the sun after he is gone?" Who indeed? The answer is easy: God.

The Lord gives meaning and purpose to life, and it is with God that the believer will find himself as the morning of eternity breaks. As I said earlier, as we examine the next chapter of Ecclesiastes, we'll discover more about the intense depression which paralyzes Solomon. Yet before we proceed, let's look at a few of the lessons of chapter 6.

LESSONS

Lesson one: *oppression is a way of life where money is concerned.* Money creates the type of environment that is a magnet for oppression. Some of us have already faced that in the business world. Another money-related oppressive situation may occur where family inheritance is involved. Otherwise loving brothers and sisters can become manipulative, greedy, and selfish as their parents' wills are probated. Settling an estate often means severing relationships.

Lesson two: *it is the love of money that creates the problems.* Christians who love money more than they love the Lord are looking for trouble (see 1 Timothy 6). God tests us concerning that which is most precious to us. It is recorded in Genesis 22 that He asked Abraham to climb to the top of a mountain and place his beloved son Isaac on the altar of sacrifice. Abraham was willing to go the distance with God. He surrendered his boy to the Lord, and God in His mercy stopped Abraham's knife-wielding hand as it began its downward stab toward Isaac's heart. Abraham passed the test; he surrendered the son for whose birth he had waited twenty-five years. God was more important to the patriarch than even his dear Isaac.

Any believer who values his finances more than his heavenly Father runs a great possibility of losing all that he or she has acquired. The Lord is the sovereign God of the universe, and He is capable of getting our attention with devastating speed whenever He wants to.

Lesson three: *wealth that is hoarded does harm to its owner.*

Four: *we cannot take our bank balances with us into the next world.*

Five: *wealth, possessions, and the ability to enjoy them are gifts from God.*

Six: *the Lord is the One who keeps us occupied with gladness of heart.*

And the final lesson, number seven: *God knows what is good for us and He also knows how many days we have left to live.*

How to Handle What We Have

In light of the reality of God's sovereignty, how should we deal with our material goods? As Solomon discovers, wealth and possessions do not give purpose to our lives. The acquisition of the extravagant should never be the chief goal of life. But there are ways in which we can handle our wherewithal and magnify Christ in the process.

You are probably thinking, "This must be the time for a message on stewardship. I'm now going to be asked to bring my tithes unto the storehouse." Don't worry. It's not my personal business what percentage of your income you give to the Lord's service. That's between you and your Lord, but I do have a few guidelines to suggest which have been taken from three sections of Scripture.

First of all, let's take a look at 2 Corinthians 9:7

> Each man should give what he has decided in his heart to give, not reluctantly or under compulsion, for God loves a cheerful giver.

Giving is a private matter. We shouldn't grudgingly sign pledge cards or yield to pressure so that our giving is something as difficult for us as sucking blood out of a turnip.

When God lays a concern and burden on our hearts, we have a responsibility to listen and act. As we purpose in our hearts, we must give, cheerfully, without hesitation.

The second passage is Proverbs 11:24-26.

> One man gives freely, yet gains even more;
> another withholds unduly, but comes to poverty.
> A generous man will prosper;
>   he who refreshes others will himself be
>   refreshed.
> People curse the man who hoards grain,
>   but blessing crowns him who is willing to
>   sell.

In Solomon's own words we see much wisdom. Men who are generous will prosper; they'll be refreshed. He who selfishly withholds and hoards will be cursed and impoverished in the long run. Being properly open-handed is ultimately to our advantage.

And the last verse I'd like to mention is Zephaniah 1:18.

> Neither their silver nor their gold will be able to save them on the day of the Lord's wrath. In the fire of his jealousy the whole world will be consumed, for he will make a sudden end of all who live in the earth.

Thinking along those lines helps us place our prosperity in correct perspective. In the end, what we've acquired won't make a difference.

Our possessions are for the here and now, and as Christians we are required to use them to God's glory. When we meet Him in eternity, we'll have to answer for the ways we have handled our marriages, our families, our finances, and our time. Those are the major responsibilities He saddles us with on earth. Even if we have abused our privileges, as believers we'll stay in the company of God, but not before we face head-on the mistakes we made while in the world.

If at mid-life—or before or after—you find yourself wrapped up in a race to acquire more and more, I suggest that you stop before the finish line and ask yourself, "Is it worth it?" If your heart longs to be right with God, you'll realize, as Solomon does, that accumulation of capital carries with it the potential for the making of madness. The following words from James Dobson's *What Wives Wish Their Husbands Knew about Women* are well worth the consideration of anyone who is in danger of becoming too enamored of dollar signs:

> I have concluded that the accumulation of wealth, even if I could achieve it, is an insufficient reason for living. When I reach the end of my days, a moment or two from now, I must look backward on something more meaningful than the pursuit of houses and land and machines and stocks and bonds. Nor is fame of any lasting benefit. I will consider my earthly existence to have been wasted unless I can recall a loving family, a consistent investment in the lives of people, and an earnest attempt to serve the God who made me. Nothing else makes much sense, and certainly nothing else is worthy of my agitation! (Dobson 1975, 108).

Questions for Personal or Group Study

1. Read 1 Timothy 6:6-17 and look once again at Ecclesiastes 5:10. Why are we frustrated when we misplace our affections by loving money above all else?

2. What does Solomon conclude about the welfare of laborers and wealthy men in verse 12? Do you agree with his opinion? Why or why not?

3. Have you ever encountered instances where wealth has been hoarded "to the harm of its owner" (5:13), or wealth has been "lost through some misfortune" (5:14)? Describe the situations, if you wish.

4. What is a gift of God, according to Ecclesiastes 5:19?

5. Against what "evil" does Solomon protest in Ecclesiastes 6:1-6? Do you agree with his conclusion that the man who fails to enjoy his prosperity is worse off than a stillborn child? Why or why not?

6. What conditions complained about by Solomon in verses 7-12 of Ecclesiastes 6 has he already mentioned in earlier chapters? Why might he be so obviously repeating himself?

8

Wisdom from the Pits

Ecclesiastes 7:1–8:17

I will never forget the conversation I held with one of the pallbearers at a funeral at which I officiated. We rode together to the graveside service that day. I sensed that beneath his composed exterior he was hurting deeply and that the sadness would have been there even if he had not been mourning the loss of his friend. The pallbearer was, by the world's standards, a very successful individual. He owned a large home, was married to a beautiful woman, and was financially secure enough to spend the rest of his days playing tennis or golf, if he chose to do so. Yet there was an emptiness inside.

I asked him there in the car if he had ever accepted Jesus Christ. At that time, he indicated that he did not have a relationship with the Lord. I didn't hear from him or of him for several months, then came a phone call from his wife to tell me that he had placed a revolver to his head and pulled the trigger. He was dead—a victim of the overpowering depression which had engulfed him and of which I had seen glimpses at that funeral months before.

"He was a little depressed," the man's wife told me, "but I never would have believed that he could have done this." Sometimes our lives seem so black because of the effects of deep depression that suicide seems the only way out. And unfortunately, it is into such dark holes of depression which many fall when the problems of middle age become overwhelming.

In his book *The Creative Years*, Reuel L. Howe makes the following observation. Although written in 1959, the parallels to today are striking:

Our crowd sure fits the description. We men are an ulcerous, tension-ridden, sex-obsessed, money-mad bunch who are too busy and too tired to enjoy life. And our women match us with their worry and diets and double chins, with the problems of modern women and modern children. Both of us are lonely and scared. We are lonely because we have lost our own youth with the hopes that we had, and we're scared because of the oncoming youth that even now is pushing us aside. I guess we are afraid life is over for us . . . (Howe 1959, 13).

The problems of isolation, fear, exhaustion, and compulsion pointed out by Howe are experienced by many of us at mid-life. It is easy to become depressed. Says Jim Conway:

One of the most common responses of the man struggling with the mid-life crisis is to drop into depression. It's the easiest escape and the one that comes most naturally. . . . Depression is the natural outcome of the conflict of forces pressing upon his life and the explosive anger, frustration, bitterness, and self-pity building within him (Conway 1979, 72).

As Conway suggests, depression often appears as an escape mechanism to the man in mid-life crisis. Sometimes it can be concealed, but as we have seen from the suicide spoken of earlier, it can make itself known with ravaging force. No one, by himself, is immune. Just consider Psalm 38 and see how its author, David, cries forth from the bottom of a well of despair.

DAVID . . . A MAN DEPRESSED

This psalm describes a time in David's life when he is emotionally desolate. His son Absalom has rebelled and seized control of the kingdom. David has been driven from Jerusalem. He is a displaced king. In his own words he tells us that he is downcast and disturbed. Absalom's disloyalty has devastatd him. "I am feeble and utterly crushed; I groan in anguish of heart," he wails in verse 8. His soul thirsts for God. "Come quickly to help me, O Lord my Savior," he implores in verse 22.

THE WHYS

What causes such intense heaviness of spirit? Though in David's case the dejection is largely brought on by Absalom's arrogance and desertion, other ingredients play a part in the making of his melancholy mind-set. I'd like to briefly mention the reasons behind David's gloom, and a few other causes of depression in the lives of many. I am not a psychologist, but I have counseled hundreds of people whose lives have been steeped in depression. These are my observations of the *whys* behind the emotional pain.

Loneliness. People who are loners are often ripe for depression. Acts of friendship—the open-hearted sharing of confidences, joys, and trials—have a way of pumping air into deflated emotions. People who have a few close, reliable friends aren't as likely as others to become depressed, because there are men and women to whom they can turn. It doesn't appear that David, in Psalm 38, has developed the kinds of intimate personal friendships which would shield him against the searing darts of depression. "My friends and companions avoid me because of my wounds; my neighbors stay far away," he laments (38:11), and we sense that he is utterly alone. No friendship has proved enduring enough, no relationship of sufficient depth, to assuage David's distress. In fact, one of his most trusted advisors, Ahithophel, has cast his lot with the rebellious Absalom (see 2 Samuel 16 and 17). And David is completely alone.

That David is a solitary man is even more apparent in Psalm 25:16, where he implores of the Lord: "Turn to me and be gracious to me, for I am lonely and afflicted." Friendless and forlorn—especially following the deaths of Jonathan and the prophet Samuel—David is a candidate ripe for depression.

Adversity. Being forced to face trial after trial after trial can make us feel sorry for ourselves, submersing us in depression. Psalm 38 gives evidence that David is weary of the fight. In his eyes, he has been pounded to a pulp by his problems. He cries to God in verses 1 and 2: "O Lord, do not rebuke me in your anger or discipline me in your wrath. For your arrows have pierced me, and your hand has come down upon me."

With Absalom's revolt, David's family has fallen apart. His kingdom is disintegrating. His popularity is at an all-time low. He mourns, "Many are those who are my vigorous enemies; those who hate me without reason are numerous" (38:20). And as he cries, "For I am about to fall, and my pain is ever with me" (38:17), it is apparent that he has been deluged with almost more than he can stand.

Criticism. Constant criticism can get us down, too. We'll especially see that as we study chapter 7 of Ecclesiastes. David also has experienced the sting of censure. "Those who would harm me talk of my ruin," he says in verse 12 of Psalm 38. "Those who repay my good with evil slander me when I seek what is good" (38:20), he also sorrowfully admits. The criticism has been constant. In the face of such nitpicking, we need thick hides so the cutting comments won't penetrate but will slide off our backs as we determine to prove the critics wrong. Yet in the meantime, being knocked down and panned is depressing.

Lack of self-worth. A poor self-image often results in depression, too. If we feel unable to make positive contributions to others, we can easily sink into a mental and emotional black hole. Driven from Jerusalem by his own son, David must have surely felt worthless—a king without a throne—when he penned Psalm 38. "I am bowed down and brought very low," he mournfully sighs in verse 6. He even blames himself for his shattered state, remarking in verse 4: "My guilt has overwhelmed me like a burden too heavy to bear." He sees himself as unable to perform even the most elementary functions. "I am like a deaf man, who cannot hear, like a mute, who cannot open his mouth," he despairs in verse 13. And he cries in verse 10: "My heart pounds, my strength fails me; even the light is gone from my eyes." In short, David considers himself good for nothing, incapable and unworthy of meeting the challenges set before him.

Inability to positively perceive the future. Finally, when there seems to be nothing to look forward to, depression results. David's capacity to gaze upward is a source of comfort to him while he is in the dumps. Even though he suffers tremendous affliction, he still recognizes the fact that God is there, able to work, capable of assuring him a future. David begs God to come quickly and help him (38:22). And with confidence in the power and faithfulness of the supreme Lord, he says this: "I wait for you, O Lord; you will answer, O Lord my God" (38:15). David is looking ahead. His simple statement of trust reveals that although he is down, he should not be counted out.

DEALING WITH DEPRESSION

Loneliness, adversity, criticism, low self-esteem, the inability to look ahead positively—these can all cause severe depression. How can the heavyheartedness be resolved? Here are a few suggestions.

First, we must examine the causes of our gloom. We've got to decide why we are depressed and then begin to deal with what has prompted the downhill slide. If there is a medical reason, perhaps a doctor can help. Sessions with a reliable Christian counselor can help us pinpoint the causes and handle the effects of our emotionally desolate state.

Second, as part of dealing with the causes, we should start to take some positive steps. This means doing what David does: turn our eyes toward God. It means feasting on the positive. How can we do that? Here's an example.

At times, one of life's adversities comes in the form of physical pain. Severe pain can cause intense depression. Whenever my aches threaten to spread from the physical to the emotional, I remind myself about the sufferings of Christ. I tell myself that I haven't been nailed to a cross yet. Turning from my pain to the Person who, as Hebrews 5:8

says, "Although he was a son, he learned obedience from what he suffered," provides relief and release. The Lord can minister to every area of our lives, including our sufferings. Looking to Him and His Word can make all the difference. And it's okay for us to confess to Him that we are depressed. We won't be telling Him anything He doesn't already know, and we'll feel much better after confiding in Him.

Third, we must fill our minds with anticipation and expectation. I am not talking about some positive-thinking placebo, but rather a realistic and healthy optimism about the future. Realizing that through our momentary troubles God will give us new indications of His will can lift us from the pits.

I apologize if these suggestions seem superficial—they have helped me climb up off the mat a time or two. The books mentioned at the end of this chapter explore the topic of depression far more thoroughly than I am able. I do know that it is important to respond with action, rather than reaction, when an emotional and spiritual cloud looms overhead.

You see, if we refuse to deal with depression, we show a lack of trust in the Lord's ability to handle our problems. In fact, depression in some ways goes hand in hand with unbelief, because it is unbelief in the power of God to take care of us which may well prompt us to slump in the first place.

SOLOMON—CLIMBING UPWARD

At the close of Ecclesiastes 6, we left Solomon about as down as a man could be—depressed and nearly irrational. We saw him erupt with bitterness and frustration from the depths of his spiritual darkness. Now we'll observe his emergence from the smoky blackness. We'll see him take action as he shifts his focus from himself onto the positive. In Ecclesiastes 7 and 8, Solomon is learning, growing, and starting to shake off the mid-life blues which have bogged him down. As he climbs upward and outward, he offers flashes of wisdom that are well worth our attention.

OF GOOD NAMES AND FINAL DAYS—ECCLESIASTES 7:1-2

> A good name is better than fine perfume.
>   and the day of death better than the day of
>   birth.
> It is better to go to a house of mourning
>   than to go to a house of feasting,
> for death is the destiny of every man;
>   the living should take this to heart.

Let's examine what Solomon says as he begins to think through the trauma. "A good name is better than fine perfume," he states in verse 1 of chapter 7. How well that speaks to the middlescent difficulties Solomon faces. Often the man in mid-life crisis forfeits his good name because of his actions. Maybe he becomes erratic in paying his bills, and finds himself the target of lawsuits. Perhaps an extramarital affair in which he engages is exposed, and his reputation is smeared by the local tongue-wagging gossips. Solomon's advice is wise indeed. A good name is more important than the most expensive fragrance; no amount of sweet-smelling oil will thoroughly cover the stench of a ruined reputation.

Solomon next observes in verse 1, "and the day of death [is] better than the day of birth." The fact that Solomon can say that and mean it shows that he is working loose from the grip of crisis. Maybe he is accepting the fact that he is inevitably looking down the final stretch of life. Perhaps his words reveal an acknowledgment of God, as he admits that death can be a far better experience than birth.

Today, only the person who knows Christ legitimately anticipates death as a wonderful event. Most people don't look at dying as something to relish. A few days ago, for example, I was watching on television as a very beautiful and popular actress was interviewed. When asked how she felt about turning forty, she replied, "Great! Anyway, it beats the alternative, doesn't it?"

We shouldn't see it that way. The thoughts of the believer shouldn't jibe with the opinion of that actress. Rather, when facing death, Christians should look at things from the perspective shown by the words on a bumper sticker I saw the other day. The sticker said, "I'm joyful, because tomorrow I might be in heaven!"

Solomon is not yet ready to agree with such a statement. Instead, he is still struggling with depression, so much so that dying does seem better than continuing the fight alive. Nevertheless, he is coming to grips with some tough issues—matters of life and death. He muses in verse 2, "It is better to go to a house of mourning than to go to a house of feasting."

Confronting the final innings of life can be scary, especially when we must pay visits to the funeral parlor. Yet when a person reaches middle age, death is frequently faced. Parents and aunts and uncles die; business associates succumb to heart attacks. One fortyish fellow told me that he had started reading the obituaries to see how old the people were who had died. He said that way he would know when to stop praising the Lord for the many years ahead and start thanking Him for the few days he had left!

As Solomon says, "Death is the destiny of every man" (7:2). That's true, and in one of his moments of wisdom he offers us some valuable advice: "The living should take this to heart" (7:2). We can deny it, we can bury it in our subconscious minds, but one day the minister at a funeral service will be talking about us and our bodies will lie—nothing more than a shell—in a coffin. "Take this to heart," Solomon cautions us all.

BEFORE IT'S TOO LATE—ECCLESIASTES 7:3-7

> Sorrow is better than laughter,
>   because a sad face is good for the heart.
> The heart of the wise is in the house of
>   mourning,
>   but the heart of fools is in the house of
>   pleasure.
> It is better to heed a wise man's rebuke

> than to listen to the song of fools.
> Like the crackling of thorns under the pot,
>   so is the laughter of fools.
> This too is meaningless.
> Extortion turns a wise man into a fool,
>   and a bribe corrupts the heart.

What else must we take to heart? Solomon says in verses 3 and 4 that "sorrow is better than laughter, because a sad face is good for the heart. The heart of the wise is in the house of mourning, but the heart of fools is in the house of pleasure." Even though he is depressed, Solomon's outlook is balanced. We learn more from sorrow than we do from laughter; we learn more from experiencing grief than we do from a lifetime of pleasurable pursuits.

Think of it this way. Like Solomon in chapter 2 of Ecclesiastes, men often deal with the problems of mid-life by imbibing from the well of worldly pleasure. They hit the bars with a few good buddies, and with jokes, laughter, and liquor, they cover up their hurts and fears. The bars close, the friends go home, and the doubts and questions surface again. All that's left is a gigantic hangover and the realization that twenty-four more pointless hours have passed. Pleasure teaches us little. But sorrow, especially at the "house of mourning," offers us so much more.

Solomon doesn't mean that we should never have fun. All that he suggests is that we can learn far more valuable lessons from the funeral than the festival. When we're confronted by death, our point of view is changed. We remember our own mortality. Our priorities are rearranged as our pride is checked. And we are prepared for the times of loss to come, as our grieving causes us to become more sympathetic toward others around us.

The great singer Enrico Caruso's favorite expression was said to be this: "*Bisogna soffrire per essere grandi.*" Translated, that means, "To be great, it is necessary to suffer" (Tan 1984, 1510). To grow, it is necessary to suffer as well. That's what Solomon tells us, from the very core of his despondency. There is no gain without pain.

He continues in Ecclesiastes 7:5-6: "It is better to heed a wise man's rebuke than to listen to the song of fools. Like the crackling of thorns under the pot, so is the laughter of fools. This too is meaningless."

His remarks supply additional insight. When attempting to deal with the hassles of middle age or other problems, it is much safer to accept the reproach of a wise man than the giddy acquiescence of fools. When we're faced with temptation and floored by depression, foolish men will always egg us on to do the wrong thing. "Leave your wife if you don't love her any more. Why bother with your kids? Quit your job. Have some fun—now... before it's too late." Such is the advice of the fool to the man wrestling with mid-life trauma.

Solomon urges us to ignore the people who throw that kind of verbal garbage in our direction. Instead, we should seek the counsel of rational, logical, wise individuals. Anything else is as transient as a bunch of thorns which, when set afire, will snap, crackle, and burn until there are only cinders left.

But it isn't easy to submit to the guidance of another. Generally, the pride of a man who is in the midst of a mid-life crisis will provoke him to do anything to avoid submission and surrender. He'll even resort to flattery, bribery, and extortion, to get his counselors to go along with him. That's why Solomon says in verse 7: "Extortion turns a wise man into a fool, and a bribe corrupts the heart." True, he is speaking in the extreme, but there is more than a tinge of reality to his words. If another person shells out advice that is hard to swallow, the typical response is to try to change his mind. Argue with him; threaten him; flatter him; bribe him. Do whatever has to be done so that his counsel will be in vain.

We read his words and wonder if Solomon hasn't swayed the hearts of his advisors to comply with his own ideas. Probably he has. Ironically, he is forced to admit the folly of the action. And despite himself, he's still in the pits, still down, still depressed.

PATIENCE INSTEAD—ECCLESIASTES 7:8-9

The end of a matter is better than its beginning,
and patience is better than pride.
Do not be quickly provoked in your spirit,
for anger resides in the lap of fools.

There is a great deal that can be learned when we've sunk to the bottom emotionally. Solomon imparts another choice bit of counsel when he says in Ecclesiastes 7:8: "The end of a matter is better than its beginning." At first glance, that may seem to be incorrect. Why should the end of a matter be better than its start? We initiate tasks with lofty ambitions, high goals, and supercharged energy. Then, by the time the job is finished, we are often drained, depleted, and drowning in compromise. In that case, the opening chords prove to be a whole lot better than the not-so-grand finale.

So when is the end superior to the beginning? It is better whenever we undergo a trial, including a mid-life crisis. In the first days, months, or even years of turmoil, we have trouble thinking of the future. We're too concerned with past regrets and present worries to look ahead. It's when we reach the end of the tunnel that we begin to step into a world of new chances and fresh possibilities. Do you remember that one of the causes of depression is the inability to conceive of the future? Solomon's comments show us that he is slowly starting to realize that there *is* life beyond middle age, that there will be an end to his difficulty.

It's important to remember what else Solomon says in verse 8 of Ecclesiastes 7. That is: while we're embroiled in trouble and even perhaps intense depression, "patience is better than pride" (7:8). When we face trauma in our lives, we often ask, "Why me? Why this? Why now?" We resent it. We tell God that we don't deserve it. "Lord, if this is the way you treat your sons and daughters, I don't appreciate it!" And we figure we have an excuse not to develop our relationship with God because He has been unfair.

What's the answer? Patience. It's the quality we need in

order to make it to the finish line without dropping in exhaustion during the race. The essential ingredient in the solution to the type of mid-life depression felt by Solomon is patience. It means making a decision not to demand, "Why me?" but to humbly inquire, "What can I learn from all of this?" It means asking God, "Please help me," and then waiting on Him. Hebrews 10:36 states, "You need to persevere so that when you have done the will of God, you will receive what he has promised." Here are the steps in the process.

THE STEPS OF PATIENCE

Step 1: *Surrender.* Turn yourself over to God so that He can work in your life.

Step 2: *Seek to understand.* Ask yourself and God what you can learn from the trauma.

Step 3: *Seek to grow.* Ask the Lord to help you learn more about Him and His ways and His will.

Step 4: *Seek to enrich.* Ask God to enable you to bear fruit in the lives of others as a result of the trials you have undergone. Actively look for opportunities.

Step 5: *Seek to glorify.* Become concerned about how you can magnify the Lord in the middle or the aftermath of your adversity.

Those steps outline a formula for recovery from the depression deadlock. Wholeness is achieved through the process of persevering. If we lay aside *pride* and embrace *patience,* we'll discover God's *purpose,* and with that knowledge will come *peace.* James writes in James 1:3-4, "The testing of your faith worketh patience. But let patience have her perfect work, that ye may be perfect and entire, lacking nothing" (KJV).

GETTING AT THE HEART OF IMPATIENCE: OWNING UP AND OPENING UP

Solomon's reflections here are wise indeed. In Ecclesiastes 7:9 he goes on to caution us, "Do not be quickly provoked in your spirit, for anger resides in the lap of fools." We must determine not to succumb to anger, for while rage persists, there is no hope of patience—only impatience. If we're dejected—tired of the struggles of mid-life or other life—and we become angry at our wives, children, even God, we're in for even more trouble. Sleeping on it won't help, because we'll wake up even madder; as Ephesians 4:26 commands, we must not "let the sun go down while [we] are angry."

Temper tantrums don't solve problems, but many of us have short fuses anyway. Blasts of temper often serve to cover the rebellious heart of a person in crisis. Letting anger seethe and smoulder until it explodes is wrong. In Solomon's words, "Anger resides in the lap of fools" (7:9).

Simply put, we mustn't allow anger to take up space within us on a permanent basis. We mustn't repress angry feelings, and yet we mustn't express them violently. So what can we do? Rather than *repress* or *express* wrongfully, we should *confess*. We should own up to God by admitting our rage to Him and to another honest person who is following Christ and who will hold us accountable. Once we *own* up, it's time to *open* up to the Lord, to His love, His truth, His Word. He'll cleanse us from unrighteousness again and again; that's His promise. As 1 John 1:9 states: "If we confess our sins, he is faithful and just and will forgive us our sins and purify us from all unrighteousness." What a guarantee!

ON LOOKING BACKWARD AND FORWARD—ECCLESIASTES 7:10-12

> Do not say, "Why were the old days better than
>   these?"
> For it is not wise to ask such questions.
> Wisdom, like an inheritance, is a good thing
>   and benefits those who see the sun.
> Wisdom is a shelter
>   as money is a shelter,
> but the advantage of knowledge is this:
>   that wisdom preserves the life of its possessor.

Another shrewd insight is presented by Solomon in verse 10. "Do not say, 'Why were the old days better than these?' " he warns. Remember that it is feasting on the positive and anticipating the future which help lift us from depression and trauma. It's doing what Paul says in Philippians 3:13: "Forgetting what is behind and straining toward what is ahead." Feeding on the past only fuels our frustration. "Those were the good old days," many people sigh, but in reality dwelling on days gone by is a waste of energy.

In fact, Solomon admonishes us that "it is not wise to ask such questions" (7:10). He reminds us that even though hindsight is generally 20/20, what might have been is simply never going to be. Why should we look back? Why then should we moan and groan phrases like these, especially at mid-life: "If I'd just known then what I know now. . . . If I'd only married her (or him). . . . If I'd simply taken that job . . ."? Winston Churchill said that when the past argues with the present, there cannot be a future. When we're immersed in crying over spilled milk or water that's been long under the bridge, we are asking to be depressed. Postmortems of the past do nothing more than dismay us.

It's looking ahead—actively, vibrantly—that Solomon recommends. And he gives us guidelines as to how we are to move forward. We are to pursue wisdom in the process. Solomon's growth is evident; he has changed his tune from earlier, when wisdom seemed of no benefit (see Ecclesiastes 2). Now he says in verse 11 of chapter 7: "Wisdom, like an inheritance, is a good thing and benefits those who see the sun."

As the old saying goes, behind every cloud there is a silver lining. The sun still shines in spite of our difficulties. Wisdom is our inheritance and supplies us with what we need to keep on keeping on. In chapter 1, verse 5 of his book, James offers the following counsel concerning responding to trial: "If any of you lacks wisdom, he should ask God, who gives generously to all without finding fault, and it will be given to him." That is the crux of Solomon's counsel also.

He continues in verse 12: "Wisdom is a shelter as money is a shelter, but the advantage of knowledge is this: that wisdom preserves the life of its possessor." Money doesn't save the life of a hiker lost in the woods during a blizzard. He can be worth millions, but only the knowledge of outdoor skills will enable him to locate a cave or dig his way into a snowbank for protection. Only sufficient know-how would have prompted him, before ever setting out, to place extra food and clothing in his backpack in case of emergency.

Likewise, as Solomon suggests, only God-given wisdom can help us survive mid-life without too many scars. We can dig our way out of a depressing crisis by surrendering to the Lord and praying for the valuable tool of discernment. It's a priceless gift, not measurable in terms of money.

WISDOM: IN GOD'S HANDS—ECCLESIASTES 7:13-14

> Consider what God has done:
> Who can straighten
>   what he has made crooked?
> When times are good, be happy;
>   but when times are bad, consider:
> God has made the one
>   as well as the other.
> Therefore, a man cannot discover
>   anything about his future.

One of the themes pulsating through the first seven chapters of Ecclesiastes has been the notion that man is given a certain lot in life and that there is a time or season for every activity. In other words, the events of our lives are, to a large extent, out of our control. We can make conscious choices, but over and above everything is God. Solomon repeats that idea when he says in verse 13: "Consider what God has done; Who can straighten what he has made crooked?"

Once again we are reminded that much of what happens to us and to those we know is beyond our jurisdiction, no matter who we are. We cannot straighten what He has made crooked (see Ecclesiastes 1:15). I remember the years when long, straight hair was in style for girls. The poor gals with wavy or curly locks tried countless methods to change "Mother Nature." A friend of mine tells me that she used to iron her hair in an effort to stretch out the curls. It worked, for a little while, then the strands of hair kinked up again. That's a minor example, but it speaks of a major truth. There are many circumstances in life which we must accept because they are designed by God. What, then, is the wise response in light of that knowledge?

THE WISDOM OF COOPERATION

How can we react to God's sovereignty properly, even when circumstances seem out of control? Wisdom in those instances involves cooperation.

I have told my children countless times as they've grown up: "I have only one purpose in life and that is to bless you and make you happy and help you to become a successful adult. Now if you can argue with my purpose, you can be disobedient." These words also reflect God's intentions in our lives. He wants us to hand Him the reins of our lives, letting Him place us where He wants us to be. He desires to do *in us* and *to us* what is necessary so that He can work *through us* to bear fruit. It's that simple. All we need to do is to be available and cooperative.

And the means of cooperation is expressed clearly by Solomon in Ecclesiastes 7:14. "When times are good, be happy," he declares, "but when times are bad, consider: God has made one as well as the other. Therefore, a man cannot discover anything about his future." When we're beset by the blues—a younger man is promoted unexpectedly at work; our marriages seem dull and unchallenging; our kids have grown all too fast; our friends appear distant; our careers seem to be at a standstill; we're losing hair and teeth and eyesight—the answer is "consider."

We must consider what God has done. He has allowed the bad times as well as the good. And as we ponder, we must also cooperate. This means searching for the lessons we can learn from Him in the process. When we figure out what He is trying to teach us, it becomes easier to climb up from the black hole.

IN ALL THINGS, MODERATION—ECCLESIASTES 7:15-18

> In this meaningless life of mine I have seen both of
> these:
>> a righteous man perishing in his righteousness,
>>> and a wicked man living long in his
>>> wickedness.
>> Do not be overrighteous,
>>> neither be overwise—
>>> why destroy yourself?
>> Do not be overwicked,
>>> and do not be a fool—
>>> why die before your time?
>> It is good to grasp the one
>>> and not let go of the other.
>>> The man who fears God will avoid all
>>> extremes.

We see Solomon inching his way out of his melancholy. The advice he offers during the procedure is practical and solid. But he's not at the end of his turmoil yet. He is still bothered by a few things; he still questions *why*, even as he absorbs the lessons God intends for him to learn.

A certain situation especially rankles him. He is disturbed when he sees "a righteous man perishing in his righteousness, and a wicked man living long in his wickedness" (7:15). Solomon questions the fairness of God in allowing such circumstances. His comments indicate that although he is beginning to turn to God, he is not yet wholly trusting in Him.

Why do righteous men sometimes die young? Many times it is because the Lord doesn't want to be separated from them any longer. Enoch walked with God, and the Lord took him home. Their fellowship was too rich for

Enoch to remain earthbound. The death of a righteous man is no tragedy. (See Genesis 5:22-24.)

Neither is the longevity of a wicked man. Often the wicked are allowed long lives so that they will have opportunities to respond to God. Many old reprobates make it to age seventy, eighty, or ninety, without ever handing their lives over to Christ. The Lord's mercy allows them to make it that far without being consumed. Patiently He waits. 2 Peter 3:9 states: "The Lord is not slow in keeping his promise, as some understand slowness. He is patient with you, not wanting anyone to perish, but everyone to come to repentance."

While We Wait

Subject as we are to God's sovereignty, what choices should we make as to how to conduct our lives? Solomon answers that question in the next few verses. "Do not be overrighteous, neither be overwise—why destroy yourself?" he advises. Is it possible to be overrighteous? Yes, indeed.

The overly righteous are the legalistic "saints" who generally tout their own sinlessness. They don't drink, smoke, or dance, and they don't go with the girls or guys who do! They're happy to reveal how much of their income they give to the church, and they enjoy describing in detail the specifics of each sacrifice they've nobly made. The person puffed up with too much self-righteousness is nothing more than an overinflated balloon, waiting to be popped.

Yet Solomon says also that we must not be "overwise." That means we must not second-guess God, plunge ahead, and steer our lives as we see fit. We're likely to crash when we do so.

Our lives should be well-balanced. Solomon goes on to urge us, "Do not be overwicked, and do not be a fool—why die before your time?" This doesn't mean that a little bit of evil is okay. Yet the cold, hard fact is that we are all going to sin. As we avoid being "overwicked," we must honestly seek to be aware of the areas of glaring weakness in our lives. We need to ask God to operate, excising the flaws as He works to make us more like Christ.

Finally, Solomon sets forth an important principle: "The man who fears God will avoid all extremes" (7:18). We must watch that we don't become so pious and zealous that we're full of self and stuffed with pride. We must deal with sin in our lives. "It is good to grasp the one and not let go of the other," says Solomon in verse 18. In other words, we must strive for righteousness while retaining a healthy awareness of our own shortcomings. That way, we keep ourselves and God in proper perspective, realizing that only He can change us and keep us in check when necessary.

NOBODY IS PERFECT—ECCLESIASTES 7:19-22

> Wisdom makes one wise man more powerful
>   than ten rulers in a city.
> There is not a righteous man on earth
>   who does what is right and never sins.
> Do not pay attention to every word people say,
>   or you may hear your servant cursing you—
> for you know in your heart
>   that many times you yourself have cursed
>   others.

God-given wisdom is the key to unsnarling confusion, even mid-life depression, in our lives. We have seen that it implies cooperation. Its rewards are immense also. As Solomon says in Ecclesiastes 7:19: "Wisdom makes one wise man more powerful than ten rulers in a city." That sounds like more than an even exchange, doesn't it?

It does, yet it's good for us to remember the old adage, "Nobody's perfect." People usually say that when they've made some sort of mistake, but it is true all of the time. No matter how much wisdom we attain, we will never achieve the standard of perfection set and met by Jesus Christ; it's impossible. Solomon puts it this way: "There is not a righteous man on earth who does what is right and never sins" (7:20). His thoughts span the centuries to speak vividly to us today.

Solomon's words in Ecclesiastes 7 mirror those later written by the apostle Paul. In Romans 3:10-11, Paul states: "As it is written: 'There is no one righteous, not even one; there is no one who understands . . . .'" And in Romans 3:23 he says: "For all have sinned and fall short of the glory of God." Only by God's grace may we have a relationship with Him. Today that grace is offered to us through the sacrifice of Christ on the cross.

Follow Solomon's earlier advice and consider what God has done. He sent His Son to die so that the penalty for our sins might be paid. Our deeds outside of Christ are abominations in the sight of the Lord—He stamps "rejected" on anything we try to give Him that we've accomplished on our own. We can never be perfect. We can never bat 1.000.

The fact that Solomon, in the midst of his struggles, comes up with a fair assessment of man's condition, indicates that he is willing to look to something or someone greater than himself for answers. We all like to learn, but everybody hates to be taught, so this is a big step for Solomon! He is reaching an important milestone both on the road to recovery from his mid-life crisis and in the quest for wisdom.

CONSIDER THE SOURCE

Yet along that path, obstacles often present themselves. Solomon points out a few of these in the verses that follow. "Do not pay attention to every word people say," he cautions in verses 21 and 22 of chapter 7, "or you may hear your servant cursing you—for you know in your heart that many times you yourself have cursed others." We can't let criticism, which will inevitably be tossed in our direction, get us down and keep us grounded. Listening to the nit-pickers, and believing what they say, will only submerge us deeper in dejection.

When we're in trouble, on come hordes of devoted do-gooders to dress us down with warnings, sermons, psalms and songs, poems and prayers. "My, my, what you must have done to deserve what you're going through!" they imply. "We'll pray for you," they say. After spitting pious venom at us, they beat hasty retreats. Their task is finished, and they won't be around to pick up the pieces or help us work through the pain.

Even worse are the people who refuse to criticize us face-to-face. Their backstabbing remarks anonymously filter in our direction as we hear reports like: "Everyone is disappointed, offended, hurt, angry, shocked, dismayed, disgusted with you. So-and-so-thinks you're such-and-such. We all feel it best that you quit, leave, change," and so on. Indirect shots hurt as much, maybe more, than hand-delivered darts because there is no opportunity for us to defend ourselves to our accusers.

When confronted with such dubiously helpful advice, the best response is to ignore it. We must seek counsel from those who are wise, caring, and compassionate. And we should accept open, honest, heartfelt guidance that is lovingly given. It is entirely different from criticism.

Criticism weighs us down. We're all susceptible. We even come to expect it. I recall sitting down with a certain couple and enjoying a fantastic steak dinner that the wife had prepared. I decided to try out an experiment I had heard of earlier, so I asked my hosts, "Where did you get that steak?" The husband responded, "At the Safeway," but the wife inquired in a worried tone of voice, "Why, is it too tough?" Isn't that typical? She expected to be criticized! Solomon warns us not to live life like that or we'll be miserable. Like David in Psalm 38, we'll be downtrodden by the foes who mercilessly taunt us.

None of us has been so high, mighty, and holy that we haven't dropped a few derogatory comments about others along the way, either. As Solomon says in verse 22: "For you know in your heart that many times you yourself have cursed others." Someone has said that if each person knew what another had said about him, there would not be two friends left in the world. I think that's fairly accurate. Let's watch it, and be sure to reject any unfounded and malicious barbs which come our way.

Who Can Discover It?—Ecclesiastes 7:23-29

All this I tested by wisdom and I said,
  "I am determined to be wise"—
Whatever wisdom may be,
  it is far off and most profound—
  who can discover it?
So I turned my mind to understand,
  to investigate and to search out wisdom and
    the scheme of things
and to understand the stupidity of wickedness
  and the madness of folly.
I find more bitter than death
  the woman who is a snare,
whose heart is a trap
  and whose hands are chains.
The man who pleases God will escape her,
  but the sinner she will ensnare.
"Look," says the Teacher, "This is what I have
discovered:

"Adding one thing to another to
  discover the scheme of things—
  while I was still searching
  but not finding—
I found one upright man among a thousand,
  but not one upright woman among them all.
This only have I found:
  God made mankind upright,
  but men have gone in search of many
    schemes."

Part of wisdom entails knowing when *not* to pay attention to people. We shouldn't make ourselves vulnerable to the caustic comments of others. We must learn to ignore more than the cynical critics.

Realizing he must reject snide, unfounded remarks, Solomon questions where he *can* turn for wisdom. He says in verses 23-24: "All this I tested by wisdom and I said, 'I am determined to be wise'—but this was beyond me. Whatever wisdom may be, it is far off and profound—who can discover it?" And in his frustration, Solomon tells us, "So I turned my mind to understand, to investigate and to search out wisdom and the scheme of things and to understand the stupidity of wickedness and the madness of folly" (7:25). He continues the attempt to find knowledge which will lift him out of his black, mid-life depression. What are his alternatives?

Where he should not turn is mentioned in the next verse. "I find more bitter than death," says Solomon, "the woman who is a snare, whose heart is a trap and whose hands are chains" (7:26). When I teach this passage in classes, I sense indignation swelling among the ladies in the audience as that verse is read. Let's set the record straight. Solomon is not advising men to stay clear of women. He is not implying that all females are floozies who work their charms to entrap men and lead them astray. Rather, Solomon is personifying earthly wisdom as a fast, loose woman—a prostitute.

The world has many forms of "wisdom" to offer. Man-made philosophies, non-Christian religions, and scientific theories serve up platters full of possibilities as to why we are here and what life is all about. Such thinking is essentially godless. If we base our beliefs on the secular instead of the sacred, it is as if we have succumbed to the lure of a tawdry, seductive woman. There is no wisdom in that, only much foolishness.

So where is the essence of wisdom? "Adding one thing to another to discover the scheme of things," Solomon goes on to say, "while I was still searching but not finding—I found one upright man among a thousand, but not one upright woman among them all" (7:27-28). The few upright men to whom he refers are, as Leupold points out, the worthy men of God in Scripture (Leupold 1978, 177). Solomon has found that the fellows like Abraham, Isaac, Jacob, Joseph, Moses, and Samuel are the only ones who have found the answers to the perplexing intricacies of life. And of course, they have been given the answers by God Himself. They form a select group of men, to whom such names as Peter, Paul, Mark, Matthew, Luke, John, and James may be added, along with others. They are the men who served as the original subjects of God's Word, some even penning the Scriptures themselves under the inspiration of the Holy Spirit.

"This only I have found," Solomon adds in Ecclesiastes 7:29, "God made mankind upright, but men have gone in search of many schemes." Evolution, humanism, fatalism—these and other devices serve to separate man from the simple truths of Scripture. The "many schemes" which men have pursued have historically not provided enduring answers to the problems of the human condition. The solutions are only available straight from the source of all creation: the God of the universe.

DISCOVERING WISDOM—ECCLESIASTES 8:1-6

> Who is like the wise man?
> Who knows the explanation of things?
> Wisdom brightens a man's face
>   and changes its hard appearance.
> Obey the king's command, I say, because you took
> an oath before God. Do not be in a hurry to leave the
> king's presence. Do not stand up for a bad cause, for
> he will do whatever he pleases. Since a king's word is
> supreme, who can say to him, "What are you doing?"
> Whoever obeys his command will come to no
>   harm,
>   and the wise heart will know the proper time
>   and procedure.
> For there is a proper time and procedure for
>   every matter,
>   though a man's misery weighs heavily upon
>   him.

Genuine God-given wisdom sheds light in life's dark recesses. It changes a man's countenance—in Solomon's words: "Wisdom brightens a man's face and changes its hard appearance" (8:1). The metamorphosis extends beneath the skin as well, for outlooks and attitudes are also altered when wisdom finds a place in someone's life. We have seen earlier that it is necessary to cooperate with the Lord in order to become wise. Solomon underscores that truth in the verses which follow.

"Obey the king's command . . ." he cautions (8:2). Ultimately, we must learn to be submissive to the Lord, the King. "Do not be in a hurry to leave the king's presence," he also states (8:3). Stay in touch with God, communicate regularly, sincerely, and meaningfully with Him. Worship Him, for He is worthy.

Not only is He worthy of worship, but He is also worthy of respect, because He is all-powerful. As Solomon says in the second part of Ecclesiastes 8:3: "Do not stand up for a bad cause, for he will do whatever he pleases." How well that describes the Lord! He will do as He pleases. We can't fight Him; we only "win" by joining up with Him.

"Since a king's word is supreme, who can say to him, 'What are you doing?' " (8:4). We can't justifiably question God, but we can rest assured that "whoever obeys his command will come to no harm, and the wise heart will know the proper time and procedure." (8:5). He will care for us if we are careful to correctly acknowledge Him. He will even reach down into the shadows of a depressive mid-life crisis, if necessary.

STUBBORN SURRENDER

Solomon continues: "For there is a proper time and procedure for every matter, though a man's misery weighs heavily upon him" (8:6). Simply put, a man is miserable in proportion to his resistance to God's sovereignty and God's will. It is such resistance which leads to crisis. When man pulls his own strings he cannot avoid entangling himself, causing himself no end of trouble. Severe mid-life trauma, with all of its ramifications, has its roots in resistance to God's authority when wisdom demands that we submit to Him.

Solomon pinpoints our problem: our misery weighs heavily upon us because we refuse to surrender. We can be so stubborn. We act just like I did after a visit to the eye doctor a few years ago. I had worn contacts for years when it became difficult for me to see so I assumed I just needed a new prescription.

"Anderson," the doctor said, "you're going to have to wear bifocals."

"I won't wear those things—they're for old people!" I protested.

"Anderson—face the facts—you're maturing," said the doctor.

So I selected some frames and had the prescription filled. When the glasses were ready, I picked them up, paid for them, and wore them out of the office. But I didn't wear them home. They sat on the car seat. When I arrived home, I marched right into the bedroom, opened the top dresser drawer, and placed my bifocals at the back. I didn't plan on wearing them again. Well, maybe I'd put them on when I was in the study—alone. Otherwise, I'd make do without them.

Then I realized how stubborn I was being. The doctor—a man trained to recognize my visual needs—wanted to help me solve my problem, and I was too vain and stubborn to take his advice. I had a choice: submit to the doctor's authority or do things my way instead.

We treat the Lord very much like I treated my optometrist. We don't listen; we don't yield to His authority; we don't ask Him for directions till we're half-blind from groping in the dark; we don't lean on Him till we are exhausted from supporting ourselves.

Always Fair?—Ecclesiastes 8:7-13

> Since no man knows the future,
>   who can tell him what is to come?

No man has power over the wind to contain it;
  so no one has power over the day of his
    death.
As no one is discharged in time of war,
  so wickedness will not release those who
    practice it.

All this I saw, as I applied my mind to everything done under the sun. There is a time when a man lords it over others to his own hurt. Then too, I saw the wicked buried—those who used to come and go from the holy place and receive praise in the city where they did this. This too is meaningless.

When the sentence for a crime is not quickly carried out, the hearts of the people are filled with schemes to do wrong. Although a wicked man commits a hundred crimes and still lives a long time, I know that it will go better with God-fearing men, who are reverent before God. Yet because the wicked do not fear God, it will not go well with them, and their days will not lengthen like a shadow.

Supporting ourselves is awfully hard to do, especially at mid-life when the problems seem insurmountable. It's much easier in the long run to submit to God's authority. Solomon is reaching that point of surrender in Ecclesiastes 8.

He reminds us in verses 7 and 8 that man is powerless to control much of his life, particularly his future. Man is even powerless of his own accord, to escape the hammerlock with which wickedness can entrap him, as Solomon tells us in verse 8. We know that it is difficult to do the right thing even some of the time, much less all of the time. It is doubly hard to shrug off the influence of false religions and philosophies, if that is where we have been searching for truth.

Such is man's condition. In verses 9-11, Solomon mentions various evil situations he has observed: wicked people receiving praise during their lifetimes, and the scheming hearts of men and women who do not fear justice. And yet

look at Ecclesiastes 8:12-13 and witness what he has con-
cluded from all of this:

> Although a wicked man commits a hundred crimes
> and still lives a long time, I know that it will go better
> with God-fearing men, who are reverent before God.
> Yet because the wicked do not fear God, it will not go
> well with them, and their days will not lengthen like
> a shadow.

What about that? Solomon says that there will be ac-
countability in God's time, and that no matter what goes on
in the world, it is best to fear and worship the Lord. He has
come to the point where he can honestly say that only God
gives meaning and purpose to life. He is starting to trust. I
can't help but think of the words of Psalm 1:

> Blessed is the man
>   who does not walk in the counsel of the
>   wicked
> or stand in the way of sinners
>   or sit in the seat of mockers.
> But his delight is in the law of the LORD,
>   and on his law he meditates day and night.
> He is like a tree planted by streams of water,
>   which yields its fruit in season
> and whose leaf does not wither.
>   Whatever he does prospers.
> Not so the wicked!
>   They are like chaff
>   that the wind blows away.
> Therefore the wicked will not stand in the
>   judgment,
>   nor sinners in the assembly of the righteous.
> For the LORD watches over the way of the
>   righteous,
>   but the way of the wicked will perish.

AND ALWAYS KIND

God is always just to deal with us as He says He will if we follow Him. An excellent illustration of this was given at the funeral of little three-year-old George, of whom I've spoken earlier. Another minister and I officiated. I remember that the preacher made the following statement at the beginning of the service: "God is not fair."

I thought to myself: I don't like that! But he went on to explain himself. "God is not fair," he said, "but God is always kind." And then he used the parable told by Jesus of the workers in the vineyard as an example. In Matthew 20:1 we read: "The kingdom of heaven is like a landowner who went out early in the morning to hire men to work in his vineyard." The landowner agreed to pay the laborers a set fee, a denarius, for their work. He returned three hours later to the place where he had hired the original men and offered others the chance to work. He did the same thing three times more—at the sixth, ninth, and eleventh hours. At the end of the day, he paid all the men an identical wage, even though those who had been employed early in the morning had sweated in the fields all day, and those who had hired on latest had put in but an hour's labor. It wasn't fair, from man's perspective. But it was ever so kind of the landowner.

That's how it is with the Lord. God is God and He can do what He wants to do. Who are we to say how He spends His funds, how He orders our lives, how He works out the details? Like Solomon, we must come to the place where we can admit the truth of the principle that God is always kind and that His way is best.

THE AUTHOR OF HAPPINESS—ECCLESIASTES 8:14-17

There is something else meaningless that occurs on earth: righteous men who get what the wicked deserve, and wicked men who get what the righteous deserve. This too, I say, is meaningless. So I commend the enjoyment of life, because nothing is better for a man under the sun than to eat and drink and be glad. Then joy will accompany him in his work all the days of the life God has given him under the sun.

When I applied my mind to know wisdom and to observe man's labor on earth—his eyes not seeing sleep day or night—then I saw all that God has done. No one can comprehend what goes on under the sun. Despite all his efforts to search it out, man cannot discover its meaning. Even if a wise man claims he knows it, he cannot really comprehend it.

Such an admission means that Solomon has come a long way. It's true that much of what occurs in life is meaningless, such as the final example he gives in the chapter of the righteous getting what the wicked deserve, and vice versa (Ecclesiastes 8:14). Life isn't "fair," from our point of view. There will be marital conflict, career upheaval, the aches of aging, the pain of watching the kids leave the nest. And all of these can combine with other sources of trouble to form the basis for severe depression, particularly at mid-life when much of the dissatisfaction often gels into a sticky crisis.

Let's avoid the difficulty if we can. If not, let's deal with it. Solomon tells us how in the last verses of Ecclesiastes 8. "So I commend the enjoyment of life," he declares, "because nothing is better for a man under the sun than to eat and drink and be glad." Why? Solomon continues: "Then joy will accompany him in his work all the days of the life God has given him under the sun" (8:15). In short, God creates happiness and joy. By turning loose each area of our lives in which we are resisting Him, we find a way out of depression. Anything else is foolish.

Besides, as Solomon concludes the chapter, "When I applied my mind to know wisdom and to observe man's labor on earth . . . then I saw all that God has done. No one can comprehend what goes on under the sun" (8:16-17). We'll never fully understand the human condition anyway, no matter how hard and long we search. "Despite all his efforts to search it out, man cannot discover its meaning" (8:17). Life will remain a puzzle to the wisest of us, at least until we get to heaven and are able to get the answers directly from the Lord. And then we probably won't care anyway! In the meantime, Solomon states with finality, "Even if a wise man claims he knows, he cannot really comprehend it" (8:17).

Let's therefore not agonize over the perplexities and seeming injustices of life. God is in charge. He is in control. Our job is to enjoy the existence He has given, trusting in Him, hoping in Him—and not worrying about what we cannot change and cannot understand.

LESSONS

That perhaps is the most important lesson to be learned from Ecclesiastes 7 and 8, but there are many more. Let me mention them briefly.

Number one: *at the bottom of depression is unbelief in God's ability to handle things.*

Two: *patience is better than pride.* From pride we progress to patience. We see God's purpose, then we receive His peace. The process is from pride to patience to purpose to peace.

Three: *tempers should be controlled.* Short fuses are bad news.

Four: *we never need to say, "Where are the good old days?"* There's no looking back.

Five: *the man who fears God will avoid all extremes.*

Six: *we mustn't pay attention to every word people say.*

Seven: *God made man upright, but man has gone in search of many schemes.* The Lord made us to have hearts for Him; there is no other answer.

Lesson eight: *wisdom brightens a man's face and changes its hard appearance, while misery weighs heavily upon him.*

And lesson nine: *no one can fully comprehend what goes on under the sun, but God is always kind.*

RESOURCES

If you find yourself grappling with depression, maybe even the sort from which we have just seen Solomon emerge, then there are a few good books I'd like to recommend. Don Baker's *Depression* (co-authored by Emery Nester) has already been mentioned. *Spiritual Depression* by Martyn Lloyd-Jones is a classic—well worth the reading. And there is another well-known work, *Happiness Is a Choice,* by Paul Meier and Frank Minirth, which can be an invaluable aid.

The writers of *Happiness Is a Choice* offer a select bit of advice on handling depression. I'd like to close with a few of their thoughts, coupled with my own. One of the characteristics of depression is that it is easy to say, "I can't." I can't be happy; I can't confide in a friend; I can't look forward to work; I can't love my wife; I can't shake these blues. And there's the worst: I can't look to Christ.

How do we escape the "I can't" mentality? We do so by changing all of the "I can'ts" to "I won'ts." That's what it's all about anyway. What we're really saying is: "I won't be happy; I won't shake these blues; I won't place my trust in Christ" (Meier and Minirth 1978, 132). Next step? If we change the "I won'ts" to "I wills," we'll begin licking the problem, especially as our resolve is strengthened through communion with God.

And may I say this? Each of us *will* survive our mid-life periods of unrest. Those of us who change our "I won'ts" to "I wills" will escape the most life-shattering aspects of a mid-life crisis. The ball is in our court. God is always waiting to work.

Questions for Personal or Group Study

1. Why is it better to go to the house of mourning than to the house of feasting, according to Ecclesiastes 7:2-4? Do you agree? Why or why not?

2. Describe a situation from your own experience in which patience has proved better than pride.

3. According to chapter 7, from what sort of people should we seek counsel, and whom should we ignore?

4. Why should we never ask, "Why were the good old days better than these?" (7:10).

5. Part of becoming wise means considering what God has done (Ecclesiastes 7:13-14), and then cooperating with His plan. Will this formula help you deal with any situations in your life right now? If so, and if you wish, explain.

6. What, according to Ecclesiastes 7:18, will the man who fears God do?

7. Solomon says that "men have gone in search of many schemes" (7:29), while looking for truth. What are some of these "schemes"? Can they explain the meaning of life?

8. What does Solomon recommend that we do in verse 15 of chapter 8?

9. Do you agree with what Solomon says in Ecclesiastes 8:17—that even the wisest among us will never fully understand what goes on under the sun? Why or why not?

9

Eat, Drink, and Be Merry

Ecclesiastes 9:1–10:20

I heard once that mid-life is a lot like standing in line to vote in California during the 1980 presidential election, after the polls had closed back east. As you'll recall, Jimmy Carter conceded the race to Ronald Reagan before the polls had shut down in the West. Any Californian who stayed in the voting line after hearing of Carter's concession was merely going through the motions. The decision had already been made.

Sometimes it seems that during middle age, we're doing nothing more than going through the motions, too. We're stuck doing all the things we ought to do: supporting the family, the church, the community. We're unable to do what we think we'd like to do. It's frustrating, all the more so because we also realize how little input we truly have in the final scheme of things. Will our kids turn out all right? Will the company we work for be sold and our positions lost? Will our neighborhoods decline? Will our best friends still be around to play golf with us at retirement time? Since there is not a great deal we can do to determine the future, we (sometimes painfully) are forced to realize our limitations as we pass the mid-point of life.

Becoming aware of the areas in which we are vulnerable can be depressing, but it can also be constructive. In fact, even a mid-life crisis can be a positive experience if it causes us to reevaluate our relationship with the Lord and make a new or renewed commitment to Him through Jesus Christ. In the last two chapters of Ecclesiastes we have witnessed Solomon confronting middle age and becoming more aware of God. We see him gain a clearer understanding of the Lord's purpose and power as he edges his way out of the black hole of mid-life depression.

On his way up and out of the pit, remember that Solomon gives us several warnings. Among these, he cautions us not to worry about "the good old days." Facing the future is far more important than dredging up the past. He also tells us not to pay attention to everything other people say about us, since criticism is extremely effective in making us slide into a slump. Finally, he closes Ecclesiastes 8 by pointing out that we are not capable of fully comprehending all that goes on under the sun, so we shouldn't agonize over why events happen the way they do. Instead, no matter what our lives hold, it will go better for us if we fear God.

What sound, practical advice Solomon offers as he works his way out of crisis! In chapters 9 and 10 of Ecclesiastes, we'll observe him as he continues the process of recovery. He supplies other pieces of sage counsel, urging us to make the most of what we have while we are around to enjoy life. And believe me, that outlook on life beats drowning in depression any day!

In a comic strip, one pudgy, respectably-dressed middle-aged fellow is depicted philosophizing to another: "Live each day as if it were your last . . . and someday you'll be right." That is some of the best advice I've ever read; it also happens to be one of the main thrusts of Solomon's writings in Ecclesiastes 9 and 10. Let's examine what he says and watch him make a renewed, if shaky, beginning at mid-life. Thank goodness there is light at the end of Solomon's tunnel—and thank God that it is *not* the headlight of an oncoming train about to knock Solomon down again!

WHAT ABOUT LIFE IN GOD'S HANDS?—ECCLESIASTES 9:1

> So I reflected on all this and concluded that the righteous and the wise and what they do are in God's hands, but no man knows whether love or hate awaits him.

Solomon tells us in verse 1 that he "reflected on all this"—meaning, all that he had written about in the first eight chapters of his book. He then reveals that these are his conclusions: "The righteous and the wise and what they do are in God's hands, but no man knows whether love or hate awaits him" (9:1).

A prominent insurance company assures us that we're "in good hands" when we sign on with one of their agents. I'm not saying that's not true, but the best hands in which we can be do not belong to any insurance firm; they are the hands of God. He controls the destinies of His children. Solomon is correct when he remarks that "the righteous and the wise and what they do are in God's hands" (9:1).

A similar comment is made by Christ during His earthly ministry. In John 10:27-29—perhaps the greatest statement in the Scripture about eternal security—Jesus says:

> My sheep listen to my voice; I know them, and they follow me. I give them eternal life, and they shall never perish; no one can snatch them out of my hand. My Father, who has given them to me, is greater than all; no one can snatch them out of my Father's hand.

When we do the most intelligent thing we can do and commit ourselves to Christ, obtaining His righteousness, we're placed securely in the Father's hands forever. His reputation is at stake . . . and He never lets go of His own. We're safe.

So in his journey to uncover the meaning of life, Solomon makes the discovery that the only way to go is with the God of his father, David. He realizes that his life and times are in God's secure grasp. In acknowledging the Lord's sovereignty—against which we have seen him struggle previously—he overcomes an important obstacle in dealing with mid-life trauma. Yet he still retains a few misconceptions about what God's purpose is in the lives of His followers. The pieces of the puzzle aren't yet entirely in place.

Look at Solomon's next observation: "But no man knows whether love or hate awaits him" (9:1). Think about that a moment. Since all things are in God's hands, then what Solomon is suggesting is that the Lord doles out the good and the bad in our lives in proportion to how much He loves or hates us. Is that true?

Not at all! Consider the words of Romans 5:8: "But God demonstrates his own love for us in this: While we were still sinners, Christ died for us." The Lord of all the universe worked out a flawless plan for our redemption—at unfathomable cost to Himself. John 3:16 says that "God so loved the world that he gave his one and only Son, that whoever believes in him shall not perish but have eternal life." The Lord has made a commitment to love us unconditionally, totally, equally, sacrificially. He wouldn't rain hatred on some and shower others with love. That isn't His style.

What is flawed is not God's purpose but rather Solomon's perception of it. For the past eight chapters of Ecclesiastes, he has been pointing out injustices in the world, some of which—like corporate oppression—he has suffered himself. Now he equates love and hate with the circumstances God has permitted in his life. Solomon assumes that when things have gone well, when he has received what he has wanted, when his prayers have been answered with a resounding "Yes!"—then God has been expressing His love. On the other hand, when adversity has struck, when the Lord has said no to petitions, it seems to Solomon that God has been venting His anger and hatred. But that is not the way it works.

God loves us unconditionally. When He disciplines us, it does not mean that He is angry with us or that He even dislikes us. Instead it means that He wants us to grow. We don't give our own children everything their hearts desire, do we? We know that if we do, we'll spoil them. Likewise, the Lord shows us His love when He gives us what we *need*, in addition to what we want. Solomon has trouble accepting the fact that God manifests His love by sometimes denying certain requests. His reaction to God resembles that of an angry little child, about to grab his toys and go into the house because he hasn't gotten his way!

When traumatic circumstances come into our lives, we must not think that the Lord is in a white-hot rage, ready to brand us as outcasts from His kingdom. When we're beset by problems, folks will often try to make us feel that way—shaking fingers at us and implying that we must have sinned horribly to deserve such punishment from the hand of God. Maybe we *are* reaping what we have sown, but perhaps the difficulties have been permitted so that we will learn to depend on the Lord even more.

The point is, we've got to rise above the notion that God allows us to undergo tough times because He hates us. He cares immensely—enough to give His own life for us. At mid-life, Solomon still has a great deal to learn about the nature of God . . . but he is coming along. He is making steady progress.

A COMMON DESTINY?—ECCLESIASTES 9:2-3

All share a common destiny—the righteous and the wicked, the good and the bad, the clean and the unclean, those who offer sacrifices and those who do not.
  As it is with the good man,
    so with the sinner;
  as it is with those who take oaths,
    so with those who are afraid to take them.
This is the evil in everything that happens under the sun: The same destiny overtakes all. The hearts of men, moreover, are full of evil and there is madness in their hearts while they live, and afterward they join the dead.

Solomon continues reflecting on the Lord's purpose, making what at first seems to be a surprising statement. "All share a common destiny—the righteous and the wicked, the good and the bad, the clean and the unclean, those who offer sacrifices and those who do not," he says. "As it is with the good man, so with the sinner; as it is with those who take oaths, so with those who are afraid to take them" (9:2). Does this mean that we all "share a common destiny" whether or not we have been made righteous in God's eyes? Is the Lord going to change His mind and invite us all inside the gates of heaven one day—Christians and non-believers alike? Is that our "common destiny"? Will He say to the person who has rejected His plan of salvation, "Well, now, that's all right. You tried. You did the best you could. Come on up and we'll find a place for you in the mansion anyway"? No!

What Solomon does mean is that God has a sovereign purpose that we're all going to come up against somewhere along the way as we live our lives (see Ecclesiastes 3:1-15). All of us face that. It is our "common destiny." The pilot of an airplane charts the course, determines the destination, and flies the plane. So it is with God, whose eternal purpose overrides all that we do. We cannot truly comprehend the extent of His control.

Solomon as much as admits that in verses 1 and 2 of Ecclesiastes 9. He reflects on the events that occur in men's lives, and he finds that he cannot explain why things happen the way they do. It doesn't seem to matter if men are worthy or unworthy—or if God is expressing what in Solomon's eyes is love or hatred. A sovereign and everlasting purpose affects each area of life, regardless.

But God is not to blame for the problems that men encounter, Solomon also realizes. The fault lies in the very nature of man himself. In Solomon's words in verse 3: "This is the evil in everything that happens under the sun: The same destiny overtakes all. The hearts of men, moreover, are full of evil and there is madness in their hearts while they live, and afterward they join the dead."

The opening words of the old radio show *The Shadow* went something like this: "Who knows what evil lurks in the hearts of men? (Pause) The Shadow knows!" In some ways, things haven't changed very much from the days when listeners sat spellbound, ears tuned to the audio adventures of The Shadow. Evil *still* lurks in the hearts of men, even as it did in Solomon's day and as it has in every age following the fall of Adam.

If you don't think so, take a peek at the shelves in your

favorite drug store. Medicines are now boxed in tamper-proof packages which encase their childproof caps. The pharmaceutical companies have had to take this measure because people cannot be trusted in an age when anonymous killers sabotage capsules with cyanide. You might also wander through the local airport and observe the security precautions now necessary because of the wave of terrorism bombarding the world. As Solomon maintains, there truly is "madness" in the hearts of men while they live.

"Surely I have been a sinner from birth, sinful from the time my mother conceived me," David laments to the Lord in Psalm 51:5. He succinctly sums up the state of humankind. In middle-age, his son Solomon draws the same conclusion about the wretchedness and wickedness of the human heart.

After men have wreaked havoc upon the earth, "they join the dead," Solomon proclaims in verse 3 of Ecclesiastes 9. It is as if he is expressing the thoughts which would later be recorded by the apostle Paul in Romans 6:23: "For the wages of sin is death . . . ." Paul finishes the verse with these words: ". . . but the gift of God is eternal life in Christ Jesus our Lord." Solomon, in acknowledging both God's sovereignty and man's weakness, gives evidence of much growth. He is moving onward, approaching the point where he will rise completely from the shadows of crisis and step into the center of God's will.

THE DEATH MARCH—ECCLESIASTES 9:4-6

> Anyone who is among the living has hope—even a
> live dog is better off than a dead lion!
> For the living know that they will die,
>   but the dead know nothing;
> they have no further reward,
>   and even the memory of them is forgotten.
> Their love, their hate
>   and their jealousy have long since vanished;
> never again will they have a part
>   in anything that happens under the sun.

Two of the most important lessons which Solomon has learned as he has struggled with the hassles of mid-life are these. First, he has recognized the fact that it is lonely fighting against God's eternal purpose. It is better to submit as the Lord plots the course and retains the controls. Second, Solomon has been forced to face the reality of death. Yet to his way of thinking, where there is life there is hope.

"Anyone who is among the living has hope," he says in verse 4 of chapter 9. "Even a live dog is better off than a dead lion!" Even the most skinny, flea-bitten mongrel who lives among the garbage cans in the alley has it better than the regal king of the beasts who has died. Why? It is a matter of hope.

Solomon continues in verse 5: "For the living know that they will die." Those who are alive have the opportunity to prepare for death, to make arrangements, to ready themselves and their loved ones. It is partly the knowledge that death is imminent which has fueled Solomon's mid-life turmoil. He still shrinks from the idea of dying. He has made some headway in dealing with the reality of middle age, but he is not yet able to admit that life beyond the grave can be much better than life under the sun.

We know these are his sentiments because he says in verse 5 that "the dead know nothing; they have no further reward, and even the memory of them is forgotten." How much those remarks resemble Solomon's words in Ecclesiastes 1. He still complains that the grave is the end and that nobody will remember him after he is gone. The depressing attitudes which have formed the foundation of his mid-life crisis remain at least partially intact. How in the world can Solomon proclaim God's sovereignty, even His goodness, and still continue to think of life as only *under the sun*? It is a mystery . . . or is it?

Do We Really Look Ahead?

Before we judge Solomon too harshly, let's consider how many of us, as believers in Christ, feel exactly the same way deep inside. In our mind's eye we conceive of heaven, but our hearts never rise above earth, until we die. We accept Jesus as Lord and Savior, we even study His Word, but we never genuinely anticipate death as the gateway to something far more wonderful than life. We are not honestly able to look expectantly beyond the grave. We rarely even admit to ourselves that death will claim us.

Other people will die, yes—but not us, or our friends and family! And so we neglect to prepare ourselves and those we love for what must come. When close Christian friends do die, we are not ready. We fall apart in our grief and bitterness, forgetting that a funeral procession full of people is watching to see how our faith stands the test. As death becomes more of a reality at mid-life, so does our fear of the end.

How differently the apostle Paul saw death! "Where, O death, is your victory? Where, O death, is your sting?" he could boldly inquire in 1 Corinthians 15:55. And ten years later in Rome, sitting in a worm-infested sewer known as the Mamartine prison, waiting for Nero to order the fall of the executioner's ax, the apostle could write these words:

> I have fought the good fight, I have finished the race, I have kept the faith. Now there is in store for me the crown of righteousness, which the Lord, the righteous Judge, will award to me on that day—and not only to me but also to all who have longed for his appearing (2 Timothy 4:7-8).

Paul genuinely looked forward to death. He knew that when absent from the body, he would be instantaneously present with the Lord—and it was a coming experience which he eagerly anticipated.

"I desire to depart and be with Christ," the apostle wrote to the church at Philippi in Philippians 1:23. While in college, I made a study of the word "depart" in that verse. Paul uses a term which means to pull up the tent stakes, fold up the tent, and go to the house. It is as if he means that we are on vacation during our time on earth. One day God will call us, and we'll have to return home.

The research mentioned above was done as part of an assignment immediately following the Christmas holidays one year. I'll never forget that semester break. Something which we might call a tragedy happened, and riveted my attention on the idea of departing to be with God.

It was my first Christmas away from home. I had to stay at school because I was playing varsity basketball and several games were scheduled over the holidays. Most of the students had left campus. My best friend and I were shooting some baskets in the gym. Afternoon approached, and he too left to be with his family for Christmas . . . but he never made it. He died that very evening in an automobile accident. One of our professors had these words of comfort to say, "Saints are immortal, until their work on earth is done." Enroute to his earthly home, my friend was unexpectedly taken to his real home—his heavenly home.

It happens, and we've got to be ready. We must prepare our children; we must prepare ourselves. That way we won't have such a rough time in middle age, when death looms as inescapably real, when it truly is not so far away.

No Looking Back

In Ecclesiastes 9, Solomon obviously does not have the full picture concerning eternity. For the Christian, the hour of death is the time of reward, the time of finishing the race, the time of gazing at the Savior. It is when the Lord will say, "Well done, good and faithful servant. Now I have some new assignments for you. Enter in to the joys I have prepared for you."

What Solomon does grasp is the finality of death. In speaking of those who no longer live, he says in Ecclesiastes 9:6: "Their love, their hate and their jealousy have long since vanished; never again will they have a part in anything that happens under the sun." At death the game is over; the gun has sounded; the race is finished. Never again do we "have a part in anything that happens under the sun." Most importantly, our chances to receive and serve a living Savior end the moment we breathe our last.

THE THREE-POINT JOB DESCRIPTION—ECCLESIASTES 9:7-10

> Go, eat your food with gladness,
>   and drink your wine with a joyful heart,

for it is now that God favors what you do.
Always be clothed in white,
   and always anoint your head with oil.
Enjoy life with your wife, whom you love, all the
days of this meaningless life that God has given you
under the sun—all your meaningless days. For this is
your lot in life and in your toilsome labor under the
sun. Whatever your hand finds to do, do it with all
your might, for in the grave, where you are going,
there is neither working nor planning nor knowledge
nor wisdom.

Solomon has talked about two topics thus far in chapter
9 of Ecclesiastes. They are *determination,* the idea that God
exercises sovereign control, and *death,* an unavoidable
event, preplanned for us all. How then are we supposed to
live, considering that God determines our circumstances
and that death is an everpresent reality?

We could become hopelessly depressed, but Solomon advises against that. Instead, he tells us that, in view of determination and death, the best we can do is to delight ourselves in the *present.* In verses 7 through 10, he gives us a
three-point job description outlining our duties and responses.

Point One: Eat, Drink, and Be Merry

Solomon first tells us: "Go, eat your food with gladness,
and drink your wine with a joyful heart, for it is now that
God favors what you do" (Ecclesiastes 9:7). We mustn't get
depressed because God has our path mapped out. We
shouldn't lapse into the blues because of our oncoming
demise. Instead we ought to enjoy life while it lasts and
while we can. That means living it up, rather than letting
ourselves be dragged down. The command is to have a
good time: to eat, drink, and be joyful. The process involves
cultivating proper attitudes.

As in dealing with depression, we are instructed to dwell
on the positives instead of dawdling with the negatives.

Say what you will about the rash of positive-thinking pro-
ponents, but the truth of the matter is that a biblically-
based positive attitude is pleasing to the Lord. It is evidence
that we believe His promises and look forward to what He
has in store for us. It beats being negative in every situation.

We must develop a *Christ-centered* positive outlook on
the situations in our lives. Paul exhorts the Christians at
Philippi with this message: "Finally, brothers, whatever is
true, whatever is noble, whatever is right, whatever is
pure, whatever is lovely, whatever is admirable—if anything is excellent or praiseworthy—think about such
things" (Philippians 4:8). He continues with these words:
"Whatever you have learned or received or heard from me,
or seen in me—put it into practice. And the God of peace
will be with you" (4:9). What a promise—given only to
believers in Christ. And as part of Christ-centered thinking,
we must look ahead expectantly, to Him. The apostle Peter
writes: "Therefore, prepare your minds for action; be self-
controlled; set your hope fully on the grace to be given you
when Jesus Christ is revealed" (1 Peter 1:13).

Those are some very positive statements—straight from
Scripture. We can't do anything about yesterday, so let's
forget it. Let's move on to today and make it something
special as we look to the Savior, dwelling on Him and on all
that is perfect and lovely and true.

A similar message is transmitted sporadically by Solomon throughout Ecclesiastes. As we thumb through the
text of the book, we see Solomon slowly awakening to the
fact that it is best to tackle the events of life optimistically.
Interspersed in Ecclesiastes are little jewels of wisdom
which give glimpses of ways to resolve a mid-life crisis by
placing emphasis on the positive. Let's review a few of
these verses:

> "A man can do nothing better than to eat and drink
> and find satisfaction in his work" (2:24).
> "I know that there is nothing better for men than to be
> happy and do good while they live" (3:12).

"So I saw that there is nothing better for a man than to enjoy his work, because that is his lot" (3:22).

"Then I realized that it is good and proper for a man to eat and drink, and to find satisfaction in his toilsome labor under the sun during the few days of life God has given him—for this is his lot" (5:18).

"So I commend the enjoyment of life, because nothing is better for a man under the sun than to eat and drink and be glad" (8:15).

Point one of our job description for life simply is to eat, drink, and be merry—an idea Solomon banters about in the first part of Ecclesiastes, then firmly grips at the end. Nothing else that he has tried has made much sense.

If we are to be content, it is indispensable that we savor the life which the Lord has given us. Yet at the same time Solomon warns us: "Always be clothed in white, and always anoint your head with oil" (Ecclesiastes 9:8). The white garments to which he refers are symbols of purity and festivity, and the oil represents joy. As Christians we should enjoy life but must maintain a sense of wholesome purity about our actions. We must be moderate. The mentality of the world is such that illicit sex, occasional drunkenness, and constant extravagance are okay. After all, the bombs may fall tomorrow, so it's smart to grab for what we can today! Such joyriding can only leave us empty and cold, just as it has Solomon in his mid-life search for meaning.

But Christians can have fun! Jesus Himself says in John 10:10: "I am come that they might have life, and that they might have it more abundantly" (KJV). That verse clearly applies to us, especially if we are cooperating with God's sovereign purpose. The Lord is not a joy-robber who delights in removing every bit of bliss from our lives as we surrender to Him. On the contrary, the reverse is true.

As a Christian, I get to play racquetball, run marathons, ski, fish, hike, climb mountains, ride horses, and travel extensively. I meet hundreds of wonderful people each year. I sometimes say, tongue-in-cheek, to the participants in one of our camps or conferences: "Isn't it terrible to be a Christian? It is just incredible what the Lord has taken out of our lives!" I make those comments at a moment when we're having a terrific time, so that my point will be effectively illustrated. God's flock shouldn't consist of a bunch of somber sheep who have nothing good to bleat about! Instead, the Lord encourages us to take pleasure in life.

POINT TWO: ENJOY LIFE—WITH A WIFE

Not only are we to enjoy life, but in verse 9, Solomon gives us a guideline as to how we are to accomplish this. "Enjoy life with your wife, whom you love, all the days of this meaningless life that God has given you under the sun—all your meaningless days," he says. "For this is your lot in life and in your toilsome labor under the sun" (9:9). Point two of our job description is to delight ourselves in a wife.

When I teach this passage in class, the single men in the audience begin to squirm a bit. Sometimes an unmarried fellow will say, "I can't fill that requirement!" Yet the Hebrew text of verse 9 actually says to enjoy life with *a* wife—so the challenge to each unmarried man is to get out there and find her!

It is ironic that at mid-life, many men tire of the women they have married. As we have seen, affairs with other women are common but do not provide lasting answers to the crisis. Separation and divorce are not viable options, either. The command is to take delight in *a* wife.

And ladies, may I offer a few suggestions as to how you can function effectively in your husband's life? Number one, be *bearable!* Be patient with his shortcomings and mistakes. Avoid excessive nagging and complaining (even if self-motivation is not your husband's strong suit). Number two, be *beautiful.* Be the loveliest you can, inwardly and outwardly. Try to dress attractively and neatly, even if kids and carpools, trips to the grocery store, the dentist, and the doctor, consume an inordinate amount of your time. Don't neglect the inner self, either. Beauty beneath the skin counts a whole lot more than what's on the surface. Through prayer and the study and application of God's Word, allow Christ to transform you into His image. If you are bearable and beautiful, then you're guaranteed to be a *blessing* in your husband's life.

Remember the three B's: be bearable, beautiful, and a blessing. They spell out how you can help your man as he encounters trouble spots. Don't misunderstand—your husband *is* ultimately responsible for his actions, but there are ways in which you can assist him. Over the years, I've seen many cases where wives have become so involved in the activities of school, community, church, and career, that they've had little time left over for their men. They've volunteered to serve everybody but their husbands, and it's no wonder that the men have often become dissatisfied with their marriages.

So wives, please do not forget that your place in your husband's life must never be taken for granted. Life with his wife should be the one area a man can consistently enjoy. Do what you can to give your husband high priority; your relationship with him ranks second only in importance to your relationship with God. And men—you ought to be doing the same for your women. That is the Lord's design . . . and it works!

POINT THREE—GO FOR IT IN YOUR WORK!

Men are to eat, drink, and enjoy life—preferably with a godly wife. What's next? The third point of the job description laid out for us by Solomon in Ecclesiastes 9 is this: "Whatever your hand finds to do, do it with all your might, for in the grave, where you are going, there is neither working nor planning nor knowledge nor wisdom." In other words, we should "go for it" in our work! We must endure enthusiastically the tasks God gives us during our years on earth.

I am not talking about workaholism. Extensive projects in and of themselves brought Solomon no happiness, as we recall. Our vocations should never become more important to us than God or our wives and families, but the Lord desires for us to find satisfaction in our labor. He wants us to work! In view of the coming of Christ, many of the saints at Thessalonica took early retirement in anticipation of His imminent return. Concerned about this lack of action, Paul wrote these words to them:

> In the name of the Lord Jesus Christ, we command you, brothers, to keep away from every brother who is idle and does not live according to the teaching you received from us. For you yourselves know how you ought to follow our example. We were not idle when we were with you, nor did we eat anyone's food without paying for it. On the contrary, we worked night and day, laboring and toiling so that we would not be a burden to any of you (2 Thessalonians 3:6-8).

We should pursue our occupations wholeheartedly and energetically. The recipe for harnessing such enthusiasm is found in Colossians 3:23-24: "Whatever you do, work at it with all your heart, as working for the Lord, not for men, since you know that you will receive an inheritance from the Lord as a reward. It is the Lord Christ you are serving."

I teach the young people who attend our camps that there is no division between the sacred and the secular. I tell them that they are no more spiritual while sitting in a Bible class than they are riding and caring for the horses which have been assigned to them for the week. Of course they love that philosophy . . . and it's true, because whatever they do in their lives should be done to the glory of God; whatever task they perform should be completed with God in mind. The Lord is, in a sense, the employer. We all work for Him, from the child asked to clean his room, to the housewife sorting the laundry, to the corporate executive analyzing market trends and setting sales quotas.

Vying for that contract, pushing that product, driving that bus, designing that building, filling that tooth, hammering that nail—whatever we do, let's do it for God. That makes it possible to endure enthusiastically over the span of an entire career. Satisfaction comes not from striving toward material goals, but from working for a very special person: Jesus Christ. Looking at things from that perspective makes it easier for us to labor with all our might, as Solomon recommends.

In the process, let's take care to keep the sequence straight. We are instructed to eat, enjoy life with a wife, and endure the job enthusiastically. Some men get it mixed up. They *endure* their home lives, but they *enjoy* their vocations, preferring job to home front. Such a tangled arrangement threatens to cause confusion at mid-life, when a fellow's career may reach a standstill and when the shallowness of a man's personal relationships may become disturbingly apparent. Keeping priorities unsnarled is, of necessity, a lifelong concern.

TIME GOES ON—ECCLESIASTES 9:11-12

> I have seen something else under the sun:
>   The race is not to the swift
>   or the battle to the strong,
>   nor does food come to the wise
>   or wealth to the brilliant
>   or favor to the learned;
>   but time and chance happen to them all.
> Moreover, no man knows when his hour will come:
>   As fish are caught in a cruel net,
>   or birds are taken in a snare,
>   so men are trapped by evil times
>   that fall unexpectedly upon them.

If we follow the three-point job description set forth by Solomon in Ecclesiastes 9:1-10, we'll be making the most of our time. Doing so makes good sense—the years march relentlessly on and we might as well enjoy ourselves in godly fashion while we can. If we maintain balanced priorities, our chances of being crushed by a mid-life crisis will be sharply lessened. We really have no other legitimate, workable alternative, since so much in life is out of the control of even the most talented among us, as Solomon once more reminds us in verse 11 of chapter 9.

"I have seen something else under the sun," he remarks. Then he mentions five observations which he has made, saying first of all that "the race is not to the swift." A person doesn't have to enter many track events to recognize the truth of that comment. At the sound of the starting gun, some runners blast off like titan missiles, only to falter and fizzle like bottle rockets before they near the home stretch. Marathons aren't won by the speedy so much as by the steady contestants who pace themselves, mile after mile after mile.

As the race does not always go to the swift, neither does "the battle [go] to the strong," Solomon next declares in verse 11. "Nor does food come to the wise or wealth to the brilliant or favor to the learned," he continues. There are no certainties regarding human performance. An All-American college fullback may be a wash-out in the pros. A renowned biochemist with seventeen registered patents may die in debt. On the battlefield, a masterful general may be outmaneuvered by a green lieutenant. What *is* predictable is the unpredictability—from our point of view—of the human experience. As Solomon concludes in Ecclesiastes 9:11: "Time and chance happen to them all."

Time marches inexorably on. As the years pass, our strength is depleted. Our priorities are revealed. We let go of goals we have set for ourselves, because it becomes apparent that we cannot achieve them. In confronting the reality of the passage of time, we can thrash about, protesting the meaninglessness of life as we have seen Solomon do. Or, we can submit by eating, enjoying, and enduring. The latter choice is by far the better. Struggling in personal turmoil squanders precious weeks, months, and years. The luxury of wasting time is something we really cannot afford.

Our lifespans are not long enough to allow us to putter away segments of them in pessimism. Solomon reflects in verse 12: "Moreover, no man knows when his hour will come: As fish are caught in a cruel net, or birds are taken

in a snare, so men are trapped by evil times that fall unexpectedly upon them." We don't know what lies around the
corner. During the eight weeks of one of my tours (in
which I was teaching the book of Ecclesiastes), several
unexpected events took place. I conducted the funerals of a
little boy and a forty-three-year-old man; Princess Grace
passed away at age fifty, after suffering a stroke and crash-
ing a car; a tiny baby was crushed in a crib by the family's
pet python. Such tragedies fall upon us with awesome sud-
denness and we, like netted fish or snared fowl, can offer
no explanation. Yet the wisest among us realize that God is
in complete control.

A WISE RESPONSE—ECCLESIASTES 9:13-18

> I also saw under the sun this example of wisdom
> that greatly impressed me: There was once a small
> city with only a few people in it. And a powerful king
> came against it, surrounded it and built huge
> siegeworks against it. Now there lived in that city a
> man poor but wise, and he saved the city by his
> wisdom. But nobody remembered that poor man. So I
> said, "Wisdom is better than strength." But the poor
> man's wisdom is despised and his words are no longer
> heeded.
>> The quiet words of the wise are more to be
>> heeded
>>   than the shouts of a ruler of fools.
>> Wisdom is better than weapons of war,
>>   but one sinner destroys much good.

The wisest of men and women also hold the key to
dealing with the mysteries of life: they manage to remain
rightly related to God's eternal purpose. They cooperate
with the Lord. In their schedules, they reserve the place of
highest importance and urgency for Him. They spend time
in meaningful communion with Christ and in purposeful
study of His Word. They emphasize family over fame,
people over power, relationships over temporal rewards.
They find the strength to confront mid-life and other life

concerns by leaning on the Lord. That is the ideal. And not surprisingly, they are often laughed at, ignored, or forgotten by the rest of the world.

In verses 13 through 16 of chapter 9, Solomon tells us the story of an incident in which a man who is truly wise is quickly forgotten. It is the tale of "a small city with only a few people in it," against which a powerful king deployed a large army and constructed "huge siegeworks" (9:14). Within the besieged city was an impoverished man with a keen mind. So intelligent was he that "he saved the city by his wisdom" (9:15). After this blaze of glory, the "hero" was rapidly discounted by the citizens he had saved. Solomon draws the following conclusion from the experience: "Wisdom is better than strength. But the poor man's wisdom is despised, and his words are no longer heeded" (9:16).

Even today we are more impressed by strength than we are by wisdom. If you are inclined to disagree, consider what these two sets of initials mean: NFL and PhD. Millions of fans view NFL games each year. Do the same attendance figures apply to lectures given by PhDs? Hardly! I do not mean to imply that football players lack intelligence, but the fact of the matter is that most of us value displays of brawn more than we do shows of brainpower. And many of us will encounter difficulties at mid-life or before or after because we'll refuse to seek wise answers. It is safe to say that the percentage of people looking for meaning by embracing what the world offers far outweighs the number who genuinely commit their lives to Christ in a time of crisis.

Solomon closes chapter 9 with two admonitions. "The quiet words of the wise are more to be heeded than the shouts of a ruler of fools," he cautions in verse 17, reinforcing the notion that recovery comes from employing God-given wisdom. The words of James 3:14-18 complement this counsel:

> But if ye have bitter envying and strife in your hearts, glory not, and lie not against the truth. This wisdom descendeth not from above, but is earthly, sensual,

demoniacal. For where envying and strife are, there is confusion and every evil work. But the wisdom that is from above is first pure, then peaceable, gentle, and easy to be entreated, full of mercy and good fruits, without hypocrisy. And the fruit of righteousness is sown in peace by them that make peace (KJV).

It is far better to pay attention to the "quiet words of the wise" than the noisy, raucous, often bitter advice of the world.

Solomon's final warning to us in chapter 9 is this: "Wisdom is better than weapons of war, but one sinner destroys much good" (9:18). The presence of sin in our lives must be dealt with if wisdom is to have its proper influence. Part of wisdom entails handing areas of disobedience to God. As a lone arsonist can set fire to a building and destroy in minutes what took months or years to design and construct, so may a little wickedness manifest itself with catastrophic consequences.

This principle becomes vivid when we recall that a crisis at mid-life is often the result of a lifetime of improper attitudes, misplaced priorities, misused time. If a man either never places God at the top of the list or neglects to keep Him there, he almost certainly insures that he will one day become disenchanted with life. Ignoring God becomes a habit, and what starts as a small amount of sin burgeons into destructive trauma.

Flies in the Ointment—Ecclesiastes 10:1-3

> As dead flies give perfume a bad smell,
>   so a little folly outweighs wisdom and honor.
> The heart of the wise inclines to the right,
>   but the heart of the fool to the left.
> Even as he walks along the road,
>   the fool lacks sense
>   and shows everyone how stupid he is.

A smattering of evil may have devastating effects. So may a small bit of foolishness. Solomon observes in Ecclesiastes 10:1: "As dead flies give perfume a bad smell, so a little folly outweighs wisdom and honor." Not only may a crisis at middlescence crop up because of unchecked sin, but even a little bit of carelessness in one's life can be dangerous.

After all, how did the dead flies of which Solomon speaks manage to drop into the perfume bottle in the first place? Surely nobody intentionally placed them there—no one would want to transform a jar of delicate fragrance into a pot of foul-smelling oil. The answer is that somebody got careless. Someone forgot to cap the jar, and a splendid scent became an unbearable stench.

As we are to beware of overt sin, so are we to be on the lookout for signs of carelessness in our lives. I am reminded of what Solomon says to his bride, Shulamith, in chapter 2, verse 15 of the Song of Solomon. His words are these: "Catch for us the foxes, the little foxes that ruin the vineyards, our vineyards that are in bloom." The "little foxes" to which he refers represent all of the minor irritants, trivial in and of themselves, which can combine to threaten a relationship. Solomon feared that a number of "little things" would escalate into big things and spoil the vine of love that was blossoming before them. That could only happen if the couple became inattentive, taking each other for granted, forgetting to protect and nurture their love.

Solomon recognized the dangers of carelessness as a young man, but it is apparently a lesson he forgot as he grew older and found it necessary to search for significance by pursuing other women (see Ecclesiastes 2). In middlescence, he finds his marriage unsatisfying. In truth, he had probably been letting the "little foxes" run roughshod over his relationship with Shulamith for years. The flies had long since buzzed their way into the perfume pot.

Many times mid-life marital problems have their roots in exactly this type of lack of caution. I remember, as I was preparing this series on Ecclesiastes, walking into my wife's office and seeing a paper on her desk entitled, "Pearl's Ecclesiastes." I thought, oh no, she's having a mid-life crisis! Then I picked up the page, which had not been left there merely by chance. I read the message Pearl wanted me to see. It began with a sentence: "Home isn't the way it used to be." Listed underneath that statement were three phrases: "Running, racquetball, hundreds of activities." I got the point.

Home was not what it used to be because I was allowing little things to become big things, permitting unimportant pastimes to become primary pursuits. And I was neglecting Pearl in the process. The dead flies were causing a tremendous stink.

THE DIFFERENCE BETWEEN RIGHT AND WRONG

Several years of outright sin or less obvious carelessness may well provoke a crisis at mid-life. Whatever the cause, the issues of right and wrong will surface at some point. The mid-life man must make choices concerning how to respond to the conflict he feels. So far, Solomon has reacted to his disillusionment with life by lunging in many different directions. That he has matured from the experience is obvious in the next two verses of Ecclesiastes 10.

"The heart of the wise inclines to the right, but the heart of the fool to the left," he states in verse 2. Conservative politicians sometimes misquote this verse to support their right-wing positions, but Solomon isn't talking politics! What he means is that the wise man lives comfortably with authority. He possesses an obedient heart. He desires to follow the standards of right and wrong established by God.

The fool, on the other hand, persists in struggling in resistance to authority. At his core is a spirit of disobedience and rebellion. Such a fellow, Solomon says in Ecclesiastes 10:3, lacks sense and "shows everyone how stupid he is," even by the way in which he walks down the road.

OF PATIENCE, PERSPECTIVE, AND PREPARATION— ECCLESIASTES 10:4-11

> If a ruler's anger rises against you,
>   do not leave your post;

calmness can lay great errors to rest.
There is an evil I have seen under the sun,
   the sort of error that arises from a ruler:
Fools are put in many high positions,
   while the rich occupy the low ones.
I have seen slaves on horseback,
   while princes go on foot like slaves.
Whoever digs a pit may fall into it;
   whoever breaks through a wall may be bitten
     by a snake.
Whoever quarries stones may be injured by
     them;
   whoever splits logs may be endangered by
     them.
If the ax is dull
   and its edge unsharpened,
more strength is needed
   but skill will bring success.
If a snake bites before it is charmed,
   there is no profit for the charmer.

If wisdom provides the solution to handling mid-life conflict, how do we incorporate it into our daily lives? In most of the remaining verses of chapter ten, Solomon answers that question. He elaborates on living life wisely, pointing out practical guidelines for conducting ourselves properly, even in the face of frustration, injustice, and gross incompetence.

In verse 4, he advises us how to intelligently respond to worldly authority. "If a ruler's anger rises against you, do not leave your post; calmness can lay great errors to rest," Solomon instructs. We are cautioned not to panic—and to avoid hasty reactions. Wisdom's strength lies in maintaining control, not in flying off the handle. Even in tense situations, we'd better remember that a leap out of the frying pan will only make us end up sizzling in the fire.

It isn't always easy to remain calm, cool, and collected when someone in authority becomes upset with us, but that is the wise response. When called on the carpet at work, for example, we shouldn't holler and scream and storm out the door, yammering, "I quit!" as we slam it behind us. That is a foolish reaction. With an attitude of calm control, we should listen to the boss, and then rationally present our side of the story. We'll at least gain his respect for our restraint! Calmness *can* "lay great errors to rest."

It is especially tough to exercise control when we tangle with authority figures whom we consider incompetent. By the time we reach middle age, most of us have run into quite a few of these characters. Solomon speaks of the undeserving powerful in verses 5, 6, and 7 of Ecclesiastes 10, remarking that he has seen yet another "evil . . . under the sun." That injustice is "the sort of error that arises from a ruler" (10:5). It happens when "fools are put in many high positions, while the rich occupy the low ones" (10:6). In fact, as Solomon reveals in verse 7, he has even seen slaves riding on horseback, "while princes go on foot like slaves."

That authority is misused and abused is a fact of life. It isn't fair—and unqualified people should be removed from their posts whenever possible. Yet even in dealing with inept officials, we must curb our tempers and muzzle our mouths. Wisdom demands discretion, moderation, and control. In the words of James 1:19-20: "My dear brothers, take note of this: Everyone should be quick to listen, slow to speak and slow to become angry, for man's anger does not bring about the righteous life that God desires." Huffing and puffing on our part plainly do not fit into the Master plan.

Blowing our stacks is a waste of energy which in the long run won't change very many situations. Once again we are reminded that much of life lies beyond our jurisdiction, as Solomon mentions in verses 8 and 9: "Whoever digs a pit may fall into it; whoever breaks through a wall may be bitten by a snake. Whoever quarries stones may be injured by them; whoever splits logs may be endangered by them." A portion of wisdom calls for us to remember this, so that we'll keep events in perspective.

And naturally, living wisely also involves being prepared. "If the ax is dull and its edge unsharpened, more strength is needed but skill will bring success," Solomon asserts in verse 10. I can't help but think that it would be much easier for the woodcutter if his ax were sharpened before he began using it to chop kindling. It is a matter of preparation.

In the same sense, "If a snake bites before it is charmed, there is no profit for the charmer," as Solomon remarks in Ecclesiastes 10:11. Any snake charmer who values his life will train his fanged cohorts before they perform in the marketplace. If proper preparations aren't made, then the charmer's wisdom would be questionable indeed.

How can we ready ourselves to meet life head-on? Our sharpest weapon is the "two-edged sword" of the Word of God (Hebrews 4:12). Our best education is familiarizing ourselves with the Scriptures and with the God portrayed therein. That is the formula, pure and simple.

MORE PRINCIPLES FOR PRACTICAL WISDOM—ECCLESIASTES 10:12-20

> Words from a wise man's mouth are gracious,
>   but a fool is consumed by his own lips.
> At the beginning his words are folly;
>   at the end they are wicked madness—
>   and the fool multiplies words.
> No one knows what is coming—
>   who can tell him what will happen after
>   him?
> A fool's work wearies him;
>   he does not know the way to town.
> Woe to you, O land whose king was a servant
>   and whose princes feast in the morning.
> Blessed are you, O land whose king is of noble
>   birth
>   and whose princes eat at a proper time—
>   for strength and not for drunkenness.
> If a man is lazy, the rafters sag;
>   if his hands are idle, the house leaks.

> A feast is made for laughter,
>> and wine makes life merry,
>>> but money is the answer for everything.
> Do not revile the king even in your thoughts,
>> or curse the rich in your bedroom,
>>> because a bird of the air may carry your
>>> words,
>>>> and a bird on the wing may report what you
>>>> say.

Solomon continues to offer practical insights for intelligent living in verses 12 through 20 of chapter 10, expounding in particular on what types of behavior we ought to avoid. He uses some strong language, describing the words of a wise man as "gracious" but declaring on the other hand that "a fool is consumed by his own lips" (10:12). Foolish men and women are in danger of choking during attacks of foot-in-mouth disease. They talk too much, and the excess blabbing often gets them in trouble. In light of that, maybe it isn't a bad idea for us to strive to become the "strong, silent types" made popular by the media.

And there is progression—probably better labeled regression—in the vocabulary of the fool. "In the beginning his [the fool's] words are folly," Solomon says in verse 13, but "at the end they are wicked madness." To make matters worse, the words of the fool are also "multiplied" (10:14). He never knows when to zip his lips or bridle his tongue!

A foolish man lacks direction and purpose in his vocation, as well. His work "wearies him," observes Solomon in verse 15. Why, the fool doesn't even know how to *follow* directions—he cannot even find "the way to town" (10:15). It is bad enough when such idiocy and sloth are obvious in the life of an average citizen. It is positively indecent when these qualities characterize a group of rulers.

"Woe to you, O land whose king was a servant and whose princes feast in the morning," Solomon cries in verse 16. He's talking about lazy leaders who use their power and privilege for personal advantage and, ultimately, for their own pleasure. Here the king's sons prefer debauchery to duty. The princes are worthless.

But blessed is the land "whose king is of noble birth and whose princes eat at a proper time—for strength and not for drunkenness," Solomon exclaims in Ecclesiastes 10:17. The virtues of responsible leadership are extolled. It is idleness which is condemned as unwise living at its worst.

"If a man is lazy, the rafters sag," continues Solomon. "If his hands are idle, the house leaks" (10:18). That verse became real to me one summer when Pearl and I were staying in a missionary cabin in the Northwest. I was speaking at a conference that week, and we had been housed in a cabin for the duration. I converted one of the four bedrooms into a study, spreading my notes on Ecclesiastes across a plywood-topped bed which was serving as my "desk." Outside, a few sprinkles began softly falling. Within a few minutes, water was pouring out of the sky in a terrific deluge. Soon I noticed that the rain wasn't content to remain outside. Water was dripping from various spots in the ceiling of my study and the other rooms. Frantically I thrust pots, pans, bottles, and buckets under the leaks. When every raindrop had a safe place to land, I returned to work.

You guessed it! The next verse I came to was Ecclesiastes 10:18. I had been treated to a first-hand experience of that passage. I can personally testify to the fact that rafters sag and ceilings spring leaks when care is not constant. Wise living demands careful maintenance. (Incidently, the leaky cabin has long since been repaired.)

And finally, living intelligently means honoring those in authority. As Solomon cautions in verse 20: "Do not revile the king even in your thoughts, or curse the rich in your bedroom, because a bird of the air may carry your words, and a bird on the wing may report what you say." Derogatory comments and snide, critical remarks have a way of boomeranging on us. Once we toss them out, even in privacy, they spread. They do what damage they can, then they return to condemn us. The person about whom we have spoken somehow finds out. Even comments made in strict confidentiality manage to return to the sender. Wise living demands discretion.

LESSONS

Six lessons emerge from chapters 9 and 10 of Ecclesiastes. Let's look at them in capsule form.

Number one: *the righteous and the wise are in God's hands. Our lives are determined according to His eternal purpose.*

Number two: *we should eat our food with gladness, enjoy life with a wife, and endure our careers enthusiastically, performing our jobs with all our might.*

Lesson three: *nothing is predictable.* We don't know when the emergency will hit, when the day of trial will arrive, when the hour of death will occur.

Lesson four: *the quiet words of the wise are more important than the raucous ramblings of fools.*

Number five: *a little folly can spoil an entire life,* as the dead flies ruin the perfume.

Lesson six: *we must not revile the authority that is above us.* Rebellion against earthly authority actually reveals resistance to heavenly authority.

In a Nutshell

The significance of Solomon's message in Ecclesiastes 9 and 10 may be summarized in a nutshell. Briefly, it is this: *The solution to the mid-life crisis comes when we submit to the determinations of a sovereign God who is working out our lives for the greatest good. How do we submit? We pursue wise living; we enjoy and endure; we trust.*

I'd like to close by telling of a fellow I know who accepted Christ several years ago when attending one of our Bible studies. He was, at that time, a vice president of a savings and loan company in a West Texas city. I did not hear from him for a couple of years following his conversion to Christ, then from across the miles came a very special letter.

He had been through a great deal during those years.

Career problems had sparked a struggle of sorts with God. It is beautiful to read in his words how that conflict ended at the moment of surrender to the Lord's purpose. I've included below an excerpt from that letter:

Dear Don,

It has been a long time since we last talked—almost two years. I'm not sure if you even remember who I am, but even if you don't, it is not really important. During your visit to [name of city], I gave my life to Christ. I had a long way to go, but fortunately the Lord is patient and was willing to spend some time on me. Sometimes, I think, the Lord has to run us into a brick wall to knock some sense into our head. At least that is the way it happened with me.

About three months ago, after months of struggling with my job, I was fired. It was a devastating experience, and frankly, I felt like the Lord had deserted me. I suffered through a couple of weeks until I realized that in all of my prayers I was trying to manipulate the Lord. I was disappointed when things didn't go my way, which at the time I thought was the only way. Finally, I hit my knees and asked for forgiveness. I asked that the Lord's will be done, regardless of what I thought about it. I pledged to trust in Him no matter what happened.

From that moment I have experienced a peace that I have never experienced before. A few days after that, I took a job selling real estate. I haven't sold anything yet, and I am flat broke, but I am working hard and I have never been happier. The Lord is with me, He loves me, and He provides for me.

Isn't that a marvelous testimony? My friend came to the point where he could ask "that the Lord's will be done, regardless of what [he] thought about it." That is surrender. He pledged to trust in Christ, no matter what. That is submission. And even flat broke, he is supremely happy—for perhaps the first time in his life. That is the reward of obedience.

Questions for Personal or Group Study

1. Keeping Solomon's reflections in Ecclesiastes 9:1 in mind, do you believe that God doles out the good and bad in our lives, according to whether He loves or hates us? Why or why not?

2. Is the nature of man, according to Solomon, basically good or evil? (See Ecclesiastes 9:3.)

3. In what ways, to Solomon's way of thinking, are the living better off than the dead? (See 9:5-6.) In your opinion, are the living *always* better off than the dead? Explain.

4. What is the "three-point job description" for living a God-pleasing life, as recommended by Solomon in Ecclesiastes 9:7-10?

5. Do people generally value wisdom, especially if it is not "attractively packaged"? Reread Ecclesiastes 9:13-17 before determining your answer.

6. What can be learned from the remark in verse 1 of chapter 10 that, "dead flies give perfume a bad smell"?

7. What principles does Solomon give us in verses 4-7 for properly responding to authority, even inept authority?

10

Meeting Up with Mortality

Ecclesiastes 11–12

A bewildered patient is depicted confessing to his wide-eyed psychiatrist in a comic strip: "I came out of my mid-life crisis and ran smack into my second childhood." After chuckling at that cartoon, I reflected a moment on its truth. For many people, that's much the way it happens. Often the fear of growing old combines with other concerns of middle age to generate a crisis in a man's life—he may languish in depression and turmoil for years. Recovery may, in fact, come just in time for our hero to face old age!

At this writing, I am fifty-three years old. The era for Geritol and golden anniversaries is not very far away. I don't often admit that—and you'll notice I didn't mention retirement, Social Security, *Modern Maturity* magazine, or any other reminders of the decades from sixty-five on. But I know that, barring my death, I'll be taking advantage of senior citizens' discounts within a few short years. In the meantime, old people are looking a lot younger to me than they used to!

At a recent Bible study, one of the members of our board shared a laughable list of definitions of old age. I'd like to include a few of them here:

Old age is when:

> . . . everything hurts—and what doesn't hurt, doesn't work.
> . . . your little black book contains only names ending in "M.D."
> . . . your children begin to look middle-aged.

    . . . your mind makes contracts your body can't meet.

    . . . you walk with your head high, trying to get used to your new bifocals.

    . . . you sit in a rocking chair and can't get it going.

    . . . your knees buckle and your belt won't.

    . . . your back goes out more often than you do.

    . . . the little gray-haired lady you help across the street is your wife.

    . . . you have too much room in the house and not enough room in the medicine cabinet.

    . . . after painting the town red, you have to take a long rest before the second coat.

    . . . you sink your teeth into a steak, and they stay there.

There are some classics in that list! But, all kidding aside, growing old is a mentally, emotionally, and physically uncomfortable process. In the book *Necessary Losses*, Judith Viorst quotes a gerontologist who makes this comment: "Put cotton in your ears and pebbles in your shoes. Pull on rubber gloves. Smear Vaseline over your glasses, and there you have it: instant aging" (Viorst 288, 1986).

CONSIDERING THE ALTERNATIVE

Aging is a process from which there is no escape other than the grave. In the words of Ralph Waldo Emerson: "Old age brings along with its ugliness the comfort that you will soon be out of it" (Whicher 1960, 404). We don't *recover* from old age . . . at least not till we're *covered* by the dust of the earth. Indeed, old age is like a disease for which there can be no cure.

The initial pangs of aging generally strike in middlescence—as a fellow's hairline recedes and his blood pressure rises. It's no wonder, therefore, that Jim Conway identifies a man's own body as the first major "enemy" confronting him at mid-life (Conway 1979, 65). In our forties and fifties, we become sharply aware of physical limitations, perhaps for the very first time.

And as we advance in years to the brink of old age, we are forced to face our own mortality. Death becomes tangible—more like an after-dinner companion than an afterthought. Comments Jim Conway:

> Intellectually, we all know that people die, but before mid-life we tend to think of death in terms of *other* people. Suddenly, in mid-life some event or thought causes us to realize that death is going to happen to us (Conway 1979, 267).

I have found Conway's observation to be true. As a minister who preaches at churches attended by many retirees, I am called upon often to conduct funerals. Death is no stranger to me. Yet at the same time, it was rather easy for me to think of death as an event associated most often with the over-seventy set. It *was* easy, that is, until the death of my friend Doug, who passed away while in his early forties.

Doug was nearly a part of our staff. He donated the services of his printing company to produce the Ministries' newsletters and study guides. At least once a week for years, I would make a trip to his print shop in the industrial sector of Dallas, so that we might discuss formats, deadlines, covers, and quantities.

Our relationship extended beyond business. We played golf and racquetball; we went camping and fishing; we talked about dreams for the future, and shared concerns of the present.

Although Doug's death followed a series of health problems, I wasn't prepared for it. And even though I knew he had merely beaten me to heaven and that I'd see him once again someday, his passing was hard to get used to. For months following the funeral, I'd find myself absent-mindedly steering the car toward the location of his print shop. It was as if I couldn't quite accept the fact that he was gone.

With Doug's death came a heightened awareness of my own mortality as well. I was in my forties at the time—and suddenly seventy seemed awfully close. What was more, it became obvious that there was nothing "safe" about the preretirement decades; death could happen at any time. Doug hadn't lived to see his forty-fifth birthday. Who was to say that my experience would be any different?

We know the death knell is not a dreaded summons for anyone who knows Jesus Christ. Instead it is the opening of a heavenly world of unimaginable beauty. We can catch a glimpse of this future glory by reading Revelation 21. Yet in all honesty, I became intensely afraid that I would be missing out on something life had to offer—some experience, some opportunity—if God chose to call me home any time soon.

Several years have gone by since Doug has died. With God's help I have come to grips with the notion of dying. I feel that I am ready whenever He wants to take me. I shall, however, always remember the disquieting experience of confronting my own mortality at mid-life.

SOLOMON'S ANGLE

In the final two chapters of Ecclesiastes, Solomon concludes the chronicle of his mid-life crisis by imparting wisdom of a most practical nature. He comes to terms with growing old and with dying. As he collides with the inevitable, he also manages, with God's help, to rid himself of the personal turmoil which has characterized his middle years. He quits searching for answers to the meaning of life because he fully recognizes that, in God, he has the source of all the answers he needs. He emerges from crisis as a survivor—not unscathed, but certainly far wiser.

Remember that in Ecclesiastes 9, Solomon urged us to eat, enjoy, and endure. Let's look now at the insights he supplies in chapters 11 and 12, as he continues to tell us how to live . . . and also, how to die.

LIVING WITH THE REALITY OF DIMINISHED TIME—
ECCLESIASTES 11:1-2

> Cast your bread upon the waters,
>   for after many days you will find it again.

> Give portions to seven, yes to eight,
>> for you do not know what disaster may come
>> upon the land.

The approach of old age and death sets off sirens of alarm in the hearts of many at mid-life. Daily routines seem mundane, relationships stifling, while the fear of missing out on the fullness of life is overwhelming. A middle-aged man, in particular, may believe that his 9:00 to 5:00 job and family responsibilities are preventing him from enjoying high (or even moderate) adventure. If he has reached forty-eight and has never climbed a mountain, shot a grizzly, parachuted from a plane, sailed the Atlantic, or even skiied down a slope, our man will want desperately to make the most of the time he has left. He'll want to milk his remaining years for all they're worth, before the onset of illness or senility makes it impossible to engage in even the mildest forms of excitement. He will intensely desire to carve out some lasting accomplishments so that his life will have counted for something.

There is, however, an art to living wisely when faced with the reality, as we all are, of diminished time at mid-life. There are methods to insure that, after we are gone, our lives will have mattered. Solomon opens Ecclesiastes 11 by suggesting how we should act, even though the final countdown seems to have started before we were ready.

"Cast your bread upon the waters," he advises in verse 1, "for after many days you will find it again." The heart of his counsel is for us, as we face old age, to reach out to others. The words of Jesus in the Sermon on the Mount are reminiscent of Solomon's command: "Give, and it will be given to you. A good measure, pressed down, shaken together and running over, will be poured into your lap. For with the measure you use, it will be measured to you" (Luke 6:38).

Casting our "bread upon the waters" means we must stop thinking *selfishly* and start thinking *socially.* We must shift our focus outward: reaching to assist others, considering their needs rather than our own. Instead of wallowing in self-pity because of the limitations our mid-years have brought, we should find our fulfillment in doing what we can for the people God has placed in our lives. That means investing time in our families—spending significant hours with our children, our spouses. It can mean praying for the needs of others, cutting the lawn of the fellow who is recovering from back surgery, offering to change the oil in an elderly gentleman's car, taking a teenage boy fishing. It can mean opening our homes for Bible studies, leading a businessmen's prayer breakfast, or asking God for opportunities to witness for Him—and then freely telling others about Jesus Christ as those chances become available.

As we thus cast our bread upon the waters, we're guaranteed that we "after many days . . . will find it again" (10:1). The blessings will come, as will the satisfaction with life. The affection of others is an added benefit. Think about it, and you'll realize that the people who are most loved are those who unselfishly serve other folks. They aren't motivated by the thought of receiving love, but by the idea of *giving* it.

Miss Lucy was an example of just such a person. She attended our church at Hide-A-Way Lake for years, in fact, until her death not too long ago. Miss Lucy was in her nineties when she went home to be with her Lord. Up until that time, she served others faithfully. She stayed busy with her needles: tatting crosses and knitting booties. Even as she grew more frail and became unable to minister in more concrete ways, Miss Lucy served by praying faithfully for the needs of others. Reading her Bible and writing letters of encouragement were her specialties. My wife Pearl paid her this heartfelt compliment the last time we saw her: "Miss Lucy, I want to grow old just like you."

On her ninety-third birthday, Miss Lucy made a list of ninety-three things she was thankful for. She never owned a car or went swimming but she learned that life at its best is lived in serving and giving. She was the epitome of unselfishness—a lovely servant of our Lord. And we miss her at Hide-A-Way! How strange it feels for me to look out over the congregation and not see her on the right-hand side of the church. She was the sort of person who enriched the lives of all she touched.

So we must cast our bread upon the waters. And yet there is more to living wisely in the face of diminished time. We must also, as Solomon instructs in verse 2, "Give portions to seven, yes to eight, for . . . [we] do not know what disaster may come upon the land." We should give of ourselves and of our resources generously, not sparingly. We need to spread out the blessings. Not only will more people's lives be positively affected, but we will benefit also. In time of personal disaster, those whom we have helped will surround and support and sustain us. By investing our time in individuals, we shall reap enormous dividends. Our lives will be purposeful. They will have meaning.

CONTEMPLATE, COMMIT, AND DIVERSIFY—ECCLESIASTES 11:3-6

> If clouds are full of water,
> > they pour rain upon the earth.
> Whether a tree falls to the south or to the
> > north,
> > in the place where it falls, there will it lie.
> Whoever watches the wind will not plant;
> > whoever looks at the clouds will not reap.
> As you do not know the path of the wind,
> > or how the body is formed in a mother's
> > womb,
> so you cannot understand the work of God,
> > the Maker of all things.
> Sow your seed in the morning,
> > and at evening let not your hands be idle,
> for you do not know which will succeed,
> > whether this or that,
> > or whether both will do equally well.

Constructively contributing to the lives of others involves making commitments. It means extending ourselves, stretching our resources. It is essential, if our lives are to have substance. But we must be careful not to overextend.

Before we make a commitment of time or money or self, we must evaluate the situation thoroughly and realistically. That is what Solomon means when he states, "If clouds are full of water, they pour rain upon the earth" (11:3). If the clouds are black and heavy with moisture, we don't have to be weathermen to predict a downpour. All we need to do is examine the sky.

Similarly, if a commitment we plan to make seems like it will be time-consuming, the chances are that it will be. We must determine to meet the obligations we make. That means not promising fishing trips to teenage boys if we don't have any intention of blocking out the time in which they'll take place. It means not starting a neighborhood Bible study, if we won't also schedule the hours necessary for weekly preparation.

Likewise, says Solomon, "Whether a tree falls to the south or to the north, in the place where it falls, there will it lie" (11:3). After a tree is felled, it is difficult to move without breaking some branches and scraping off some bark. Once we have made a commitment, it's tough to untangle ourselves from the obligation gracefully, without doing damage somewhere. The time to consider the cost of an enterprise is *before* the project is launched, before the contracts are signed, before the cement is slapped on and allowed to dry.

Essentially that is what Jesus teaches us in Luke 14. In verses 28 through 30, He asks the following of the crowds traveling with Him:

> Suppose one of you wants to build a tower. Will he not first sit down and estimate the cost to see if he has enough money to complete it? For if he lays the foundation and is not able to finish it, everyone who sees it will ridicule him, saying, "This fellow began to build and was not able to finish."

We shouldn't conduct our lives by leaving in our wakes strings full of partially-completed projects and unfulfilled promises, like so many half-built towers. It is important for us to evaluate the costs prior to breaking ground on some new venture. For one, we might appear foolish if we begin something that we cannot finish. We may also find ourselves in danger, as Jesus further informs His audience in Luke 14:

> Or suppose a king is about to go to war against another king. Will he not first sit down and consider whether he is able with ten thousand men to oppose the one coming against him with twenty thousand? If he is not able, he will send a delegation while the other is still a long way off and will ask for terms of peace. In the same way, any of you who does not give up everything he has cannot be my disciple (Luke 14:31-33).

The king contemplating an attack must first consider his assets and liabilities. The price of battle is not likely to be nominal, so it is smart to analyze the situation beforehand. Jesus draws a parallel as He enumerates, in verse 33, the tremendous cost of truly becoming His disciple. That doesn't mean that we should shrink from making the commitment to Him. It does mean that we should proceed with open eyes, a clear head, and a deliberate heart.

Two old sayings give a good picture of the manner in which we should make meaningful commitments in our lives. The first is, "Anything worth doing is worth doing well," and the second is, "Nothing is free." We increasingly discover the truth of those statements as time passes. Involving ourselves in a significant way in the lives of others does not come cheaply, but it is definitely worthwhile.

"GETTING A ROUND TUIT"

After we have weighed the consequences of involvement, we must act. We must take the plunge, for, as Solomon says in Ecclesiastes 11:4: "Whoever watches the wind will not plant; whoever looks at the clouds will not reap." If we wait for perfect conditions before we begin to give of ourselves, we'll be doomed to inaction. While we're looking for "pie in the sky," we'll miss the real opportunities for service which surround us. Exactly the right time to do something will probably never exist.

So many folks contemplate death and vow to do something significant for God with their money and talents before it's too late. I have had conversations with numerous individuals who have learned they have fatal illnesses. More often than not, these people have expressed a desire to accomplish something for the Lord. Maybe it's talking about Christ to an unsaved family member; perhaps it's donating a parcel of land to a church for a youth camp; possibly it's setting up a scholarship fund at a Bible college or seminary; sometimes it's as simple as speaking to a Sunday school class about how the Lord has proven faithful over a lifetime.

Whatever the intentions, most of the time the people never get around to acting. They're dead before the deed gets done. I am thinking about purchasing a stockpile of nickel-sized wooden disks with the words "A Round Tuit" stamped on each, so that I might hand them out as reminders that we must make provision to take action! We must get around to it—whatever *it* happens to be. I fully intend to buy those wooden nickels . . . if I ever get around to it, that is!

It is in human nature to procrastinate. We are adept at watching the wind and gazing at the clouds; we're not as good at planting and reaping. We put off following through on the resolutions we make. We know we need to exercise, register for night school, paint the house, recover the sofa, take the family camping, but we shove anything not included in our daily routine onto the back burner whenever possible.

Of more eternal importance, we put off receiving Christ as Savior, forgetting the urgency with which these words of Paul were written in 2 Corinthians 6:2: "Now is the time of God's favor, now is the day of salvation." Even if we are already believers, we delay in loving and serving the Lord as effectively as we might. Yet the foundation of the meaningful life is not built on procrastination but on execution, not on setting goals but in striving for them.

Proverbs 27:1 instructs: "Do not boast about tomorrow, for you do not know what a day may bring forth." Only

God knows that. In a similar vein, Solomon goes on to advise in Ecclesiastes 11:5: "As you do not know the path of the wind, or how the body is formed in a mother's womb, so you cannot understand the work of God, the Maker of all things." We cannot fully comprehend the methods of the Lord who is the Creator of all the universe. What we can depend upon is that He will meet our needs. He will reap the results for us, if we only take steps to cast our bread upon the waters for Him. And it is essential that we include Christ in that process.

What we do under our own steam, apart from Jesus Christ, appears as nothing more than "filthy rags" to God (Isaiah 64:6). But when we trust Christ to control our lives, when we seize the chances for service which He places in front of us, when we actively pursue a closer relationship with Him through prayer and study, our lives will count for something! We won't lie on our deathbeds and mourn what might have been.

DIVERSIFICATION

Solomon gives us another clue as to how to meaningfully invest the days of our lives. He recommends the following in verse 6 of Ecclesiastes 11: "Sow your seed in the morning, and at evening let not your hands be idle, for you do not know which will succeed, whether this or that, or whether both will do equally well." It's wise to diversify.

My friends who play the market caution against acquiring only one kind of stock. They advise purchasing shares in different sorts of companies. That way, if a recession hits in one industry, the other investments should still be in good shape. And I can see the wisdom of their perspective.

Diversification makes sense—in the business world and also in the Christian realm. I believe an example of this is evident in our Ministries. We have diversified, and the results have been different than we would have ever imagined. Let me explain.

When our nonprofit corporation was set up, we had to decide upon three reasons for incorporating. The first was easy: camping. My family and I had been involved in Christian camping for ten years, and loved it. Actually, the original purpose for forming the Ministries was so we might purchase some land and set up a first-class campground. Our second reason for incorporating was counseling. I like being involved with people, and counselors get plenty of opportunities to help others. We had to have a third reason to incorporate, so we selected teaching.

At first, I figured that I would teach some Bible classes—and maybe speak at a few conferences, just to keep bread on the table. All of this teaching would take a back seat to establishing our camp and providing our counseling services. Frankly, I really didn't want to sit on a stool and teach Bible classes. God, however, seemed to keep opening opportunities for me to do just that. He seemed to bless each study series, so that my "occasional" teaching became quite regular. I now go on tour nine months out of the year, teaching Scripture.

Fourteen years ago, when we incorporated, I would have never believed it possible. After all, we were going to create a camp! And do you know what? We still don't own any camping facilities. The family and youth camps are held at rented locations. And counseling . . . I rarely have the time any more to counsel anyone in depth. The others on our staff devote a larger portion of their time to this than I do. God chose teaching as the area of my personal ministry that He desired to bless. I have found that I am happy doing what He tells me to do, and I'm miserable when I stop paying attention to Him.

You, too, can find fulfillment through diversification in your personal ministry. And don't worry! You do not have to attend seminary. You certainly do not have to become a fulltime professional Christian worker. Your life for Christ can be terrifically successful even if you do not possess a list of divinity degrees and a resume full of the names of evangelical organizations for which you've worked.

Try your hand, for example, at teaching a Sunday school class. Sing in the choir at church. Lick envelopes at the campaign office of a Christian politician. Read Bible stories to your children. Hold family devotions. Pray regularly with your spouse. Make it a point to become friends with your neighbors and co-workers. Take an interest in their lives. Invite them to come to your home for dinner. Ask them to go hunting, bowling, or golfing with you. Search for opportunities to tactfully and naturally bring the good news of Jesus Christ into your conversations with them; they need the Savior. Also, stay busy. "Sow your seed in the morning, and at evening, let not your hands be idle" (11:6). Always remain in close contact with the Lord, letting your relationship with Him develop and mature. And never let your deeds eclipse in your heart the One for whom they are done.

TAKE DELIGHT, BEFORE DARKNESS SHROUDS—ECCLESIASTES 11:7-10

> Light is sweet,
>   and it pleases the eyes to see the sun.
> However many years a man may live,
>   let him enjoy them all.
> But let him remember the days of darkness,
>   for they will be many.
>   Everything to come is meaningless.
> Be happy, young man, while you are young,
>   and let your heart give you joy in the days of
>   your youth.
> Follow the ways of your heart
>   and whatever your eyes see,
> but know that for all these things
>   God will bring you to judgment.
> So then, banish anxiety from your heart
>   and cast off the troubles of your body,
>   for youth and vigor are meaningless.

There will be wonderful, joyous days for us as we serve the Lord. As Solomon says in verse 7 of Ecclesiastes 11: "Light is sweet, and it pleases the eyes to see the sun." Life lived for God is satisfying and full. Yet rain falls, even in the sunniest and warmest of seasons. As one of my friends puts it, "Sometimes it seems that behind every silver lining there's a cloud!"

There will be days—plenty of them—when the land-scape of our lives will seem bleak, when it will appear as though God has pulled the shades to shut out the light and capture the darkness. Some days, nothing will go right!

I think of the story about the airman who was about to parachute for the first time and was scared to death of the prospect. His instructor told him, "Settle down. There's nothing to this. All you do is jump out, count to ten, then pull the rip cord on your main chute. It'll open, and you'll float to the ground. Now in case it doesn't work, you've got an emergency chute—pull the cord on that and it'll pop out, and you'll be okay. A truck will be waiting below to pick you up and take you back to the base."

The rookie paratrooper did as instructed. He jumped out of the plane, counted to ten, and pulled the cord of his main chute. Nothing happened. Still calm, he reached over and yanked on the rip cord of his reserve chute. But again—nothing happened! The last words he was heard to exclaim while plummeting to the earth were, "And I suppose the truck won't be down there either!"

That fellow had a day when nothing went right. And just like that hapless paratrooper, we'll experience times when the best part of the day takes place before our morning alarm clock rings. Occasions like that happen with increasing frequency as we approach old age. The older we get, the more there is to go wrong! Aches, pains, the deaths of friends, separations from family members, loneliness, failing health—growing older is a bed of roses with few blossoms and an awful lot of thorns. Solomon conveys that idea in Ecclesiastes 11:8: "However many years a man may live, let him enjoy them all. But let him remember the days of darkness, for they will be many. Everything to come is meaningless."

How do we live wisely, in light of that dreary reality? Solomon gives that answer in verse 9:

> Be happy, young man, while you are young,
>   and let your heart give you joy in the days of
>   your youth,
> Follow the ways of your heart
>   and whatever your eyes see,
> but know that for all these things
>   God will bring you to judgment.

I have heard parents take that ninth verse and hurl it at their teenaged and college-aged kids as some kind of fire-and-brimstone-packed warning. "Go ahead and live it up, Junior," threaten Mom and Dad, "and someday you'll be sorry! God is going to judge!" But that is not how the verse ought to be interpreted.

Instead, Solomon is contending in Ecclesiastes 11:9 that wise living within the limited space of a man's life calls for him to enjoy himself. We should particularly make the most of our youth, partaking of the wholesome pleasures of life while we can. Solomon doesn't advocate lawlessness or immorality—just plain and simple enjoyment of God and His goodness and His gifts.

And what is more, Solomon says, "But know that for all these things God will bring you to judgment" (Ecclesiastes 11:9). What are "all these things" for which we'll be brought to "judgment"? It is simple. As believers, we will not be condemned for having fun, for savoring the years God grants us. "All these things," to which Solomon refers, are all of the questions, the concerns, the trials, the puzzles, the emptiness, the oppression, the tragedies, which we encounter during our threescore and ten upon the earth. Someday God will explain it all to us, when He renders judgment. We won't need to ask, "Why me? Why this? Why now?" because we'll know the reasons, thanks to Him. (See 1 Corinthians 13:12.)

So keeping our future rewards in mind, what must we do? Solomon advises each of us in verse 10: "So then, banish anxiety from your heart, and cast off the troubles of your body, for youth and vigor are meaningless." We need to quit worrying! Three times in the Sermon on the Mount

Jesus says to His listeners, "Do not worry" (Matthew 6:25,31,34). We must rid our hearts of all alarm.

Persistent worry in the life of a believer means one of two things. Either we are not trusting the Lord to handle the situation about which we are concerned, or we have not turned the circumstance over to God yet. In Ecclesiastes 11:10, Solomon is telling us that the Lord will handle our old age and physical death when they come; He'll take care of us. We shouldn't be bothered by the fact that, at mid-life, we are closer to our death days than we are to our birth days. We must "cast off the troubles" of our bodies and realize that God has some exciting things in store for us in the days that remain. As Christians, we always have something to look forward to, even as we prepare to die, *especially* as we prepare to die!

Recall that Solomon closes chapter 11 with this statement: "For youth and vigor are meaningless." That is why we must stop worrying about growing old. Just because a man is young and strong does not mean that he is happy or that he holds the answers to the perplexities of life. More than likely he is too busy trying to build a reputation to even take notice of such things.

OF DEAD ROSES AND TROUBLED DAYS—ECCLESIASTES 12:1-8

> Remember your Creator
>   in the days of your youth,
> before the days of trouble come
>   and the years approach when you will say,
>   "I find no pleasure in them"—
> before the sun and the light
>   and the moon and the stars grow dark,
>   and the clouds return after the rain;
> when the keepers of the house tremble,
>   and the strong men stoop,
> when the grinders cease because they are few,
>   and those looking through the windows grow
>   dim;

when the doors to the street are closed
    and the sound of grinding fades;
when men rise up at the sound of birds,
    but all their songs grow faint;
when men are afraid of heights
    and of dangers in the streets;
when the almond tree blossoms
    and the grasshopper drags himself along
    and desire no longer is stirred.
Then man goes to his eternal home
    and mourners go about the streets.
Remember him—before the silver cord is
        severed,
    or the golden bowl is broken;
before the pitcher is shattered at the spring,
    or the wheel broken at the well,
and the dust returns to the ground it came
        from,
    and the spirit returns to God who gave it.
"Meaningless! Meaningless!" says the Teacher.
"Everything is meaningless!"

In his book on Ecclesiastes, *The Art of Staying Off Dead-End Streets,* Richard de Haan tells a story about a very wise lady named Mrs. Mack. It seems that one evening Mrs. Mack sat waiting in the car while her husband ran into a drugstore to make a few purchases. Two young ladies, one of whom Mrs. Mack knew, walked by the parked car, chattering noisily. Mrs. Mack heard the girl she knew say that she planned to become a Christian some day, but she wanted to have a good time first. She was an attractive young woman, and her words gave Mrs. Mack a most fitting idea.

About a week later, the young woman received a package sent by Mrs. Mack. She untied the ribbon, lifted the lid and discovered to her surprise that the box contained nothing but wilted roses. She assumed that there had been a mix-up in the delivery, but soon learned that there had been no mistake. Spying Mrs. Mack walking along the street, the young lady thanked her for the roses, making no mention of their distressed condition. Mrs. Mack's reply astonished her.

"I'm glad you liked them," Mrs. Mack said. "I cut them last Monday and enjoyed them all week, but this morning when I noticed they were beginning to get old and faded, I thought of you and had them delivered to your door." Seeing the girl's puzzled and hurt expression, the older lady went on to explain that she had overheard the conversation in the drugstore parking lot. The young girl was, pointed out Mrs. Mack, behaving selfishly by withholding her heart from Jesus while she was youthful, charming, energetic, and attractive. She was treating the Lord no better than she had been treated when Mrs. Mack intentionally sent her the wilted roses. She planned to offer herself to Christ only after the bloom of youth had long vanished. The older lady's lesson was not lost on the younger woman. She soon accepted Jesus Christ and began to effectively serve Him (De Haan 1974, 148-149).

Solomon's message in Ecclesiastes 12:1 is not unlike that delivered by Mrs. Mack to the girl. "Remember your Creator in the days of your youth," he urges us, "before the days of trouble come and the years approach when you will say, 'I find no pleasure in them.' " Our best recourse is to give our lives to God while we are young—preferably at the first opportunity we have. Letting Him control our lives early on saves us a great deal of heartache. When we wait, we may end up offering Him only leftovers. Besides, the "days of trouble" are approaching.

The Days of Trouble

And what are those "days of trouble" to which Solomon refers? They are the years of old age. Using a series of poetic symbols Solomon gently paints a vivid portrait of growing old in verses 2 through 8. He speaks with tender realism—that he is able to do so should not surprise us. His father David was fifty-two, in the prime of mid-life, when Solomon was born. With the impressionable eyes of youth,

Solomon witnessed firsthand the aging of his father. David's death at seventy came when Solomon, present at the deathbed scene, was but eighteen years old (see 1 Kings 2:1-10). No wonder that he can so accurately depict in Ecclesiastes 12 the days of growing old!

We must remember the Creator in the days of our youth, "before the sun and the light and the moon and the stars grow dark." Old age is the time when the lights grow dim, right? Gray days seem even drearier, nights longer. Gloom and depression settle in. The moon does not appear as bright, and certainly not as romantic, as it once did. It's harder to drive after dark—even the street lights seem to do little to illumine a night-drenched stretch of freeway.

Not only does the world appear to be enshrouded in darkness, but Solomon also observes in verse 2 that as one grows old, "the clouds return after the rain." Troubles, particularly physical difficulties, drop on us like bucketfuls of rain as we grow older. One elderly gentleman I know fell and broke his hip while recovering from the first of two cataract surgeries. The broken hip and bandaged eye were good for something: they made his arthritis and rheumatism seem mild in comparison! Of course he also worries about his wife, who can't get around as well as she used to. And there are concerns about the doctors' bills, which the insurance company may or may not pick up entirely. As he has aged, this man has been showered with one cloudburst of hardship after another, and it does seem as though each rain is followed by still another brewing storm.

Old age is also, as Solomon comments in verse 3, "when the keepers of the house tremble, and the strong men stoop, when the grinders cease because they are few, and those looking through the windows grow dim" (12:3). One of my favorite gospel tunes is the song, "This Old House." The lyrics speak of a dilapidated structure, getting "shaky" and "old," having seen less ramshackle days in years past. And the message is clear: our bodies eventually become like that old house, run down and creaky, sagging and squeaky. Whoever wrote that song must have had Ecclesiastes 12:3 in mind, where Solomon describes the Geritol era as the time when "the keepers of the house tremble." The "keepers of the house" are simply the arms and the legs. Once strong and reliable, they become wrinkled, gnarled, and shaky as the years go by.

Solomon also observes that in old age "the strong men stoop" (12:3). The "strong men" are the shoulders, and one doesn't have to see many elderly folks to know that most do not walk about erect. Instead, their shoulders are rounded, their bodies hunched forward, their frames bent down as if wearied from decades of lugging around a tremendous weight.

Not only do the shoulders of the elderly sag but also "the grinders cease because they are few" (12:3). There just isn't much left of the uppers and the lowers by the time most of us reach old age! We have to avoid steak and settle for hamburger. As one fellow in his seventies moaned, "Every night I put my eyes on the table, my teeth in the glass, and my hearing aid in the drawer. I'm beginning to worry about what else might have to come off before I can get to sleep!"

My grandchildren will be giving me a large-print Bible, for old age is also, as Solomon reflects, the period when "those looking through the windows grow dim" (12:3). In other words, it becomes harder to see.

The eyes do begin to fail us as we grow older. How many over-sixty people do you know who do not wear glasses, at least part of the time? Not many, I would guess. More often we become like the dear elderly lady who was a guest at the same dinner as I. She was seated across the table from me, and I sat amazed as she reached for the sugar shaker and began pouring the white stuff on her salad. She thought she had grabbed the salad dressing! She just couldn't see clearly any longer . . . and on that evening she ended up with awfully sweet lettuce as a result.

What is more, old age also marks the era "when the doors to the street are closed and the sound of grinding fades; when men rise up at the sound of birds, but all their songs grow faint" (12:4). Our eyesight fails, and so does our hearing. The noises outside seem to fade. Conversations between others cannot possibly be overheard. Words, phrases, and fragments of speech meld into an indiscernible hum. "What's that you say, my boy? I can't hear you. Been listening to my kids' music too long!" we joke. But the reality is that it is more difficult to distinguish individual sounds as we grow older. Even loud noises, like "the sound of grinding," seem to be lowered in volume and intensity.

For the elderly, "all their songs grow faint" (12:4). I think of some of the older women who want to sing soprano in the church choir. Every choir has one or two of these. They used to be soloists. They never miss a practice. And their voices break and crackle and squeak like chalk on a board. They've lost their ability to sing. Their songs have grown faint as their vocal chords have been weakened by age.

In addition to being a time of sensory impairment, old age is also characterized by increasing fear. In Solomon's words, it is "when men are afraid of heights and of dangers in the streets" (12:5). "Be careful on that ladder, son!" exclaims the elderly father to his middle-aged boy who is climbing to the roof. My own dad still isn't afraid to mount a ladder. (Sometimes I wish he were!) He gets up on top of the house to repair a damaged TV antenna or patch a small hole. But will my mom and he fly in an airplane? Certainly not! That's too high!

Heights are not all older people frequently are afraid of, either. As we progress in years, it gets scary to walk the streets. There are dangers to be avoided. Muggers and purse snatchers prey especially on the Social Security set. It even becomes difficult to *drive* the streets. Traffic grows heavier with each passing season, and accidents more common. An elderly person responds more slowly than a younger driver. It becomes simpler and safer to run errands between rush hours, and never after dark. My parents dislike driving after dusk any more, and they live in a fairly safe, small community. But nighttime is when it is harder to see and the crazy drivers who cause accidents are loose. At the root of my folks' reluctance to venture out after dark is evidence of lost confidence in their ability to handle the unexpected.

Old age is also, according to Solomon, the occasion when "the almond tree blossoms and the grasshopper drags himself along and desire no longer is stirred" (12:5). The blossoms of an almond tree are white, as is the hair on the heads of many elderly men and women. As it becomes harder for us to walk while growing older, we drag ourselves along like crippled grasshoppers. We use walkers or canes. We move very slowly, barely able to carry the lightest of burdens.

And worse than all of that—old age is the time when "desire no longer is stirred"! Food and drink lose their savor. The idea of working holds little appeal. Sex loses its scintillating lure. Solomon's own father, David—very aware of the presence of a beautiful woman when young—spends his final days with Abishag, the beautiful virgin . . . dies and leaves her that way (see 1 Kings 1:3-4).

And eventually, when the aging process is complete, "Then man goes to his eternal home and mourners go about the streets" (12:5). We die, but we do not face nothingness or encounter oblivion. As believers, we come into the presence of the Maker of the universe. Mourners may visit the funeral parlor and follow the hearse to the cemetery, but they'll really have no reason to grieve. When deceased, we'll be freer and happier than ever before, as God erases the suffering, tears, and pain of our earthly lives. Paul puts it this way in 2 Corinthians 5:8: "We are confident, I say, and would prefer to be away from the body and at home with the Lord."

Yet when a loved one dies, it's best to do as Solomon recommends in Ecclesiastes 12:6: "Remember him—before the silver cord is severed, or the golden bowl is broken; before the pitcher is shattered at the spring, or the wheel broken at the well." The "silver cord" represents the spinal cord; the "golden bowl," the head or brain. The "pitcher" symbolizes the lungs, the "wheel," the human heart. Each major organ must function, or else we die . . . when they quit, we do, too.

When the organs cease to operate, our bodies are useless. Then "the dust returns to the ground it came from, and the spirit returns to God who gave it" (12:7). After death, our physical beings decay, no matter how much embalming fluid has been pumped into our veins. Like worn-out garments, our bodies become as dust. They are shells which disintegrate, while our spirits live on in eternity.

What is life, then? "Meaningless! Meaningless! . . . Everything is meaningless!" cries Solomon in Ecclesiastes 12:8. His words are nearly identical to those uttered in Ecclesiastes 1:2. Why the repetition? Hasn't Solomon learned anything from his mid-life trauma? Why does life still appear "meaningless" to him?

It is because he has discovered that physical life *is* meaningless. It is empty. Our bodies ultimately fail us, as we have seen so vividly illustrated in Solomon's prose. While we live, our eyes are filled with tears. When we die, the hulls which have encased us are reduced to ashes. Eternity lies ahead of us; that is what matters.

Ironically, Solomon finds meaning in mid-life by deciding that life on earth is meaningless—without God, that is. Life above the sun far overshadows in importance anything that takes place below. Coming to that conclusion makes all the difference in the present world, and in the world to come.

FINAL WORDS—ECCLESIASTES 12:9-14

> Not only was the Teacher wise, but also he imparted knowledge to the people. He pondered and searched out and set in order many proverbs. The Teacher searched to find just the right words, and what he wrote was upright and true.

> The words of the wise are like goads, their collected sayings like firmly embedded nails—given by one Shepherd. Be warned, my son, of anything in addition to them.

> Of making many books there is no end, and much study wearies the body.

> Now all has been heard;
> here is the conclusion of the matter:

> Fear God and keep his commandments,
>   for this is the whole duty of man.
> For God will bring every deed into judgment,
>   including every hidden thing,
>   whether it is good or evil.

Solomon concludes the chronicle of his search for significance in life with a few final, and infinitely wise, remarks. He again describes his quest, claiming to have "imparted knowledge to the people . . . [and] pondered and searched out and set in order many proverbs" (12:9). He reminds us that he "searched to find just the right words," and that his writings were "upright and true" (12:10). In his journey, he came to value the "words of the wise" who possess God-given insight (12:11). To these only must we listen, as Solomon admonishes in verse 12, "Be warned, my son, of anything in addition to them." And he includes a statement which my own children love to hear: "Of making many books there is no end, and much study wearies the body" (12:12).

In his final words, Solomon reveals "the conclusion of the matter" (12:13). It is a succinct summary of the heart of wise living at any age. It particularly speaks to the man in mid-life who finds his earthly existence unsatisfying. Solomon's words contain the crux of the answer to the crisis.

"Fear God and keep his commandments," he says, "for this is the whole duty of man. For God will bring every deed into judgment, including every hidden thing, whether it is good or evil" (12:13-14). The solutions are threefold. Let's briefly discuss them.

Number one: *Fear the Lord.* Surrender to the sovereign purpose of God; respect Him; believe Him; resolve to discover His intentions for your life—and the sooner, the better.

Number two: *Keep His commandments.* Submit to His Word. Be obedient once you discover His purpose for your life.

Number three: *Remember that God will bring every deed*

into account. Realize that you'll stand in judgment. There is a day of reckoning, and it is an awesome yardstick against which to measure our obedience.

A LAST LOOK

Let's look at a capsule review of Solomon's journey through crisis. We first learned about the foundation of his trauma. We then watched as he imbibed of pleasure and poured himself into projects. We saw him rub up against the sovereign purpose of God. We viewed his entanglement in the corporate squeeze, and his preoccupation with what money can buy. We witnessed his struggle with depression. Eventually we saw him begin to live for the present: eating, enjoying, and enduring. Finally we watched him come to grips with the ideas of growing older and dying. We have seen him come full circle—from complaining about the meaninglessness of life beneath the sun in Ecclesiastes 1, to acknowledging the meaningfulness of life above the sun in Ecclesiastes 12. He has come a long, long way.

LESSONS

Only two lessons need be brought into focus as we conclude our study of Ecclesiastes.

Number one: *Any non-Christian who is experiencing crisis in his or her life must first receive Jesus Christ as Savior before there can be any hope of proper resolution.* The ultimate end of God's sovereign purpose is to save the soul of each individual through the precious blood of Christ, through faith in His finished work on Calvary. Before we can find answers, it is essential that we come to the cross.

Number two: *Any Christian in crisis must get on track with God through submission to His instructions in His Word.* We may not want to hear what God says, but we'd better sit up and take notice. He calls for us to be renewed, brought into His likeness.

THE WORLD'S EYE VIEW

Perhaps the most important thing which Solomon has done during his search for significance in mid-life is that he has come to grips with the notion of dying, and with the idea of eternity. Remember he says in Ecclesiastes 12:7 that at death "the dust returns to the ground it came from, and the spirit returns to God who gave it." There *is* hope beyond the grave, and that truth is of immense comfort to believers who face the latter part of life. In John 16:21 Jesus compares the coming agony of His death on the cross with that of a woman in labor. In childbirth and death there is pain, yet at the end of the suffering there is an arrival. For the woman in travail, it is the birth of a long-awaited child. For the Christian encountering death, it is a birth of a different sort—an arrival into an eternity which will be spent with a gracious and loving heavenly Father. Seeing death as an opportunity for "birth" is not, however, the world's eye view.

I'd like to quote from Judith Viorst's book, *Necessary Losses*. In the chapter called "The ABC of Dying" Viorst expresses an outlook on death which is shared by many today:

> For awareness of our mortality may heighten our love of life without making death—our personal death—acceptable. Looking death straight in the eye, we may hate it a lot. And although our sense of finitude may be the mother of beauty, the frame of the picture and even the yolk of the egg, it may make a mockery of our works and our days.
> By assaulting our feelings of personal significance.
> By rendering all of our enterprises meaningless.
> By tainting our deepest and dearest attachments with transience.
> By taunting us with the question Why were we born if it wasn't forever? By taunting us with the question Why is there death? (Viorst 1986, 307).

Does death, as Ms. Viorst asserts, assault "our feelings of personal significance"? Not if we are Christians. True, death is the "great leveler"—all of us will die, no matter what our positions and accomplishments in life have been. Yet the Christian who dies goes to be with the Father. And this miraculous journey is only possible because two thousand years ago God the Father sent Jesus Christ the Son to hang on a cross and pay the penalty of our sins for us. How much more "personally significant" can we be? After all, God cared enough to send His Son, providing for our salvation and extending us an invitation to move in with Him when our lives on earth are done! Death is a promotion for us, because the Lord loves us.

Death also, according to Viorst, renders "all of our enterprises meaningless." That is correct of course, to an extent. Like Solomon, the project we've started and properties we've acquired will be in someone else's care, for better or worse. Most of our worldly enterprises will lack importance after we are gone from the scene. But the hours we have spent in cultivating relationships, teaching our children, serving our spouses, ministering to others—these will still count for something even after the eulogies have been delivered. We'll be given crowns of glory in eternity for what we have done through God's strength and in His name. As Peter writes to the elders of the church in 1 Peter 5:2-4:

> Be shepherds of God's flock that is under your care, serving as overseers—not because you must, but because you are willing, as God wants you to be; not greedy for money, but eager to serve; not lording it over those entrusted to you, but being examples to the flock. And when the Chief Shepherd appears, you will receive the crown of glory that will never fade away.

And does death, as Viorst suggests, taint "our deepest and dearest attachments with transience"? In a sense, yes, as Christians we will not be spending eternity with any of our contemporaries who have died without receiving Jesus Christ as Savior (John 14:6). Yet at the point of death, there will be but a temporary interruption in our relationships with fellow believers. Soon they'll join us, as they also cross into the presence of God.

And as for the questions: "Why were we born if it wasn't forever? . . . Why is there death?"—they represent misconceptions. You see, life *is* forever, even though life on earth is not. Death exists as a curiously vital passage, the gateway to life everlasting.

Coming to terms with mid-life necessitates grappling with the notions of old age and death, as Solomon has done in Ecclesiastes 11 and 12. In the process, we see him make good his escape from crisis. It is essential that we, too, come to grips with the death which, even as I write, is drawing nearer. We all face what Solomon did. The choices are ours, and the decisions will have neverending significance.

Before the Curtain Falls

Effectively handling middle age, old age, and death means that we must acknowledge our frailties. If we're honest, we'll also admit that we need some outside help in handling the last segment of our lives.

In 1973 the low rumblings of Watergate were escalating into the vicious roar of a scandal which would eventually topple a presidency. Charles Colson had resigned as White House Special Counsel, a position less flatteringly known as Richard Nixon's "hatchet man," and had returned to private law practice.

Stories in the *Washington Post* had linked him with the Watergate break-in. Daily his home in McLean, Virginia, was surrounded by an army of reporters. Stripped of prestige, hounded by accusers, fearful of the future, Colson writes of his experience:

> To the outside world I preserved the tough-guy facade, but there were moments when my own weakness

now surprised me. I often woke up in the middle of the night with a sick feeling in my stomach, my heart beating rapidly and wild fantasies racing through my mind—scenes of jail, cold cement floors, iron bars, and men in gray denim marching along steel hallways (Colson 1977, 100).

During the summer of 1973, real and unfounded charges against Colson continued to make headlines each day. Government officials leveled accusations against him on national television. The incredible pressure mounted. Chuck Colson was a man in the midst of a crisis of meaning. He felt empty. He needed answers.

How much the fact that he was in his early forties contributed to the hollowness Colson felt in 1973, I do not know. I do know that he was searching for significance. He contacted his friend Tom Phillips, the president of Raytheon Company and a committed Christian.

In his book *Born Again,* Colson describes an evening spent in the Phillips home. It was an evening in which Tom Phillips explained that worldly success was meaningless without a relationship to God through Jesus Christ. The reality that the sin of pride had infected his life hit Colson with devastating force as Phillips read from C. S. Lewis's *Mere Christianity.* With a copy of *Mere Christianity* under his arm, Colson left for the evening. He was not a changed man . . . yet (Colson 1977, 107-116).

Charles Colson recounts the experience of moments later sitting in his car outside the Phillips home:

> Outside in the darkness, the iron grip I'd kept on my emotions began to relax. Tears welled up in my eyes as I groped in the darkness for the right key to start my car. Angrily I brushed them away and started the engine. "What kind of weakness is this?" I said to nobody . . . .
>
> As I drove out of Tom's driveway, the tears were flowing uncontrollably. There were no streetlights, no moonlight. The car headlights were flooding illumina-

tion before my eyes, but I was crying so hard it was like trying to swim underwater. I pulled to the side of the road not more than a hundred yards from the entrance to Tom's driveway. . . .

With my face cupped in my hands, head leaning forward against the wheel, I forgot about machismo, about pretenses, about fears of being weak. And as I did, I began to experience a wonderful feeling of being released. Then came the strange sensation that water was not only running down my cheeks, but surging through my whole body as well, cleansing and cooling as it went. They weren't tears of sadness and remorse, nor of joy—but somehow, tears of relief.

And then I prayed my first real prayer. "God, I don't know how to find You, but I'm going to try! I'm not much the way I am now, but somehow I want to give myself to You." I didn't know how to say more, so I repeated over and over the words: *Take me.*

I had not "accepted" Christ—I still didn't know who He was. My mind told me it was important to find that out first, to be sure that I knew what I was doing, that I meant it and would stay with it. Only, that night, something inside me was urging me to surrender—to what or to whom I did not know.

I stayed there in the car, wet-eyed, praying, thinking, for perhaps half an hour, perhaps longer, alone in the quiet of that dark night. Yet for the first time in my life, I was not alone at all (Colson 1977, 116-117).

In the middle of a deserted road, bathed in darkness and washed in his own tears, Charles Colson arrived at the point of surrender to God. But his was not a foxhole decision, made only to ward off the bursting flak of Watergate. For Colson, the next days would be spent in studying Scripture, in reading the arguments of C. S. Lewis, in confronting the claims of Jesus Christ (Colson 1977, 120-130).

In John 10:30, Christ states emphatically: "I and the Father are one." Not a mere prophet or teacher—Jesus Christ was and is God the Son, sent to earth in mortal form to live a perfect life, and to die the death of atonement for us. He paid the penalty. He cancelled the debt. Now we, through recognition of our sin, and faith in His Godhood and in His finished work on the cross, can enter into a relationship with Him. Eternal life is the believer's, yes, but so also is the vibrant, day-to-day reality of friendship with God.

All that, Charles Colson embraced when he uttered these words days after the episode outside the home of Tom Phillips: "Lord Jesus, I believe You. I accept You. Please come into my life. I commit it to You" (Colson 1977, 130).

And that, my friends, made every tear, every moment of anguish, every trial experienced by Colson, magnificently worthwhile.

As we struggle with the uncertainties of life—especially of mid-life—we too are free to voice such words: "Lord Jesus, I commit everything to You."

Questions for Personal or Group Study

1. What are we commanded to do in Ecclesiastes 11:1-2? What are some practical ways in which we can "cast [our] bread upon the waters"?

2. In what ways does the statement, "Whoever watches the wind will not plant; whoever looks at the clouds will not reap" (11:4), poignantly speak to the person facing old age?

3. According to Ecclesiastes 11:6, is it wise to diversify? What are some of the ways in which a believer may diversify in his personal ministry?

4. What is the all-important counsel given by Solomon in Ecclesiastes 12:1?

5. In verses 2-5 of chapter 12, at least fifteen characteristics of old age are described. Are these observations accurate of the elderly today? Explain your answer.

6. What is "the conclusion of the matter," according to Solomon in Ecclesiastes 12:13-14? In what ways do these verses reveal the solution to the mid-life crisis? Explain.

11

When the Dust Has Settled

Much like the prodigal son in the far country in a pigpen of his own making, who finally comes to his senses, so does the man in mid-life crisis. When he does, the fiercest part of the mental, emotional, physical, and spiritual battle is over. But our man must still work out the details of the peace treaty he has got to make with himself and with his God.

How can he do it? How can he put his life back together again, even if it seems hopelessly fragmented? That is the question we'll address in this final chapter. For the prodigal, the answer was contained in a statement of determination: "I will go home to my father and say, 'Father, I have sinned against both heaven and you'" (Luke 15:18 TLB). And thus the process of rebuilding the rubble begins.

> Humpty Dumpty sat on a wall
> Humpty Dumpty had a great fall.
> All the king's horses and all the king's men,
> Couldn't put Humpty Dumpty together again.

Rebuilding the rubble is rarely easy. Look at poor old Humpty Dumpty. He gets a little careless, loses his balance for a time, and ends up splattered across the sidewalk. All the king's men can't glue him back together. (I have yet to figure out why the horses were even given a shot at it.) Humpty is destroyed—one good egg gone because of some moments of carelessness.

The mid-life crisis is a product of careless moments, careless months, and careless years. It happens because we misplace our priorities concerning God, our wives, our families, our work. As we emerge from the fires of crisis, we may feel as shattered as Humpty Dumpty after the fall. Our vision vanished, our dreams ditched, our castles crumbled, we simply want to know, "Is there any hope?" The reply to that is, "Yes!"

THREE TO GROW ON

It is good for the man recovering from crisis to remember three very important principles. Here they are:

Number one: *Life's greatest challenge involves what we're going to do with the time that is left.*

Number two: *We can ruin the rest of our lives by refusing to let go of the past.*

Number three: *God is the master potter who is famous for transforming cracked vessels into beautiful ones which bring glory and honor to Him.*

TIME TO GROW UP

Keeping those principles in mind, it becomes time for our man to grab hold of reality. It is time to grow up. Judith Viorst writes:

> Growing up means letting go of the dearest megalomaniacal dreams of our childhood. Growing up means knowing they can't be fulfilled. Growing up means gaining the wisdom and skills to get what we want within the limitations imposed by reality—a reality which consists of diminished powers, restricted freedoms and, with the people we love, imperfect conditions.
>
> A reality built, in part, upon the acceptance of our necessary losses (Viorst 1986, 161).

As the author suggests, growing up means admitting weaknesses, experiencing losses, learning to live with dwindling powers and imperfect people. Although Viorst's is a secular perspective, the truths she expresses apply also to believers. As we grow—through childhood to adolescence, from young adulthood to middlescence and beyond—we are forced to release unrealistic expectations.

Yet thank God that He enables us, His children, to grasp firmly a plan designed by Him. His is no second-rate reality, something we merely "settle for" or resign ourselves to. For in God's scheme our lives—even post-crisis—can be peaceful, happy, productive, full, and glorifying to Him. Growing up is worth every growing pain, in the end.

The Living Bible paraphrase of Paul's message in Philippians 3:11-14 is one of my favorites:

> So, whatever it takes, I will be one who lives in the fresh newness of life of those who are alive from the dead.
>
> I don't mean to say I am perfect. I haven't learned all I should even yet, but I keep working toward the day when I will finally be all that Christ saved me for and wants me to be.
>
> No, dear brothers, I am still not all I should be but I am bringing all my energies to bear on this one thing: Forgetting the past and looking forward to what lies ahead, I strain to reach the end of the race and receive the prize for which God is calling us up to heaven because of what Christ Jesus did for us.

Look at Paul's words. "I am still not all I should be." That can apply to each of us; we're not all that we should be. But Paul also says that he is bringing his "energies to bear" on some specific areas. He is "forgetting the past and looking forward to what lies ahead"; he is straining "to reach the end of the race and receive the prize for which God is calling us up to heaven because of what Christ Jesus did for us." Essentially, he is doing three things . . . and they are steps which also ought to be taken by the Christian emerging from mid-life trauma who hopes to make a complete recovery.

Here, briefly, are the stepping stones to wholeness, some practical suggestions for rising above the ruins:

Step one: *Look to the past.*
Step two: *Look to the present.*
Step three: *Look toward the future.*

At first glance, these may seem trite. And without further explanation, they would be superficial indeed. Practically speaking, though, I know of no better remedy for reconstructing a life. Let's take a closer look at these ideas.

Looking to the Past

Paul states in Philippians 3:13 that he is in the process of *forgetting* the past. That means he is allowing it to remain where it belongs: behind him. He refuses to let what has happened before color his present or his future. Those are big words coming from Paul, because before he met Jesus Christ on the Damascus road, he delighted in persecuting Christians. His first taste of that ungodly work occurred at the murder of Stephen.

Paul guarded the cloaks of those who stoned the young man, the first martyr of the church. He looked on in sadistic and self-righteous approval while Stephen's body was crushed and his blood spilled (Acts 7:54–8:2). Then Paul set off on a rampage of his own. Acts 8:3 tells us that he "began to destroy the church. Going from house to house, he dragged off men and women and put them in prison." After meeting the Lord, Paul was a changed man, from the inside out. Yet he still had much to be sorry for. He had a past of which nobody calling himself a Christian would be proud. But he was able, with God's help, to overcome it.

The same thing may be said for the man coming out of a mid-life crisis. During the years of trauma, he may have said and done some stupid things, leaving a trail of broken relationships and wounded people in his wake. The guilt he feels seems overwhelming. The past relentlessly rears its dragon-like head to affect the present—to keep him in bondage, to prevent him from making a clean start.

It doesn't have to be that way. But before he can conquer

the past and put it in its place, he'll have to face it honestly. The dragons must come out in the open before they can be slain.

If we need to bump off some dragons of days gone by, let's get busy! That means looking to the past—realistically. It involves examining the damage, candidly and fairly appraising it with eyes observant enough to belong to the most meticulous insurance claims adjuster. Whom have we hurt? In what shape is our career? With whom must we sever relations? What is left of our formerly good reputation? How have we sinned against God? Against man? What, if anything, can be salvaged?

Besides appraising the damage, we must also consider the causes of the trouble. Much as F.A.A. inspectors descend upon the site of a plane crash to poke through the charred wreckage for clues as to why a disaster happened, so should we look at the fragments of our lives to determine the reasons behind the trauma we've experienced. What areas of our lives have we permitted to overshadow our relationship with the Lord? Have we focused on acquiring things rather than knowing people? In what areas have we rebelled against God's purpose? What has caused us to plunge to the ground rather than soar above the clouds?

And, lest we get too depressed, we should also take an honest and revealing look at the good things of the past. Where have we succeeded? Have we, except for the years of crisis, been a good manager . . . a faithful husband . . . a reliable provider . . . a loyal employee? Have we been any of these during the crisis? What have been our strong points? Are we intelligent, strong, personable, articulate, efficient, athletic, or kind—to name a few? What have been the bright spots in the past?

Once the past has been dissected to our satisfaction (or dissatisfaction), then we must begin earnestly to leave it behind. To do so, it is necessary to look at the present, for only in the here-and-now may anyone operate actively to remove the influence of yesterday.

LOOKING AT THE PRESENT

Picking up the pieces—As mid-life survivors who have already looked to the past, we have determined how we have failed during the crisis. We know if we have injured our wives, our kids, our friends. We know if we have shortchanged our employers or employees. We know if we have not measured up spiritually. Now, in the present, we can do something about it. We can pick up the pieces.

Our first aim must be to get right with God and with man. Sin, Satan, and selfishness have been involved in the crisis, and they must be handled. It is essential to seek God's face for forgiveness and renewal. That means talking to Him, perhaps praying as David did in Psalm 51:10-12:

> Create in me a pure heart, O God,
>   and renew a steadfast spirit within me.
> Do not cast me from your presence
>   or take your Holy Spirit from me.
> Restore to me the joy of your salvation
>   and grant me a willing spirit, to sustain me.

And when we honestly repent and ask for His forgiveness and cleansing, the Lord will respond to us gently, and with love. If you're not convinced, recall how tenderly Jesus deals in John 8 with the woman caught in adultery. "Then neither do I condemn you. . . . Go now and leave your life of sin," the Lord tells her, compassion undoubtedly filling His voice.

The apostle Paul declares before the governor Felix: "So I strive always to keep my conscience clear before God and man" (Acts 24:16). We should do no less. Getting right with God comes first. Then, it's time to make amends with man.

The man who has been caught up in a mid-life cisis must act in the present to resolve the human havoc his behavior in the past has wrought. That means apologizing when necessary, making restitution where possible, confessing when appropriate . . . and always remaining sensitive to situations where such soul-baring will do more harm than good. Some things are better left unsaid.

When the transgressions of the past have been brought to light, when forgiveness from God (and, where possible, man) has been sought, then the slate is wiped clean. The errors of yesterday are laid aside. The cycle of living day-by-day is set in motion.

Proceeding day-by-day—The challenge of daily living for the man emerging from crisis is to take what is left and, under God's direction and leadership, begin to build a framework for a meaningful life. Take one day at a time.

It becomes essential to rearrange priorities, according to His wishes for us. Today is the time to start. It's likely the original sparks which ignited the crisis emanated from misplaced priorities of some kind. So today, let's devote some time to prayer and the study of God's Word. Today, let's have a conversation with our spouses which extends beyond the surface. Today, let's pay closer attention to our children, observing the types of people they are becoming.

And let's realize that we can make the changes slowly, as long as they occur steadily. We must beware, as Solomon cautions in Ecclesiastes 5:2, of making rash promises and empty vows that will be binding. The key is shortening our vision slightly and asking of ourselves, "Is God faithful *today*, and can He meet my needs?" It is written in Lamentations 3:22-23: "Because of the Lord's great love we are not consumed, for his compassions never fail. They are new every morning; great is your faithfulness." As we positively affirm the truth of God's steadfast care and provision, the task is to get on with living life to the hilt, tackling one twenty-four hour period at time. The Lord's mercies are new each morning!

Prepare to persevere and to win—And while we are proceeding day-by-day and rearranging priorities, we must remember that we are precious and valuable to God. He loves us unconditionally, and He is reaching out to us to make things right with His mercy and forgiveness. Nothing we have done, even while in the rebellion of mid-life trauma, changes His love for us. After Peter had denied Him three times prior to the crucifixion, the Lord still forgave and restored him (see John 21:15-19). No indiscretion on our part can prevent the same, if we have truly trusted Christ as Savior.

Hebrew 12:1 is paraphrased beautifully in the Living Bible. It says so well what our aims for the present ought to be:

> Since we have such a huge crowd of men of faith watching us from the grandstands, let us strip off anything that slows down or holds us back, and especially those sins that wrap themselves so tightly around our feet and trip us up; and let us run with patience the particular race that God has set before us.

We are still valuable to God and, with His assistance, we are able to "strip off" the encumbrances and finish the race.

I remember running in my first marathon in Las Vegas several years ago. Believe me, I was motivated only by the desire to finish the 26.2 miles; I had no aspirations of setting any records (except maybe for the slowest time in the event). At the twenty-mile point in that race, I "hit the wall." My stomach and legs cramped. I didn't care if I completed the course. As I stopped to walk for a moment, thoughts of all the friends back home who were praying for me surfaced. How guilty I felt when I realized that I was failing them. Then a thought popped into my head. Just because I had to walk part of the way did not mean that I couldn't finish the race! And before you know it, the next 6.2 miles were behind me. The marathon was history, and I had crossed the line (without, I might add, the slowest time of the day).

My point is, we must accept the fact that the race of life set before us can be finished well, no matter what has taken place before—no matter if we stumble, fall, or have to "walk" a little.

Crossing the finish line with quiet resolve beats being pulled from the race, as Lot's wife was. In Genesis 19, Lot and his family were led out of Sodom before the city was obliterated. Lot's wife, in direct disobedience, turned her head to look at the smouldering ruins. As a result of her defiance, her blatant refusal to follow the orders of God, her foolishly rebellious heart, she became a pillar of salt.

The actions we take daily from hereon in will determine whether we will finish well or finish poorly. It's good to remember, too, that quitters never win . . . and winners never quit.

LOOKING TOWARD THE FUTURE

We've dealt with the past. We're living in the present. With these areas intact, it is healthy to look toward the future. How is that done?

It is achieved by setting some goals for the second half of life. An integral part of goalsetting involves seeking the Lord's wisdom and will and purpose. It is essential to be in fellowship with Him before proceeding any further.

At mid-life, I made a list of some practical objectives for myself. They are included here, in more general terms, so that they will be applicable to most. I hope, in the second half of life, to grow spiritually, to increase my dependence on and knowledge of the Lord. I also desire to strengthen bonds with Pearl, the children, and the sons and daughters-in-law who are being added to the family. Additionally, I want to take care of myself physically. And finally, I desire to tackle some new challenges professionally. Let me share my thoughts on the "four D's" with you.

Devotional discipline—Determine to set aside regularly scheduled time for the reading of the Word, prayer, and worship, daily. Do not let a day go by without spending some time in God's presence.

Develop depth—Work on drawing closer to significant people in your life. Establish friendships with the folks you love! Spend quality and quantity time with them. Investing in the lives of others is rewarding beyond measure.

Diet, dress, dedication to exercise—In 1 Corinthians 9:27

Paul says, "Like an athlete I punish my body, treating it roughly, training it to do what it should, not what it wants to. Otherwise I fear that after enlisting others for the race, I myself might be declared unfit and ordered to stand aside" (TLB). We must feel physically fit in order to have strength to finish the race. A good diet is essential; learn to feed your body what it needs. Exercise is important, too. Paul trained as an athlete so that his body would serve him. Besides, as the waistline shrinks, the self-image expands! Dressing neatly and attractively doesn't hurt, either. It can be a real confidence booster.

Determined direction—Set your face like a flint to follow the will of God in your life. Lay out some professional and personal goals that you are capable of reaching. Your most productive years lie ahead. You are a seasoned, experienced veteran. And as you strive, focus on the service you can provide to others in the process (see Acts 20:34-35).

FINISHING WELL

The older I get, the more I realize that heaven is the place for finishers. Remember that in 2 Timothy 4:6-7 Paul writes, "For I am already being poured out like a drink offering, and the time has come for my departure. I have fought the good fight, I have finished the race, I have kept the faith." Jesus cried out on the cross, "It is finished" (John 19:30). Fewer than eight hours before, He had prayed to the Father, "I have brought you glory on earth by completing the work you gave me to do" (John 17:4).

As *we* prepare to finish, let's determine, by God's grace, to finish well. We ought to remember along the way that our efforts will not only be judged by how few times we have fallen along the course, but also by how many times we were willing to get up off the ground, dust off our britches, and begin to run again as He would have us to. There is hope after a crisis at mid-life, and you may well discover that the fire of trial has burned away much of the chaff in your life. God has used and can use what you have been through.

As we close, let us meditate on the words of this hymn by Johnson Oatman, Jr. The Lord's way is the higher way, leading to higher ground.

> I'm pressing on the upward way,
> New heights I'm gaining every day;
> Still praying as I'm onward bound,
> "Lord, plant my feet on higher ground."
> My heart has no desire to stay
> Where doubts arise and fears dismay;
> Though some may dwell where these abound,
> My prayer, my aim, is higher ground.
> I want to live above the world,
> Though Satan's darts at me are hurled;
> For faith has caught the joyful sound,
> The song of saints on higher ground.
> I want to scale that utmost height,
> And catch a gleam of glory bright;
> But still I'll pray till heaven I've found,
> "Lord, lead me on to higher ground."

Suggested Readings

ON ECCLESIASTES

Bridges, Charles. 1960. *An Exposition of the Book of Ecclesiastes*. Great Britain: The Banner of Truth Trust.

DeHaan, Richard W. and Herbert Vander Lugt. 1974. *The Art of Staying off Dead-End Streets*. Wheaton, Illinois: Victor Books.

Foster, Robert D. *A Challenge to Men from Ecclesiastes*. Colorado Springs, Colorado: Challenge Books, Ltd.

Hubbard, David Allan. 1976. *Beyond Futility*. Grand Rapids, Michigan: William B. Eerdmans Publishing Company.

Kaiser, Walter C., Jr. 1979. *Ecclesiastes: Total Life*. Everyman's Bible Commentary. Chicago: Moody Press.

Kidner, Derek. 1976. *A Time To Mourn, a Time To Dance*. Downers Grove, Illinois: InterVarsity Press.

Leupold, H. C. 1978. *Exposition of Ecclesiastes*. Grand Rapids, Michigan: Baker Book House.

MacDonald, William. 1976. *Chasing the Wind*. Chicago: Moody Press.

McGee, J. Vernon. 1977. *Ecclesiastes and Song of Solomon*. Pasadena, California: Thru the Bible Books.

Swindoll, Charles R. 1985. *Living on the Ragged Edge: Coming to Terms with Reality*. Waco, Texas: Word Books.

ON ADULT DEVELOPMENT AND MID-LIFE

Conway, Jim, 1979. *Men in Mid Life Crisis*. Elgin, Illinois: David C. Cook Publishing Company.

Conway, Jim and Sally Conway. 1983. *Women in Mid Life Crisis.* Wheaton, Illinois: Tyndale House Publishers.

Conway, Sally. 1980. *You and Your Husband's Mid Life Crisis.* Elgin, Illinois: David C. Cook Publishing Company.

Dobson, James. 1980. *Straight Talk to Men and Their Wives.* Waco, Texas: Word, Inc.

——. 1975. *What Wives Wish Their Husbands Knew about Women.* Wheaton, Illinois: Tyndale House Publishers.

Howe, Reuel L. 1959. *The Creative Years.* Greenwich, Connecticut: The Seabury Press.

MacDonald, Gordon. 1985. *Living at High Noon: Reflections on the Dramas of Mid-Life.* Old Tappan, New Jersey: Fleming H. Revell Company.

Sheehy, Gail. 1980. *Passages.* New York: Bantam Books.

Sterner, John. 1985. *Growing through Mid-Life Crises: Thoughts from Solomon and Others.* St. Louis: Concordia Publishing House.

Swindoll, Charles R. 1984. *The Lonely Whine of the Top Dog.* Waco, Texas: Word Books.

Viorst, Judith. 1986. *Necessary Losses.* New York: Simon and Schuster.

Acknowledgments

Baker, Don and Emery Nester. 1983. *Depression: Finding Hope and Meaning in Life's Darkest Shadow.* Portland, Oregon: Multnomah Press. Used by permission.

Bloch, Arthur. 1977. *Murphy's Law and Other Reasons Why Things Go Wrong!* Los Angeles: Price/Stern/Sloan Publishers, Inc. Used by permission.

Bridges, Charles. 1960. *An Exposition of the Book of Ecclesiastes.* Carlisle, Pennsylvania: The Banner of Truth Trust. Used by permission.

Colson, Charles W. 1976. *Born Again.* Old Tappan, New Jersey: Chosen Books, Fleming H. Revell Company. Copyright © 1976 by Charles W. Colson. Used by permission.

Conway, Jim. 1978. *Men in Mid Life Crisis.* Elgin, Illinois: David C. Cook Publishing Company. Used by permission.

Crouch, Andrae. 1971. "Through It All." Burbank, California: Manna Music, Inc., copyright © 1971 by Manna Music, Inc. International copyright secured. All rights reserved. Used by permission.

David, Hal and Burt Bacharach. "I'll Never Fall in Love Again." Copyright 1968 by Blue Seas Music, Inc. and Jac Music, Inc. International copyright secured. All rights reserved.

DeHaan, Richard W. and Herbert Vander Lugt. 1974. *The Art of Staying off Dead-End Streets.* Wheaton, Illinois: Victor Books. Copyright 1974 by Radio Bible Class, Grand Rapids, Michigan. Used by permission.

Denver, John. 1981. "Seasons of the Heart." Port Chester, New York: Cherry Lane Music Publishing Co., Inc. © Copyright 1981 by Cherry Lane Music Publishing Co., Inc. All rights reserved. Used by permission.

————. 1981. "Sleepin' Alone." Port Chester, New York: Cherry Lane Music Publishing Co., Inc. All rights reserved. Used by permission.

Dobson, James C. 1980. *Straight Talk to Men and Their Wives.* Waco, Texas: Word Books, Publisher. Copyright © 1980 by James C. Dobson. Used by permission of Word Books, Publisher, Waco, Texas.

————. 1975. *What Wives Wish Their Husbands Knew about Women.* Wheaton, Illinois: Tyndale House Publishers. Used by permission.

Eareckson, Joni and Steve Estes. 1978. *A Step Further.* Grand Rapids, Michigan: Zondervan Publishing House. Copyright © 1978 by Joni Eareckson and Steve Estes. Used by permission of Zondervan Publishing House.

Feller, Dick. 1975. "Some Days Are Diamonds (Some Days Are Stone)." Nashville, Tennessee: Tree International. Copyright © 1975 Tree Publishing Company, Inc. International copyright secured. Used by permission. All rights reserved.

Fenelon. 1973. *Let Go.* Springdale, Pennsylvania: Whitaker House. Used by permission of the publisher.

Hatfield, Mark. 1976. *Between a Rock and a Hard Place.* Waco, Texas: Word Books, Publisher. Copyright © 1976 by Mark Hatfield. Used by permission of Word Books, Publisher, Waco, Texas.

Howe, Reuel L. 1959. *The Creative Years.* Greenwich, Connecticut: The Seabury Press.

Hupp, Debbie and Bob Morrison. "Gravel on the Ground." Nashville: Music City Music, Inc. Used by permission.

Jones, Charles E. 1968. *Life is Tremendous.* Wheaton, Illinois: Tyndale House Publishers. Used by permission.

Leupold, H. C. 1978. *Exposition of Ecclesiastes.* Grand Rapids, Michigan: Baker Book House.

MacDonald, Gordon. 1985. *Living at High Noon: Reflections on the Dramas of Mid-Life.* Old Tappan, New Jersey: Fleming H. Revell Company. Used by permission.

McGee, J. Vernon. 1977. *Ecclesiastes and Song of Solomon.* Pasadena, California: Thru the Bible Books.

Meier, Paul D. and Frank Minirth. 1978. *Happiness Is a Choice*. Grand Rapids, Michigan: Baker Book House.

Nixon, Richard M. 1984. *Real Peace*. Boston: Little, Brown and Company. Used by permission.

Oatman, Johnson, Jr. "Higher Ground."

Pentecost, J. Dwight, 1979. *Man's Problems—God's Answers*. Chicago: Moody Press.

Peterson, Eugene A. 1983. *Run with the Horses: The Quest for Life at Its Best*. Downers Grove, Illinois: InterVarsity Press. Copyright © 1983 by Inter-Varsity Christian Fellowship of the United States of America and used by permission of InterVarsity Press.

Scott, Clara. "Open My Eyes, That I May See."

Segal, Brenda Lesley. 1980. *The Tenth Measure*. New York: St. Martin's Press, Inc.

Sheehy, Gail. 1980. *Passages*. New York: Bantam Books.

Sterner, John. 1985. *Growing through Mid-Life Crises: Thoughts from Solomon and Others*. St. Louis: Concordia Publishing House. Copyright © 1985 by Concordia Publishing House. Used by permission.

Swindoll, Charles R. 1980. *Three Steps Forward, Two Steps Back*. Nashville: Thomas Nelson Publishers. Used by permission.

Tan, Paul Lee. 1984. *Encyclopedia of 7700 Illustrations: Signs of the Times*. Rockville, Maryland: Assurance Publishers.

Unger, Merrill F. 1966. *Unger's Bible Dictionary*. Third edition. Chicago: Moody Press.

Viorst, Judith. 1986. *Necessary Losses*. New York: Simon and Schuster, Inc. Used by permission.

Whicher, Stephen E., ed. 1960. *Selections from Ralph Waldo Emerson: An Organic Anthology*. Boston: Houghton Mifflin Company. Used by permission.

Yeager, Chuck and Leo Janos. 1985. *Yeager: An Autobiography*. New York: Bantam Books, Inc. Used by permission.

DON ANDERSON MINISTRIES

Popular pastor, teacher, and conference speaker, Don Anderson tours Texas and neighboring states giving Bible classes and business luncheon seminars during the fall, winter, and spring months. During the summer, Don Anderson Ministries staffs many youth and family camps. Don also preaches regularly at two churches staffed by the Ministries and speaks at conferences in various locations in the United States and Canada. His audiences of business and professional men and women, housewives and tradespeople testify that his refreshing teaching makes the Scriptures "come alive" for them.

Don Anderson graduated from Northwestern College in 1955 with a B.A. degree and received his Masters degree from Dallas Theological Seminary. He has been in Christian ministry for over thirty years serving as a Young Life staff member, youth pastor, program director at the Firs Bible and Missionary Conference, executive director of Pine Cove Conference Center and, since 1972, has served as director of the non-profit organization, Don Anderson Ministries, headquartered in Tyler, Texas.

Don Anderson has many audio and video cassette tapes based on his teachings which are produced by the Ministries and distributed widely. There is also a Ministry newsletter, *The Grapevine*, which reaches about eight thousand homes.

If you'd like to enhance your study of the Scriptures, the cassette tape series of *Ecclesiastes: The Mid-Life Crisis* is available from the author. If you are interested in hearing Don's teachings, please write to this address for a free audio and video tape catalog.

Don Anderson Ministries
Station A, P.O. Box 6611
Tyler, Texas 75711